C0-AUG-644

A
CHINESE
VILLAGE

A
CHINESE
VILLAGE

Taitou,
Shantung
Province

By MARTIN C. YANG

楊懋春

Columbia University Press, New York

The completion and publication of this study were made possible by funds granted by the Viking Fund, Inc., a foundation created and endowed at the instance of A. L. Wenner-Gren for scientific, educational, and charitable purposes. The Viking Fund, Inc., is not, however, the author or publisher of this publication, and is not to be understood as approving, by virtue of its grant any of the statements made, or views expressed, therein.

COPYRIGHT © 1945
COLUMBIA UNIVERSITY PRESS
NEW YORK

First printing September, 1945
Second printing November, 1945
Third printing 1947
Fourth printing 1950
Fifth printing 1959

Published in Great Britain, Canada, India, and Pakistan
by the Oxford University Press
London, Toronto, Bombay, and Karachi

Foreword

THE rise of community studies is one of the most significant phenomena in the development of the social studies. Such studies have come into being in response to certain trends which are evident in modern science in general. Scientific research began with the more or less artificial isolation of particular phenomena and their investigation without relation to the contexts in which they normally occurred. However, it became increasingly evident that there were factors of patterning and of functional interrelations between phenomena of different orders which could not be revealed by this approach. The importance of such factors increases with the complexity of the configurations into which phenomena are integrated and reaches a climax in the social situations with which sociology, anthropology and, to a lesser extent, personality psychology have to deal. The community study constitutes a frank recognition of the necessity for investigating such situations as wholes. It contributes equally to the development of pure and of applied science. It reveals, as no other type of investigation can, the interrelations of the multitudinous factors which influence the life both of the community and its component individuals. It also provides that intimate understanding of individual needs and desires without which no attempt at planned change can be successful.

How to study and describe the life of any community is, in itself, a problem of no mean proportions. While there has been a steady improvement in our perception of the wide range of phenomena which have to be observed and recorded, community studies which appeared quite adequate a few years ago fail to provide answers to many of the questions which we ask today. Most of the earlier studies were primarily enumerative and designed to provide the sort of data which would lend themselves most readily to statistical treatment. They tell us how many washing machines there were in a village at a certain time or how many villagers belonged to each of how many churches. Although the value of such data is still recognized, modern social scientists are becoming increasingly interested in discovering how washing machines or churches are integrated into the life of the community and how the people feel about them.

As long as the social scientist is dealing with American or even Western European communities, lack of information on these points is partially compensated for by a background of common understandings. Even in the absence of specific data many things can be taken for granted. However, as soon as one attempts to deal with communities whose cultures are fundamentally different from our own very few things can be taken for granted. There are, to be sure, certain common denominators of human motivation, but these are too general to provide much help in the understanding of specific situations. Between such universal factors and the overt behavior characteristic of the members of any community there lies a zone of concepts and attitudes. It is these covert elements of culture which give the overt behavior its social significance and without a knowledge of them much of this behavior will remain inexplicable.

How to penetrate the covert level of an alien culture is still one of the most difficult problems which confronts the investigator. Since most of any society's attitudes operate at the unconscious level, they can rarely be ascertained by direct questioning. Even when the members of a community are thoroughly friendly and cooperative, they are still unable to tell the investigator many things simply because they have never thought about them. The investigator will have to discover such things for himself. If he is to do this successfully he must have not only an intimate knowledge of the language but also a genuine sympathy with his subjects and a more than ordinary degree of sensibility. He must be able to perceive the emotional context of situations and to understand much that is left unsaid. Unfortunately, it is an open question whether such sensibility can be either learned or taught. At least it is vastly more difficult to acquire it than to learn a strange language or the formal techniques in recording a community's organization and activities.

Most American social scientists are fully conscious of these difficulties. They know that the best way to acquire an intimate knowledge of any culture is and always will be to be reared in it. As a result they are turning more and more to individuals who were born and brought up in non-European cultures for aid in understanding these cultures. It is much easier for such persons to acquire the necessary scientific techniques for community study than it is for outsiders to acquire the sort of knowledge of a community without which these techniques are of little value. Any individual who attempts to describe the life of his own community must, of course, approach it with a more than ordinary measure of objectivity.

However, the non-European who acquires real skill in the use of European scientific techniques can hardly fail to develop this objectivity also. Any individual who has participated intimately in two cultures is in a position to see both with heightened clarity. Every point of contrast brings into consciousness attitudes and values which might otherwise remain unconscious. "Marginal men" are in a position not only to interpret their cultures to us but also to interpret our culture to ourselves. It is safe to predict that some of the most valuable contributions to social science will come from scientists who, because of this double cultural participation, can approach both facts and theoretical formulations with detachment.

The present book shows how happy the results of such a blending of intimate knowledge and scientific training can be. Although it is not the first study of its sort, it seems to me to be one of the most successful. Dr. Yang knows his village as only a villager could, yet looks at it with scientific detachment. His descriptions are both accurate and sympathetic and will be of equal interest to the social scientist and the general reader. One finishes the book with a feeling that these are real people and people very like ourselves.

RALPH LINTON

Columbia University, New York

Author's Preface

AS the rural rehabilitation movement assumes increasing weight in China's national reconstruction program, statesmen, economists, and social leaders are coming to realize that a scientific and comprehensive study of China's rural life, past and present, is a prime necessity in the furtherance of this movement. Study of this kind can eliminate much of the waste and inefficiency which have marked the beginnings of the movement and can also prevent many tragic mistakes.

The present world situation is bringing nations increasingly into closer contact. Far-sighted statesmen and students of humanity realize that the foundation of international association lies in the ability of different nations to understand each other's cultures. It is gratefully observed that China in the past half century has had the privilege of being studied from a cultural point of view by numerous Western scholars. The writing of this book is a small part of one of these projects. The writer hopes that his work may contribute something to the cultural understanding between China and America.

The village of Taitou has been selected as the object of the first study because the writer was born and reared there, and lived there until he entered high school. Until recent years, he has returned to the village at least once each year, the periods of his visits varying from five days to several months. He has maintained his contacts with his relatives in Taitou and has kept himself informed about the daily life and significant happenings in the village. Therefore, this study is a record of facts which have been personally seen, heard, and experienced.

The great problem in a study of this sort is the selection of the best method of presentation. The usual way is to choose the important aspects in the daily life of the community—economic, social, political, religious, educational—and to describe each one in detail. The better way seems to be to begin with the presentation of the most primary group and follow through to the limits of the social range. From a dynamic point of view, a society is made up of the complicated interactions between individuals in a primary group and between groups in the larger organizations. The actual life of a society, as well as of an individual, is like a stream starting from its source and flowing toward a larger body of water. It is also a process of diffusion or radiation, the relationships being more loosely integrated the further removed they are from the primary source. An effective method for studying the life of a rural community is to start with the interactions between the individual in the primary groups, go on to those between the primary groups in the secondary group, and finally those between the secondary groups in a large area. An important consideration is that in each of these areas, the life must be presented in its entirety, not in fragmented pieces.

In Taitou we find that the family is a primary group. It is true that in a large family there may be two or three smaller basic units, such as a married son with his wife and children, who form a small exclusive group within the family pattern. But so long as all members live under the same roof and work and eat together, the family is a unified, primary group.

The village is a secondary group. Between the family and the village, there are various transitional groupings—clans, neighborhoods, the associations of families on the basis of similar social or economic status or school affiliations, and religious groups. Beyond the village is the market town, which draws all the villages together in a loose but nevertheless distinct relationship. It represents the large area, and the transitional links between it and the village are the groups of small villages and the groups of families which are of one clan but which are scattered in two or three neighboring villages. The interactions in these groups are sometimes different from those in all other kinds of groups and cannot be ignored.

Based on the above method and findings, the present study is organized as follows: first, the physical environment, the social pattern, the people who live in the community, their means of livelihood, and their standard of living are described. Thus the reader first sees the village as a static community. However, the foundations of the social life lie in the interactions of the individuals within the family. To explain the Chinese conception of the family, a typical farm family in Taitou is described in respect to the interactions between the family members, economic and ceremonial activities, the rearing and training of children, the caring for the old, and the significance of marriage.

In discussing the villagers' standard of living, our method is to describe what kinds of food the people actually eat in a year and how they prepare the three meals every day. Attention has also been paid to some conspicuous customs in relation to food consumption and to the social stratification as regards the general types of meals prepared in different families.

Since it has not been approached from a dollar-and-cents point of view, nothing has been presented in tables or charts, or, in other words, in statistics.

Beyond the family, life extends to the village; therefore, the next description has to do with village life. In this section it is apparent that the life of the village is much less significant than that of the family. Although the village is a unity with a unified life of its own, and a clearly defined leadership, it also has smaller groups within its own organization. The next section of the book, therefore, has to do with village organizations, neighborhood activities, extra-village associations, village conflicts, and village leadership. Since the clan organization plays now and then a significant role in regard to individuals as well as families, it is necessary to devote some space to its form and activities.

Rural life beyond the village is seen in relations of the village to the market town. It is also seen in the relations of the village to neighboring villages in the same market town area. No attempt is made to divide these relationships into economic, social, political, religious, or educational aspects, since the writer's purpose is to present the picture as an integrated whole.

In conclusion, the relations between the village and the places beyond the market town area are briefly mentioned, special emphasis being paid to the recently developed relationship with Tsingtao.

The writer believes that it is possible to picture the daily life of a rural community with the framework thus outlined. And to make the picture real, through the eyes of a person who actually grew up in the community and experienced most of the social life described, the study is concluded with the story of a villager's boyhood. The writer feels justified in saying that the information given in this study is reliable and that the life picture thus presented is preserved in its wholeness so far as possible; he hopes that the rural community of Taitou will be culturally understood by the readers.

However, statistical accuracy cannot be claimed in regard to the figures that have been given, except those cited from published books or articles; nor can the complete exactitude of all the information be guaranteed. This is regrettable, but inevitable, since the writing was done in a place several thousand miles away from the village and was dependent entirely upon memory.

Disagreement regarding the described economic and social conditions in the village is expected from people who are familiar, in one way or another, with rural China. Some may feel that the picture has been painted too favorably; others may accuse the writer of being too lenient with the landlords, usurers, and the crooked village gentry. Whatever the criticisms may be, the truth lies in the fact that one cannot cover all phases of China in one study. China is so huge, and its living conditions are, due to the undeveloped means of communication and transportation, so diverse from place to place that what one observes in South China may be entirely different in the north. Even in the same province, one finds quite different economic and social practices in various sections. For this reason, one cannot assume that because abuses exist in some parts of China, these must be found also in Taitou, and that if life is dark in some village, it must be the same in this one. The readers are here assured that the writer tried very hard to free himself from any significant bias. There has been no intention to exaggerate one element of the culture and conceal another. He has tried his best to recall things as they actually existed in the past and are existing today. He has also tried to explain everything in such terms that most of the villagers themselves would agree with his statements. Of course, he could not avoid including in his writing some of his own points of view.

The study was made possible by the kind sponsorship of the Department of Anthropology of Columbia University, of which Professor Ralph Linton is the chairman. Professor Linton not only supervised the whole study, but also read the manuscript with great patience several times and made numerous valuable suggestions. His genuine appreciation of the work encouraged the writer a great deal and in turn helped the accomplishment.

Acknowledgment is also due Miss Leona Steinberg, who rendered appreciable assistance throughout the work. She edited the manuscript and made many suggestions regarding the organization of the material.

Apologies and appreciation are given to the villagers of Taitou who have been referred to in the study. In no case were real names given, but since the community is one in which people know each other intimately, and, since the life described is entirely contemporary, the individuals and families cited will be easily identifiable to the present inhabitants of Taitou. What must be pointed out here is that all the citations have been made in the single purpose of scientific study; there is not the slightest personal favor and disfavor involved.

M.C.Y.

Columbia University, New York
April, 1945

Contents

Introduction

"FREEDOM from want," one of the four freedoms enumerated by President Roosevelt as a goal for humanity, has stimulated world-wide interest. The Hot Springs Conference on Food and Agriculture held in 1943 made unmistakably clear the fact that food is basic to the health and welfare of people and that great changes in the application of science to agriculture will have to be brought about if the world's populations are to be more adequately fed. The hope that science holds out for a better world is stimulating a growing interest in the development of more scientific and productive agriculture in China, India, and other densely populated nations. More and more leaders from these countries and from other parts of the world are coming to the United States to learn about scientific developments in agriculture. They do so with an interest that applies not only to science as such, but to the practical applications of science to production and living.

During the past decade we have had a remarkable development in the social sciences. We are learning that progress in one science must inevitably be followed by progress in all others. For example, many laboratory and experimental findings in the field of agriculture have been enlarged upon in medical research to the ultimate welfare of human health. In two other fields, soil conservation and human nutrition, we have only recently made considerable progress in extending through mass education, some of the findings of research. Our progress in extending these scientific truths has been made possible through researches in the social sciences, through extension education, and the raising of the educational level of the masses of our people.

If we are to make continued progress in applying the findings of science to human welfare we will need to know more about the manner, methods, and means man employs in making a living; the way he organizes to accomplish the things he considers important; the level of living he has and the standard he strives for; the ideas he has about ways of making a living; and the channels of communication with the world outside. We need to have a greater appreciation of the basic values by which people live and the processes and forces that must be effective if change is to occur.

In the field of agriculture there has not, until recent years, been an awareness of the importance of understanding "culture." Missionary workers in other countries have in general not been fully oriented to the new culture and have as a result ignored many of the cultural principles developed by the social scientist. The American people have been appreciative and sympathetic toward China. Missionaries have gone to China and rendered outstanding service. Agricultural experts from the United States have gone there and helped in many ways, and yet the impacts of scientific agriculture on China have been very slight.

It seems inevitable that many changes will take place in China after the war. Since China is a rural nation its changes in agriculture are likely to be far-reaching. Because of the stresses and strains of war, China will want to rehabilitate its agriculture as soon as possible so that its gallant people may not long suffer. To help direct these changes, China's agricultural students and technicians are now coming to the United States for training in research and Extension.

Dr. Yang's book presents a living account of rural China as seen in its cultural and social setting—a rural village. Before reading Dr. Yang's book I had read many of the books on China's agriculture which were readily available and from each learned about different segments and phases of China's agriculture and rural life. To my knowledge this book is the first of its kind to tie together the various phases of rural life in China in a thoroughly coherent and understanding story.

I cannot think of many writings which can possibly be more timely so far as China and the United States are concerned. Those who read the book will be immediately impressed with the fact that rural China has a culture vastly different from ours. We know from experience that we cannot transplant our culture to Asia. If we have a scientific basis for understanding how the culture of the Chinese works, we should be able to give to China more intelligent assistance in the task of agricultural reconstruction. Dr. Yang's book can, in my estimation, make a great contribution, which will assist us in aiding, in such ways as China may desire, in the planning and the development of a more productive and scientific agriculture; for he has laid before us a new and scientific key to an understanding of the rural culture of China.

Dr. Yang's book is important to all workers in the field of agriculture from another angle. It is a fine example of a new approach by which the methods of cultural anthropology are brought to bear in an agricultural community. I hope that more such studies will be forthcoming from other parts of the world. Such studies will be very important from the standpoint of the improvement of rural conditions throughout the world.

> M. L. WILSON
> *Director of Extension Work*
> *U. S. Department of Agriculture*

Washington, D. C.
January, 1945

The Village Site 1

THE village of Taitou is located on a stretch of level land ringed with mountains on the southwestern shore of Kiaochow Bay. Directly across the bay to the east is a small peninsula, on the southern end of which is the city of Tsingtao. This city, which has grown up in recent decades, now provides Shantung and its neighboring provinces with means of access to the outside world. It is a center of commerce, industry, and transportation and thus plays an important role in the growing trade between rural China and the manufacturing centers in distant parts of the world.

This region is one of the oldest agricultural areas in China. Its people are almost all farmers who cultivate their own land and live in compact villages. There are about twenty villages and a rural town. The town is Hsinanchen—the only marketing center for the region. Taitou is about two thirds of a mile south of Hsinanchen with which it is connected by a new highway. The communication between this area and the outside is comparatively good; there are improved land routes and modern sea vessels. When the villagers want to go to Tsingtao, for instance, they take a highway that leads south to the small port of Hsuehchiatao and from there take a steamboat across the bay. When the weather is good, there are numerous routes that can be traversed by sailing boat. To the north there is a modern motor road leading to Wangtai, a large market town, and thence to the county seat of Kiaohsien. While Taitou is politically a part of the County of Kiaohsien, observation of the network of communication shows us that it is much closer to and has more important connections with Tsingtao than it has with the county seat.

The Small Pearl, the highest of the local ranges, lies to the west. To the north lies the Long Hill stretching from west to east, while to the south is the Long Wall. These three form a horizontal arc with the eastern shoreline at one end.

There are four rivers which flow from west to east. These are small streams and not navigable. In the rainy season they are indeed obstacles to transportation and travel, for there are no bridges across them, only stepping stones which are useless at high water.

The stream that flows along the southern edge of Taitou is locally called

Taitou River. To the north the land is high and extends in a sort of platform to the base of Mt. Small Pearl. To the south it sweeps downward; the lowland is the mouth of a valley formed by the water rushing down from the mountains toward the sea to the east. The name of the

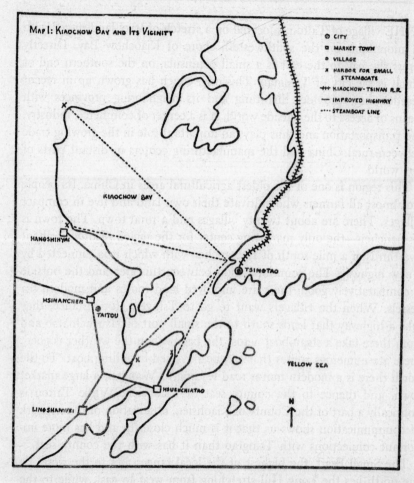

village derives from this formation: *tai* means platform or stage; *tou* means end. The low area is one of the few places in this part of China which is suitable for the cultivation of rice, although part of it is grassy or wooded swampland.

The climate of the area is good because of the proximity of the sea and mountains. No record of climate has ever been made for Taitou, but Tsingtao Municipal Government thus describes it:

It is foggy in the summer. From April to the end of July there are always one or more heavy fogs every week. From December to March of the next year, it is dry and rather cold, but there is not much snow. Therefore, the most desirable seasons in Tsingtao, so far as weather is concerned, are periods from middle of April to middle of June and from the beginning of September to the beginning of November. In Tsingtao the hottest day has not been more than 35.6 ° C. and the coldest day has not been more than 12.8 ° C. below zero.

Regarding the direction of winds, in the summer there are more winds from southeast, while in the winter more from northwest. There are more breezes than strong winds. Big storms are few. In the winter there are usually three or four periods of strong winds from Po-hai [or the Gulf of Chili], which is across the Shantung Peninsula in the north.*

In support of this general description records of the temperature of twenty consecutive years are given here in condensed form:

MONTHLY RECORD OF CLIMATE FOR TWENTY YEARS IN TSINGTAO [a]

Month	Air depression (in mm.)	Temperature (in °C.)	Monsoon	Days of fog, frost, rain, snow	Rainfall (in mm.)
Jan.	772	−2	North	2, 15, 5, 5½: 27½	8
Feb.	770	−0.1	North	4, 13, 4, 4: 25	8.4
Mar.	767	4.4	South	4, 7, 1½, 5: 17½	15
Apr.	762	10.1	South and Southeast	6, ½, 5: 11½	27
May	758	15.4	South and Southeast	Rain 7, fog 8: 15	28
June	755	19.5	South and Southeast	Rain 8½, fog 11: 19½	80.7
July	755	23.5	South and Southeast	Rain 12, fog 12: 24	96
Aug.	755	25.3	South and Southeast	Rain 11, fog 2: 13	136
Sept.	761.4	20.8	North	Rain 7.5, fog .5: 8	92.8
Oct.	765.7	15.9	North and Northwest	Rain 3, fog 1: 4	12
Nov.	779	8.0	North and Northwest	Rain 4.2, fog 1: 5.2	17
Dec.	773	1.0	North	1, 14.4, 4.4, 3.3: 23.1	15.9

[a] Kiao-Ou-Chih, Vol. II (1929), Section 6.

According to Buck,** the annual rainfall for the area is 700 mm. This

* A brief translation from Kiao-Ou-Chih ("Gazette of Tsingtao"), Vol. II (1929), Section 6.

** John Lossing Buck, Land Utilization in China (Shanghai, Commercial Press, 1937), Atlas volume, Chap. III, Maps V, XII, XIII.

is, no doubt, an average of both the continental and the coastal sections. The annual rainfall of 536.8 mm. recorded in the accompanying table is reliable. The temperatures also follow Buck's record * : in January both are 0 ° C. or a little under this; in July, Buck's is 24 ° C. while in the table the figure is 23.5 ° C. The difference is due to the greater nearness to the sea. The hot days in Taitou occur not in July but in August when the temperature is 25.3 ° C.

The quality of the soil varies from section to section. In the hilly land to the west, northwest, and southwest, the soil is sandy and yellow, while in the east, north, and northeast it is heavy and dark. In the south and southeast are areas of flood layers, swamps, and a piece of water land. The soil of the water land is very fertile and produces a fine quality of rice. Some of the flood land is alkaline, but where the thick flood soil has accumulated the land is good. However, because of the recurrent threat of flood, its price is only equal to, or even lower than, that of land containing inferior soil. The water land can command a price as high as that of a residential lot. According to a geological report in the *Gazette* of Tsingtao, the geological composition of this area is largely limestone. Buck, however, includes it in the area of brown soil.

The crop fields lie beyond and around the village (see Map II). While the boundaries of neighboring villages frequently overlap, usually the boundary line is recognizable. In Taitou the distance from the village to the boundary line varies. To the south it is very short, only several blocks beyond the vegetable gardens and threshing grounds; to the southwest it is much longer, almost one and one-half miles. To the west, northwest, north, northeast, and east the distances are much the same—about two thirds of a mile.

The village site can be divided roughly into two parts: the residential area and the immediate outskirts. The former is situated on the north bank of the Taitou River. Here the one main street follows the bowlike curve of the river, with narrower roads branching from it in both directions. A number of small lanes and paths, all running northward, connect with the main street. Most of the residences are located north of the street. The local people call the lanes and paths *hu-tung*, and, if the villagers of a certain *hu-tung* are members of a certain clan, then the name of the clan is added to the *hu-tung*'s name. But sometimes people of the western part call the lanes in the eastern part *tung hu-tung* (*tung* means east), while those of the eastern part call the lands in the western part

* *Ibid.*

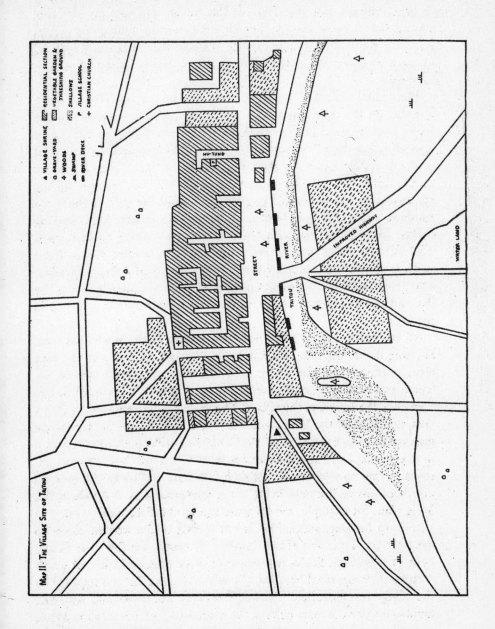

MAP II. THE VILLAGE SITE OF TAITOU

▲ VILLAGE SHRINE   ▨ RESIDENTIAL SECTION
○ GRAVE-YARD   ▨ VEGETABLE GARDEN & THRESHING GROUND
♣ WOODS   ▨ SHALLOWS
Ⅱ SWAMP   P VILLAGE SCHOOL
▬▬ RIVER DYKE   ✝ CHRISTIAN CHURCH

HU-TUNG

STREET

RIVER

TAITOU

IMPROVED HIGHWAY

WATER LAND

hsi hu-tung. Two of the lanes in the western end are really roads leading to other villages. For the safety of the village, and perhaps for other reasons, not all the *hu-tung* go through to the northern limit of the village. Recently, for defense against bandits, the southern entrances where the *hu-tung* are connected to the main street have been fortified by gates or barricades.

The central section of the main street is quite spacious. To the south it opens on the river and affords a view of the open country. On the levees built by some of the wealthier families along the riverbank grow rows of willow trees. This part of the main street is something of a social center or public square for the village. In the summer, the villagers sit on the stones or on the levees under the trees and talk through the hot afternoons. In winter, the old people relax against the walls in the warm sunshine and watch the children at play in the square. Men weaving baskets or knitting straw rain coats or perhaps working on farm tools work out here rather than in their narrow and smoke-filled homes. Some portions of this open space are the private property of different families, who often use their part as an open stable for their animals during the day and also as a place to keep manure and earth before it is moved to the field.

All the better houses are in the central part of the residential area. *Hu-tung* divide the area into four main divisions according to the four clans in the village. The first part, which is almost eight-tenths of the whole area and includes almost all the good houses, is occupied by the P'an clan, the largest in the village. The second is occupied by the Ch'en clan, the third by the Yangs, and the fourth by the Lius. On the village map (page 5) one can see that the families of each clan cluster together in one section forming a nucleus out from which the clan's territory extends. A few isolated families of each clan have settled among families of other clans or live outside the main residential area. A family of the Yang clan, for example, moved years ago to the P'an clan's section in an eastern *hu-tung*, and a P'an family moved to the western corner to live near the Yang and Hsueh families. Recently, another P'an family built in a northern field a new house of brick walls and tile roof which is completely separated from the old residences. But this was regarded by the villagers as definitely unusual. Generally, the older and wealthier families occupy the main parts of the residential area, whereas the poorer or smaller families spread into the outlying areas. In the main residential area are the village school, the Christian church, the two oil-pressing shops, and a small foundry. The village school does not have its own building, but occupies one or two rooms of a family house. The Christian church, which was built more than twenty-five years ago, is a good building, the only finer one being the new home of the P'an family.

Immediately beyond the residential area lie the vegetable gardens and threshing grounds. The first section, which belongs to the P'an clan, lies across the river to the south. Both the threshing grounds and vegetable gardens there are large and well cultivated. The second section, which is on the east side, also belongs to the P'an families. The third, on the west, belongs largely to P'an families but the Ch'en and Yang families also have some land there. The last group is on the northwest and belongs entirely to Yang, Ch'en, and Liu families.

Beyond the gardens lie the graveyards of the four clans. There is no general cemetery; each clan buries its dead on land which is believed to be favorable to the future generations of the clan. When the clan becomes large and several branches split off, each branch chooses its own ground for burial. After a number of generations small graveyards or isolated mounds are scattered everywhere around the village. It is rather strange that no graveyard here is decorated with pines or other big trees like those one would see in other parts of the country. Even those of the P'an clan are bare. Consequently, the graves look rather wild and ugly.

The southern side of the residential area is quite beautiful in summer. Along both sides of the river there are several stretches of wooded swamps. Not long ago, when the countryside was peaceful and when the P'an families were in their prosperous period, the village was admired by travelers who approached it from the south. Before one reached the edge of the river one could hardly see the village because of a thick green wall of trees. But as the traveler went on, suddenly the village burst into view before him, and in the next instant he was walking before the watching eyes of the villagers and could see the farmers hoeing in the vegetable garden or working on the threshing grounds, women washing their clothes on the river dikes while children played around them, people sitting and working under the tall willow trees, and also the big oxen and mules standing on the river bank. Unfortunately, a great part of that is gone. During the last ten years the P'an families declined rapidly. The woods have been cut, broken river levees have not been repaired, and the tall willow trees are almost gone, as are the oxen and mules.

The Taitou River is not large, but because it is close to the Small Pearl and because the river bed is shallow and there are no embankments the village is subject to floods every year during the rainy season. The current is so rapid that a great part of the water overflows both banks. Perhaps that is why people of the village have never bothered to build a permanent bridge over it. The north bank, which is the main street of the residential area, is protected by small dikes, but on the southern side great pieces of land were damaged or completely washed out about half a century ago. What is now woodland and sand was formerly all good fields. After the rainy season, the river is only a narrow and shallow stream. Sometimes people have to dig deep into the sandbed to get water.

Besides the small paths which lead to the fields, two roads lead south. One comes to the central part of the main street, another passes through the western end of the village. These are wide, improved roads. From the east there are three roads, all narrow, which lead only to other villages. On the west there is only one road. The improved highway connecting Taitou with the market town extends to the northwest.

The People	2

I T is hard to say just how large the population of the village is. Since the revival of the *Pao-chia* system,* each family must post on the top of the front door a card bearing the name, age, sex, kinship status, and occupation of the family members. However, access to this means of counting is impossible, so our estimate must be made on the basis of the size of an average family and the approximate number of families in the village.

According to Buck,** the average size of a Chinese farm family throughout the country is 5.21 persons. Buck's study is based on information collected from 269 localities over an area of 253 *hsien* (or counties) of 22 provinces. All the material was collected from 1929 to 1933, and from three sources: *Hsien* government records; well-informed local residents; and an agricultural survey conducted by a faculty group of the Agricultural College of the University of Nanking. In Shantung province, 23 *hsien* are included in the study. Although Kiaohsien, to which Taitou belongs, is not among them, Tsimo, a neighboring *hsien*, is included. Tsimo is similar to Kiaohsien in agriculture, natural resources, and social organization, therefore, what has been found true for the former can be applied largely to the latter. According to the study, the average size of a farm family in Tsimo is about 5 persons, and the average size of a household is 6.5 persons. The first of these figures is somewhat smaller and the second much larger than the average elsewhere in the country. By a farm household the author of the study means "all persons living and eating together, including non-relatives, such as hired laborers."

According to the present writer's impression, a family in Taitou cannot be as small as 4.8 persons, the Tsimo figure. It may be even larger than the national average of 5.21 persons. Ten out of thirteen families of the Yang clan number at least six persons; many of the Ch'en and P'an families also have six to ten members. Thus, it would seem more accurate to set the average at six persons, including parents, children, and grand-children.

* See pp. 244–245.
** John Lossing Buck, *Land Utilization in China* (Shanghai, Commercial Press, 1937), "Farm Population."

The number of families in the village is also difficult to estimate. More than ten years ago it was generally believed to be about a hundred but there is no doubt that the number has increased in the last decade. Many large families have broken into three or four separate units. None has moved, but a few may have died out. It seems safe to say that there are now about 120 families in the village. If we take these two estimates, then the number of the village's population should be about 720 people.

The Tsingtao Municipal Government published a census of the municipality for three consecutive years, 1924–1926.* A great part of the environs of Tsingtao is rural. The Hsuehchiatao District, for example, is an agricultural and fishing area at the southwestern side of Kiaochow Bay, close to Taitou. The three years' census shows that the average size of the family in all the medium and large villages in this district is from 5 to 6 persons. This supports both Buck's number (5.21) and our own estimate (6). But we must bear in mind that the number is variable from village to village. In some villages it is less than 5, while in others it is more than 7.

We do not know the birth and death rates, since the villagers do not officially report births or deaths, and nobody, so far, has made any survey of the relative number of male, female, old, and young. However, within the years that the writer can remember, no abnormal condition has occurred in any one of these aspects. This may be due to the fact that the village is still predominantly rural and has not as yet been greatly influenced by any conditions which might upset the old balance. Female infanticide has never existed.

According to the census of the Hsuehchiatao District, in 1926 the population of 3,629 families in 46 villages was 19,236 people; of this number 10,338 were male and 8,898 female (54 percent and 46 percent, respectively, with a male preponderance of 8 percent. In all the villages, except two, the number of women was less than that of men, and in some villages the differences were unbelievably large. There must have been quite a few mistakes in the figures. It is true in this district, as in others, that men are reluctant to report their young women to outsiders. The preliminary data of the census were undoubtedly collected by the district police stations. To many rural people, policemen are strangers, or at least suspicious persons. On the other hand, the police could have known nothing of the purpose of the census. Therefore they would make no effort to persuade the people to tell what they did not want to tell, and

* *Kiao-Ou-Chi* ("Gazette of Tsingtao"), Vol. III, Section 1, on "Population."

consequently a great number of women might not have been reported.

A few families increased significantly and expanded into several new families, while others remained about the same. A Yang family, for instance, had four sons and one daughter, all of whom were married. The first son's wife married at the age of twenty-five and her first child was born after two years of marriage. She had seven children altogether, but two died in infancy. Her last child was born when she was about forty-five years old. If she had married eight years earlier, she might have had three more children than she did. The second son's wife was 23 when he married her and she had her first child two years after marriage also. She is now forty-five years old and has five living children, two having died in infancy. She might have had two or three more children had she married some years earlier. The third son's wife was married at the age of 28 and gave birth to her first child after ten months of marriage. She bore five children altogether, one of whom died. She is now about forty years old. She might have had five or six more children had she married twelve years earlier and had she not been separated from her husband for the last three years. This woman and her husband do not believe in having many children and have practiced birth control. The fourth son's wife married at the age of twenty-three and in ten years of married life has borne four children. The daughter of the family, who married when she was 19, has given birth to seven children, five of whom are living and two of whom died. From the foregoing it would appear that the average fecundity of the women is rather high, though a number of women, because of disease or bad health, bore only a few or no children.

The death rate among children is high, about two out of every six or seven born. The villagers, for the most part, accept this as a matter of course. If a family loses more children, three out of five for example, the neighbors feel that something must be wrong; either the wife has brought bad luck on the family, or the ancestors have committed actions destructive to God and against human principles. If, on the other hand, all the children in a family live to grow up, the mother and the family are considered very fortunate and unusual. The death rate is highest among children under the age of three; it tapers off decidedly between the ages of five to ten. When a young baby dies, the body is not deeply buried and is easily dug up by wild dogs or wolves. When an old woman asks the name of a neighbor's child and is told that the child is ten years old, she will say, "Good, the child is out of the reach of dogs!"—meaning that the danger of death is past.

The average life span of adults is about sixty to seventy years. Women die earlier than men. This may be because they bear children, work hard, and usually have a diet which is inferior to that of the men. When a man of sixty or over is too ill to leave his bed for more than several days at a time, the whole family take it very seriously. But if he is under sixty, they are less concerned since the possibility of death is much less. When a person under forty dies, the death is regarded as very unusual and great grief is shown by both relatives and neighbors. When a person under sixty dies, the death is still considered unusual, but there is less grief because the deceased has grown-up children to continue the family line and to care for the infirm. If the deceased is over sixty, the death is taken as a matter of course, and only close relatives grieve. In case a person lives longer than seventy or eighty years, his death is a relief to relatives and friends. This is especially true if the family is poor and the young people are not filial. Death may also be a happiness because the deceased had lived long and had enjoyed a good life; it is good for him to die before he becomes too old to be liked by the younger generations.

The marriage system in this community as in all other Chinese communities is patrilocal—the woman goes to her husband's home. This is the chief form of population displacement; emigration and immigration are rare. Two families, Wang and Hsueh, who live at the two ends of the village, came to Taitou six or seven decades ago. They are still small and poor families. The father and a son of the Wang family were once popular carpenters in the community and might have been received as full members of it had not the daughter had a liaison with a young man of a neighboring village. Her mother, by permitting it, was considered equally blameworthy. The villagers complained because of the disrepute brought upon their home town by the affair. The father and the son, conscious of the general disfavor, went away, leaving the daughter behind. Later she was married and so the family disappeared from Taitou.

The Hsueh family also had once been favorably regarded. The father served for a time as one of the village officers, but after his death his son did not succeed him, and, because they were poor, the family was again disregarded in community affairs. Years ago, another Hsueh family moved to the village, and built a home in the southwestern outskirts of the residential section. The family is declining. These people are not treated cordially by other villagers and do not have much to do with the other families.

There is a story about the coming of the Tang clan to the village. It is

told that about two hundred years ago two poor Yang brothers lived in
Hsiahocheng, one hundred miles to the southwest of Taitou. The brothers
came to the southeastern part of Kiaohsien as farm laborers. Because they
were honest, diligent, and dependable in many ways they were continuously hired by large farm families, but they were not employed in
the same place. One worked in Hsiaochuang, only half a mile from
Taitou to the west, while the other was in a place ten miles to the northwest of the village. Each of the brothers earned enough to marry and
settle down where they worked. In a hundred years, their descendants
formed large clans. In Hsiaochuang the Yangs were the dominant clan,
numbering 80 or 90 families. The other brother's descendants formed a
village called Yang-chia Shih-liang. (Several villages in the same area were
called Shih-liang, and Yang-chia Shih-liang means the Shih-liang of the
Yangs.) Later, one of the Yang families of Hsiaochuang moved to Taitou
and by now has grown into more than a dozen separate families.

Occasionally a family has moved out of the village. Between two small
hills about half a mile away, there is a hamlet of ten or fifteen families,
the descendants of one or two P'an families who moved there sixty or
seventy years ago. The kinship between them and the P'an clan of Taitou
is still recognized. Several smaller groups in the neighboring mountains
are also descendants of some P'ans who moved out, but they are not
numerous enough to form a village. Another P'an family moved to the
outskirts of a village near Taitou, but it died out because the two sons
never married. The P'an family which moved to a village about two miles
west of Taitou became the most influential clan in the new place.

About fifty years ago a Yang family moved from Taitou to the market
town of Hsinanchen. It was believed that the move was caused by
quarreling among the married brothers and wives. After the separation,
however, relatives and kinsmen continued to make seasonal visits to them
and to give them grain, foodstuffs, and special help. The family died out
some time ago because the son did not get a wife and the parents left no
property.

On the whole the population of Taitou is stable. Families rarely leave
the village. Individuals move about and many of the young people go
to the larger towns to work, but they maintain close ties with their
relatives at home and usually come back to the village, eventually to
settle down. Any population change in Taitou is more apt to be a result
of changing birth or death rates than of shifting population.

Agriculture | 3

I N this area, as in all other parts of the country, the cultivated land has
for long been elaborately partitioned into very small fragments. A
farmer, or a family, does not own one but a number of plots, and these
are generally scattered in a number of localities. Homes are not on the
cultivated land but are in the village. To get to his farm a farmer has to
go to several different places, some of them quite distant. Each field belongs to a different owner and each owner must have some way of reaching his field, so there are numerous roads or paths crossing the land. In
the summer, or during the growing seasons, the land resembles many
small strips of different colors lying side by side.

Even within the environs of a single village, there is a wide range in the
value of the soil. The extreme fragmentation prevents ownership of all
the land of a given quality by one or a few families and thereby reduces
the possibility of complete crop failure for any one family. Since different
land is more or less suited to different crops, a family which has land in
several places can grow various kinds of food, will always get some return
from its land, and, being, therefore, self-sufficient, has less need to trade.
In former times the fields must have been larger. Since a father's holdings
are equally divided among all his sons, there is an endless process of
division and redivision. Another factor which increases the parceling is
the numerous small transactions in buying and selling land. Families buy
small bits of land from their neighbors, but seldom whole fields. It is
impossible to recombine these fragments, for that would require owners
of two or three fields to relinquish them at one time to one person. A
family does not sell land unless it absolutely has to, so that the possibility
of several families having to sell at once would be extremely rare.

The size of the fields varies greatly. The smallest may be only one tenth
of a *mow*,* while the largest may be as much as five *mow* or more. Fields
in the hills and valleys and in the water land are usually small, while those
in the level land are large. In the hilly places many tiny fields are terraced
on the slopes and bottoms. Sometimes these are just little corners—a
plot as large as a *mow* is rare among them. The water land has always been

---

* A *mow* in this area is a little less than a quarter of an acre (4.3 *mow* = 1 acre);
it is one and a half times larger than an official *mow* (240 sq. *pu*), and contains
360 sq. *pu*.

greatly treasured by the villagers, and each small piece is worth a great deal. It has been divided into many plots so that each of the well-to-do families can have one. In the north, west, and east sections of the level land few fields are smaller than one *mow*; most of them are from one to

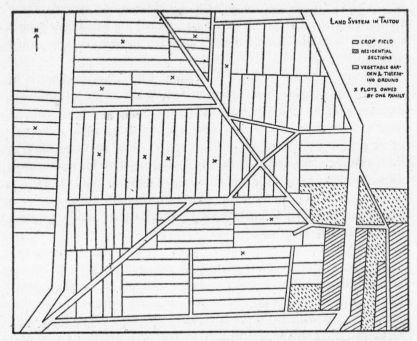

This shows the fragmentation of the crop land which belongs to families of Taitou. The fields marked with X belong to one family. The family has also a number of fields in other sections which are not shown here.

two *mow* with quite a few three-*mow* pieces. Plots as large as four or five *mow* are, as a rule, owned by well-to-do families, or families that were well-to-do not long ago, because only a wealthy family could buy so much land in one time and in one piece. The purchase would be made when a family with large land holdings was in decline. Such opportunities are few. The P'an families in the village tried hard to keep their large fields from being broken up, but the increasing number of their descendants made this impossible and finally most of the large fields were divided into small pieces.

According to Buck,* the average size of the fields throughout the country is half an acre, but in North China, or the wheat region, it is

* J. L. Buck, *Land Utilization in China* (Shanghai, Commercial Press, 1937), Chapter VI, p. 184.

over three times as large as in South China, or the rice region. "[The fields] averaged 0.12 and 0.17 acre for the Southwestern Rice and Rice-Tea Areas, as compared with 1.26 acres for the Spring Wheat Area." The neighborhood of Taitou does not conform to this. Taitou is in the winter-wheat and kaoliang area; as population is much denser here than in the spring-wheat region upon which Buck's figures are based, the fields are bound to be smaller, though they are considerably larger than those in the rice region.

A general summary of the size of family land holdings indicates four main groups: families with thirty to forty *mow*; those with twenty to twenty-nine *mow*; those with ten to nineteen *mow*; and those with holdings of from one to nine *mow*. About ten years ago there were two or three families each of whom had as much as eighty to ninety *mow*, and five or six families who had from fifty to sixty *mow*. In the last decade all these families have either broken into small units, or else been forced to sell their land because of losses inflicted by bandits or because of the extravagance of their children. At present, perhaps no family has a holding greater than forty *mow*.

The main crops are wheat, millet, barley, soybean, corn, sweet potatoes, and peanuts. A variety of vegetables are grown in the gardens: cabbage, turnip, onions, garlic, *chiu-tsai, yuan-sui*, radishes, cucumbers, spinach, several kinds of string beans, squashes, peas, and melons. There are also many kinds of fruit but none of them in quantity. While there are no orchards, one or two fruit trees may be seen on the edges of most of the vegetable gardens.

A great part of the land is good for growing sweet potatoes and peanuts, and the yield in these crops is abundant. Because most of the families own only a very limited quantity of land, they have to grow the crops which are most suited to the soil and which offer the best prospects of a good yield. From June to October, sweet potatoes, peanuts, and soybeans occupy almost 50 to 60 percent of the crop land. Next in importance is millet, to which 30 percent is given, leaving only 10 percent for other crops and vegetables. From November to June of the following year, part of the land is devoted to winter wheat and winter barley and part of it is left fallow. Families with the larger holdings grow more wheat, millet, and soybeans, while the poorer ones have to raise more sweet potatoes and peanuts. Wheat takes a longer time to grow and requires more fertilizer, and the yield is not high, but wheat flour is regarded as one of the best foods. Wealthy families like it and can afford to grow it. It is also a good cash crop. Sweet potatoes grow well in the hilly and sandy soil and do not require much fertilizer, which is an advantage. They are a much more dependable food, both in quantity and nutritive value, than wheat. Therefore, a family without much land has to grow more *mow* of sweet potatoes than other crops. Since peanuts grow well in soil that is not suitable for wheat, they are the main cash crop of the poorer families. Soybeans are important as a cash crop and also for home consumption; all families grow them in large quantities. Millet is also generally grown and is the most important staple for local consumption.

All but a few families have vegetable gardens. Some vegetables are grown in the open fields. Each family grows from one tenth to one half of a *mow* of turnips. String beans and peas are planted between the rows of the crops or at the edges of the field. A few families also raise water and honey melons. On the water land wet rice is grown. The year's harvest of this crop is not of any significance in the village's whole economy, but it is interesting to note that it gives the village some rice culture which is rare for this area.

At the end of August (about the middle of the seventh month on the lunar calendar), right after the millet and soybeans have been harvested, the emptied fields are plowed and left fallow for about a month. Sowing of winter wheat begins at the end of September. Several days before this, well prepared fertilizer is transported to the fields and dumped in heaps. When the sowing starts, three or more people go to the field with a team (an ox and a donkey or an ox and a mule), a plow, a wooden harrow, several fertilizer holders, seeds, and a certain amount of the powder made from soybean cakes. First, the seeds, the soybean powder, and the fertilizer are carefully mixed so that each handful of the mixture will contain the same proportion of seeds and fertilizer. Then, the plowman drives his team along the length of the field to make the furrows. The other two or three men fill the fertilizer holders with the mixture, and, hanging them over their shoulders, follow the course of the plow dropping handfuls of the mixture into the furrows about a foot apart. Each man covers one section of the field. This method takes more time and labor but where human labor is cheap and fertilizer and seeds are scarce, it is the preferred system. When the sowing is finished, the field is leveled with the wooden harrow, which is drawn by the team across the field. Then the furrows disappear, and the fertilizer and the seeds are well overed. In about a week, young shoots emerge from the earth and in a month they become strong enough to endure the cold weather. If the snowfall is heavy, the villagers will expect a good harvest of wheat, but if it is too dry or if there is too much cold rain, the young plants will be severely damaged. Therefore, a heavy snow covering the earth always evokes joy and the celebration of the New Year Festival takes on more warmth and color.

In April when the weather turns warm, the young plants of wheat begin to grow again. Some farmers may weed the fields, but most do not. The growing period of winter wheat lasts a little over two months, that is, from April to the first part of June. On the fifth day of the fifth month, when the winter wheat is ripe, a big festival is held, the *Tuan Wu* Festival.

In this area wheat is not harvested by the sickle. The stalks are pulled out of the ground by the roots and bound in small bundles which are then taken to the threshing ground in wheelbarrows, on animal back, or on human shoulders. The crop is threshed and the grain is dried and stored. The threshing is done by animal and human labor, with the help of simple tools. Threshing time is the first time in the year that women work out of doors. Less work is required for growing wheat than is needed for other crops, but the capital outlay is high, the soil must be fertile, and the yield is not satisfactory.

The cultivation of millet is begun in the early spring. As soon as the weather is warm, the fallow fields in which the sweet potatoes or peanuts were grown last year are plowed up or softened with a harrow. Spring plowing should not be too deep. After this, prepared fertilizer is carried to the fields. At the beginning of May when the earth has been warmed through, the millet is sown. This is very like wheat sowing, but, because the soil is soft in spring and because the young shoots will need more solid earth for support, the fields are pressed down with a stone roller after the sowing. A farmer who has no stone roller tramples the ground with his feet.

After a week or so, if the weather is favorable, the small young leaves of the crop appear just above the ground. In another week, they are young shoots; and in still another week they are about three inches high. At this time the difficult work begins. The crowded young plants must be thinned out to give them space to grow freely. This can only be done by hand with the aid of a small hoe and, consequently, it is slow and tiresome work. Differentiating healthy plants from weak ones or from the young grass must be done by experienced farmers. About a week or ten days later, the weeds are cleared out and earth is packed around the bottom of the plants so that they can stand up. This is repeated in another ten days or two weeks, and again a third and a fourth time—the more weeding the better for the crop. From the time the seeds sprout until the harvesting the farmers need not spend much time in their millet fields except what is required for pulling out the diseased or insect-ridden plants.

In this part of the country millet and kindred grains ripen in late August. Millet is harvested as wheat is. Women, especially young girls, cut the seed-heads from the stalks with pieces of sharpened iron when the crop is gathered on the threshing ground. All the women, young and old, work at this time, and girls may even work for other families and thus earn a little money for themselves. The threshing and stoning of the grain is also participated in by the women.

Peanuts are sown at almost the same time as millet, the beginning of May. Peanuts are usually alternated with sweet potatoes in the same fields. The fields are plowed and fertilized again, and carefully selected peanut seeds, which have been nurtured at home, are soaked in warm water for a while and then left in a warm place for a couple of days; when small buds appear the seeds are ready for sowing. The fertilizer is first applied in the furrows and then the seeds, about three at a time, are laid on top of the fertilizer. This is usually done by children. The field is leveled and hardened with a stone roller and is made so flat that when the young plant appears, solid pieces of earth cling to it. The first weeding is done when the tender leaves spread out and the young vines begin to extend. The second weeding comes after about fifteen days and, if the weeds grow fast, a third weeding may be needed. The field should be moist and soft from this time on so that the "needles" on which the peanut shells grow can easily penetrate the soil. When the shells have grown up and the kernels are forming, which takes about one and one-half months, dry weather is desirable, for if the ground is too wet the shells will rot. The farmers know this, and therefore they always grow this crop in hilly fields with a sandy soil.

Peanuts are harvested at the end of October. This work is so laborious, that, if peanuts were not a source of money and the vines the main source of animal feed, the crop might have been abandoned long ago. Formerly, the vines were cut and removed from the field, which was then plowed and the earth broken into a fine powder containing the peanut shells. When shaken into a sieve, made of a wooden frame and woven iron wire, the earth would fall through and the shells remain in the sieve. This method was abandoned about twenty years ago because it was too laborious. Today the whole thing is done with one tool, a hoe, and needs the labor of just one person, but the work requires much greater effort.

The farmer swings the hoe over his head and brings it down forcibly on the ground around the plant. This he does two or three times, breaking up the earth so that the entire plant can be lifted out, the shells still clinging to the roots. Any shells left in the ground are then picked up. The entire harvest is really accomplished by prolonged physical exertion. It is not even possible for several people to work together to shorten the task or to make the work less strenuous.

Women and children pick the shells off the vines, some of the girls hiring out for this kind of work. Also, girls go over the fields to pick up the remaining shells. In one day a diligent girl can collect as much as 20 or 30 pounds, which is worth a dollar or more. In ten days she can earn ten to fifteen dollars. This money will belong to her, not to the family as a whole. If the oil-pressing shops start work at this time, a girl has another chance to earn some money by working in the shops breaking the shells.

Of all the agricultural work done by these people, the cultivation of sweet potatoes is the hardest. In April the farmer begins to select, from among the fresh sweet potatoes which he has stored up during the past winter, the best ones for seed. These he buries in wet sand on a warm brick bed. After ten days or two weeks, young buds appear on the skins of the seeds. The buds put forth shoots in a short time and by now the weather is warm enough for the seeds to be planted in the vegetable garden. They are set out in rows in a nursery bed and heavy fertilizer is applied. When the young shoots grow into vines and start spreading on the ground, the nursery must be kept wet all the time.

After the wheat is harvested, the empty field is immediately prepared for the sweet potato plants. The field is plowed, and small, parallel ridges are built up. These ridges must be soft and smooth at the top. If the farmer has any fertilizer for this crop, it will be applied underneath these ridges, but usually he does not have any. Meanwhile, the farmer's wife and children are busy at home cutting the long vines in the nursery into short sections, which are then bound into bundles and carried to the field in baskets. The experienced father plants the vine sections on top of the ridges. At the same time the elder son or the hired laborer carries water by pail from a river, a pool, or a well which may be close by. The younger daughter and son pour about a pint of water into each of the small holes in which the vines have just been planted. The mother and the elder daughter fill the holes with earth, so that the whole vine section is covered except for one leaf which must be left outside. In a week, if the weather is favorable, buds come out and develop into new vines. The weeding starts then and after a few days the vines must be weeded continuously. During the rainy season when the ground is wet, small roots come out all over the long vines. They must not be allowed to grow into the soil. So, the farmer's sons turn the vines from one side of the ridge to the other after every rain. If the furrows become too small because of the frequent washings of the rapid rain, the ground between the ridges is plowed and new earth applied to the tops to protect the sweet potatoes.

Sweet potatoes are harvested at the same time the peanuts are—in October, the busiest season for the farmers of Taitou. The vines are cut, usually by the younger boy. Then the father and the elder son come to the field with hoes, baskets, wheelbarrow, and donkey. They dig sweet potatoes very much as they dig peanuts. The younger boy collects the harvest into two big baskets which are tied on the wheelbarrow. The sweet potatoes are either taken home and stored for the winter, or they are moved into another open field for processing. This is largely women's work. In the field, the daughters begin to clean the sweet potatoes and the mother prepares a small table on the ground. She cuts the clean sweet potatoes with the cutter. Thin, round slices drop down through the hole underneath the cutter into a basket. These are spread on the ground and left to dry in the sunshine. After the midday meal, which the women prepare and eat at home and the men eat in the field, the work goes on. The women stop earlier to prepare the evening meal but the men continue to dig till it is too dark to see. On the way home, everybody is tired, with sore back, stiff legs, and burning hands, but they are cheerful because the harvest is good. One of the sons must sleep in a temporary shelter built where the sweet-potato slices are drying. Another son sleeps in a hut on the threshing ground, so that he can watch the peanuts stored there and the cabbages in the adjacent garden. It takes about two weeks for the work in the field to be done.

The family spends more and more time on the threshing ground and in the vegetable garden. The harvest has now been collected from the fields and piled on the ground and must be prepared for storing. Every day the large heap of peanuts that have not yet been sold must be spread out when the sun is warm and piled up after sunset lest they rot. The sweet-potato slices must be taken care of in the same way. The dried vines of the two crops have to be chopped up with grass and stored for feed for the ox and the donkey. Cabbage and other vegetables are harvested and stored or processed. When the threshing ground is again clear, the small hut that was built only for the busy season is torn down and the materials are taken home.

The cultivation of soybeans is comparatively simple. Sowing begins immediately after the harvesting of wheat and barley. The farmer simply sows the seeds in the furrows, without having to plow the land beforehand. The seeds are dropped by a boy who follows the plow. Then the field is leveled by a wooden harrow and the seeds are covered. No fertilizer is used unless the farmer has a surplus, for it is not absolutely necessary. After three or five days, if the soil is wet enough, the young sprouts appear on the ground. The field is first weeded when the plant has three leaves and is given a second weeding within fifteen days. Rain and hot weather are needed now. When the bean shells have formed and are half-filled, the ground should not be wet and, therefore, too much rain is not desirable. When the shells are full and the beans become solid, the harvesting begins. The farmer and his elder son cut the plants with their sickles just above the ground and then transport the harvest on the back of the donkey or in the wheelbarrow to the threshing ground. Women do not participate in this at all.

It is interesting to note that within a considerable area only this village raises rice. The method of rice cultivation here is somewhat different from that seen in the rice-growing region. Our farmers do not sow the seeds first in a nursery and, consequently, they do not replant the young shoots, but simply sow the seeds directly in the field. In April or May when the water is warm and shallow, farmers plow the land by turning over a thick layer of the soil with an iron spade. The surface of the soil is warmed, small holes are dug in it and the rice seeds are sown. After several days the young shoots come out. Our farmers never irrigate their rice. Rice is considered a superior food in the village because it is so scarce. If a poor boy is asked what food he likes best, the answer always is bread of wheat flour, white rice, and pork cooked with cabbage.

Every family has a vegetable garden, no matter how small, and from early spring to winter it is in use. Since the garden is small, it is always intensively cultivated, fertilized, and watered. The harvest from a vegetable garden can usually meet a single family's needs. A great part of the cabbages raised in the garden is preserved for the winter. Turnips and string beans are also stored but a part of them may be sold in the market town. The cultivation of turnips is also much more intensive than that of other field crops. The young plants must be thinned several times and a number of weedings are needed before the ground is completely covered

is full, the contents are removed, not directly to the field out of the village, but to a place just before the front door or to the sidewalks of the streets. If rain comes before it is piled up and covered, the whole street becomes a mess of dirt. Another dangerous thing is the direct application of urine and manure to vegetables. To the farmer these are not serious objections. On the contrary, he is proud of having a large pit of dirt with three or four pigs playing in it, for this represents the prosperity of the family and helps him secure good wives for his sons. Besides, the villagers do not spend much time on matters which do not have direct reference to the economy of the family.

Recently, the Mass Education Association in Tinghsien, Hopei, made some effort to improve the condition of the privy in the farmer's home, and the universities of Cheeloo and Yenching tried to find ways of preventing it from being a source of disease in the summer. They have also tried to kill the insect germs in manure before it is used as fertilizer. An attempt was made to increase the quantity of fertilizer by mixing a certain amount of straw, earth, and greens with the manure. These efforts have brought some results, but the situation remains largely unchanged.

Oxen, mules, and donkeys are the customary farm animals. The donkey is the cheapest of these and even a family with only ten *mow* of land has a donkey. If a family owns fifteen *mow*, a small cow joins the donkey to form a team; a family with twenty *mow* can have a donkey and a large ox; a family with more than forty *mow* can have a donkey, a large ox, and a mule. A family owning less than ten *mow* cannot afford any animal and must either work without one or cooperate with a more fortunate neighbor by exchanging labor for the use of his animal.

Oxen are chiefly used for plowing and sowing, and seldom for pulling wheelbarrows or drawing the millstones. After plowing or sowing an ox remains in the barn, under the shade of the willow trees, or in the sunshine near a wall. Mules are used more frequently—for transporting harvested crops from the field to the threshing ground, pulling the millstones when the donkey is too tired, or for riding to other villages on visits.

Practically every family has a donkey. They are used for every kind of transportation and in many ways in domestic work. Housewives of the village do not often touch the ox, and never try to handle a mule, but they can control donkeys like pets. The absence of a donkey would not only hinder the small farmer in his field, but his wife at home as well.

Although agriculture is the main means of livelihood, many subsidiary occupations supplement income in the slack periods of the farm work calendar. For example, a little foundry was established by two brothers of the P'an family in Taitou. They had previously worked in a machine shop in Tsingtao and the n 'iods used in their own business were modern, although simple. Hav---ₒ made a handsome profit, the family bought several *mow* of land and built two or three better houses. The brothers receive orders for metal implements used on the farm not only from fellow villagers but also from the people of other villages in the vicinity. Once they cast a bell for the village church, which preferred to patronize a local shop.

There is also a woodworking shop where one carpenter and an apprentice make furniture parts, plain doors and windows, and a number of simple farm implements. In addition to filling villagers' orders they produce goods to be sold in the market town. There are other carpenters who do not own shops but who work in the homes of their customers. A carpenter can earn much more than a farmer. He receives both board and money, and his wage is higher than a farm laborer's. The fact that very few follow this trade, despite its pecuniary advantages, indicates the importance of farm work in the villagers' eyes and their obvious preference for it.

There are three or four cloth weavers. One of them once bought an improved loom and opened a workshop. There he worked for himself and sold his products in the market town or in other villages. Unfortunately, he had to stop because he was short of capital and also because he could not work steadily at it. All the other weavers have only old looms and their rate of production is very low. Recently they have been forced to compete with factory-made cloth which comes in to the country in daily increasing quantities. Young people prefer the fine cloth whenever they can afford it, though the old people still believe that homespun is much better—they say it lasts longer and is better-suited to rough farm work. The importation of cloth has resulted in an interesting compromise between the old and young. Many families have given up the traditional spinning of yarn from raw cotton and now they buy the factory-made cotton yarns in the market town and weave it into cloth at home. This cloth still preserves, to a great extent, the old pattern because it is woven on the old looms. The young people are temporarily satisfied with it because they cannot often afford the new relatively expensive cloth. For the time being they accept the compromise. Their elders console themselves by listening to the sound of the old loom and by seeing the familiar patterns emerge from it, taking comfort in the thought that the old traditions still exist and that the world has not yet gone to the devil. They are much concerned, however, about a new problem created by the situation—how to keep their daughters occupied during the long spring, now that they do not have to spin.

A few years ago three families owned oil-pressing shops. In the winter and spring they pressed oil from the locally raised peanuts and soybeans. One of them also opened a shop for making the baskets used as containers for shipping oil to Tsingtao. It was a profitable business and for some time supplied work for ten or more people; but, recently, due to bandit raids and heavy taxes, all the shops have been closed. They still have their equipment, however, so that when order is reestablished they may resume work.

There are five or six masons who build houses for the villagers and for people of neighboring villages. Some of them also work periodically in Tsingtao. Their earnings are as good as the carpenters' and several families whose sons are masons have attained a better standing in the community.

It is interesting to note that all these craftsmen are members of poor families. Some have bettered the family status, others have kept their relatives from starvation. Only the oil-pressing shops were owned by members of wealthy families. But we see that nonetheless very few are engaged in industry. What the local people value most is land: big land holdings and a prosperous farm are to them the real signs of prosperity and this is why no rural industry has ever developed into a business of any significance. Necessity is the only incentive, or at least it is the main one, for taking up any means of livelihood other than farming.

None of the artisans in this village makes his living entirely from his trade, with the exception of the preacher of the Christian church and the teacher of the Christian school. All the masons, carpenters, weavers, workers in the small foundry, the village schoolteacher, the crop watcher, and the several village officers work on their land with their families during the sowing and harvesting seasons or whenever they happen not to be engaged in their professional work. All artisans work for wages only part of which consists of money, the rest being in meals and, occasionally, lodging.

Independent trade ventures attract the ambitious young men. In the winter, or whenever they are not occupied on the farm, they may collect eggs and poultry, or vegetables to sell in Tsingtao, thus making a modest gain. Some go to the cities and purchase things used at the New Year celebration, or other seasonally needed goods, which they resell on special market days at a small profit. Three or four men are regular traders and make frequent buying trips to Tsingtao and neighboring market towns. Their earnings are used by their families to improve the homes or farms or to buy more land.

Fishing is not a regular occupation but is a minor source of income for women, some of whom go to the sea while the tide is receding to dig for shellfish which they sell to the villagers or to the seafood traders in the market town. An experienced woman may derive a fair income in this way. In a slack summer, young men also fish. They do not sell their catches but contribute them to the family larder.

In the winter when farmers have little to do on the farm, they collect wood or other kinds of fuel on the near-by hills. If a man is diligent, he can collect enough for the entire winter and early spring. It helps the family very much.

There are two kinds of hired farm laborers, the yearly or permanent, and the daily or temporary, laborer. Hired farm workers may also be classified according to skill and experience both in agriculture and domestic work. Some are chief laborers or farm overseers, while those who are unskilled, or have just started to work on the farm, are assistant laborers. A yearly laborer is not necessarily one who works throughout the entire year. Usually his term of employment runs from the sixteenth day of the first month on the lunar calendar up to the first day of the tenth month. Daily laborers are hired chiefly in the busy seasons, when sowing, hoeing, and harvesting have to be done. Families who have yearly laborers may also hire daily laborers for a few days to get the work done on time. During this period a group of able-bodied men carrying hoes or sickles and wearing straw raincoats and rain hats wait every morning at a corner of the main street in the market town to be hired. This is called locally the "market of laborers." Any farm family who needs help sends someone there to hire a man. There are no established rates, but usually the rate of the first engagement is maintained. The people who come to the market for employment are for the most part poor farmers from the area who take care of their own small farms, working on them either before or after the busy season, or at night when they return home. Sometimes a family asks a poorer neighbor to help. In this case they do not go to the labor market but they still follow the market rate. This may become a more or less permanent relationship between the two families. The poorer family may borrow animals, seeds, or implements from the richer one without payment, or the richer family may just send its team to plow the other's land. The wife and children of the poorer family will help on the threshing ground or in the home of the richer one when they are needed.

The engagement of a yearly laborer is usually made in the winter through a go-between. As soon as the matter is settled, the parents of the would-be laborer may ask the employer to pay them a part of their son's wage. If the arrangement is to be continued for the coming year, the laborer must be informed through the go-between before he leaves the work and his wage is decided upon at that time. On the other hand, if either or both do not want to continue, both parties must be informed before the date of departure. Besides the money wage, a yearly laborer also receives some compensation in kind; in this village the rule is two *sheng* (about sixteen pounds) of wheat, ten feet of cloth or an ordinary suit, a straw raincoat and a straw rain hat, all the tobacco that he can consume, and some food at the New Year Festival. Occasionally, a little money is given to him when he is allowed to visit a village opera or to attend the annual fairs in the market town. A hired laborer's board and room are supplied by the employer.

The hired men and the family members who also work in the field at this time usually have their breakfast and midday meal in the field. Several special meals are given a laborer throughout the working year. The first is a dinner of welcome on his first day at work. The so-called rejoicing feast occurs on the second day of the second month. A third is the *Ching-Ming* Feast, at the beginning of the third month. Then comes the *Tuan-Wu* Feast on the fifth day of the fifth month. There are also special meals in both the sixth and the seventh months. After these, the biggest one, the *Chung-Chiu* Feast, occurs on the fifteenth day of the eighth month. In the ninth month there are a number of unusual meals because the season is specially busy. The last is the farewell dinner given on the first day of the tenth month. The working year is now over and the hired men are leaving. If they have been retained for the coming year, the dinner will be more lavish.

On three occasions the meals are regular feasts, according to local custom; these are the *Ching-Ming* Feast, the *Tuan-Wu* Feast, and the *Chung-Chiu* Feast. In each of these a number of meats, eggs, fresh fish and seafood, green vegetables, and locally made whiskey are served. Generally, every family must show its hired men that it has done for them all that its economic ability permits. Otherwise, the laborers complain and broadcast the fact that the family is stingy, which would make it difficult for them to get people to work on their farms. On these three occasions, the farm hands are treated as guests; the head of the family pours wine for them and begs them to eat as much as they can. There is a common belief that to feed the hired men well is one of the prerequisites for the success of a family's farm management.

In a small family a hired man may sleep in the same room with an unmarried son; he may have a room of his own, or he may live in the small hut on the threshing ground. In a well-to-do family special quarters are built for the hired help. The rooms are simply furnished, the occupants themselves take care of them. Women are not allowed to come to such quarters. The laborers are not allowed to take along their wives, but they may visit their families several times during the year.

Relations between the family members and the hired laborers are generally congenial. Change in economic status is frequent, so that in the same generation a family who has been hiring laborers may come to the point of hiring their own members out to others. On the other hand, a number of families who were poor may become relatively well-to-do. Since mobility of this kind is great, one family cannot feel superior or inferior to another. Moreover, most of the hired men come from families who own land, though it may be but a small piece, and as long as a family owns even an inch of land they consider themselves on a par with their fellow villagers. A comparatively well-to-do family may have a son working for a neighboring family or for one in a neighboring village. This family may have, say, ten *mow* of land. Since the father, mother, and one son can take care of the land by themselves, the other son is able to work for others. By diligence and thrift small pieces of land may be added every year, so that the family is respected in the community, and no one would look down upon a hired laborer from such a family. All the hired laborers are either from the same village or from villages in the same area. The families know each other. Workers and owners all follow the same occupation and work together in the fields. All these factors tend to minimize distinctions between wage-earners and employers. But recently the situation has been changing. More disputes arise; laborers demand higher wages and better meals. The employers try voluntarily or involuntarily, to meet these demands, but they complain that it is very difficult to handle hired laborers in these days. It is not easy to make a fair judgment as to which side is right and which is wrong. The situation as a whole is unfortunate because the rising price of labor is not due to a natural shortage but to social and political chaos. Since the outbreak of civil war, with the attendant increase in banditry and local upheaval, many young people have abandoned the old tradition and have become restless. Some have joined the bandits, others have entered the militia employed by ambitious local chieftains, and others have simply disappeared.

Standard of Living	**4**

THE population of Taitou can be divided roughly into four classes on the basis of food consumption. At the lowest level is the group for whom sweet potatoes are the main item of diet; next are those who have a combination of sweet potatoes and millet; third, those who eat millet and wheat; and at the top, those who eat mainly wheat. All classes eat garden vegetables in large quantities when these are available. The first two groups rarely have animal products of any kind; the last two have them only occasionally.*

Among the poor, sweet potatoes are eaten at every meal every day throughout the year. From harvest time until the spring of the following year, they eat fresh sweet potatoes; when these are gone, they eat the stored dry slices. These are boiled, or ground into meal which is mixed with other flour to make bread or noodles. Supplementing the potatoes are, first, a kind of gruel made of barley flour and peanut powder; second, a kind of hash made of chopped turnips and soybean juice; and third, one or two kinds of pickles. Occasionally some kind of bread is served.

During the busy season food is more plentiful. Steamed millet or millet bread takes the place of sweet-potato slices, and green vegetables cooked with fat are added to the diet. On a poor family's table, meat, fresh fish, or eggs are seen only on special occasions, when guests are entertained, or for the New Year celebration. Soybean oil, peanut oil, are used in cooking, and in richer households, pork fat. A poor woman tastes sugar only when she delivers a child.

As the economic condition of a family improves, the diet is supplemented. Millet, barley, soybeans, wheat, and other kinds of cereal are added to the sweet potatoes. Food consumption varies with the seasons. In winter and early spring, when work in the field is light, foods made of sweet potatoes are important in every meal. But as soon as men get busy, the quality of the food is gradually improved. A morning meal for men, including family members and hired laborers, would consist of a combination of steamed bread made of millet and soybean powder, boiled

* "The Chinese diet comes almost entirely from vegetarian sources, in contrast to the American diet with its large percentage of calories from animal products." J. L. Buck, *Land Utilization in China* (Shanghai, Commercial Press, 1937), Chapter XIV, p. 414.

sweet potatoes, barley gruel, turnip and soybean hash, salted fish, and one or two kinds of pickle; for the noon meal, steamed millet bread, steamed wheat bread, a dish of green vegetables cooked with fat, gruel of millet and rice, salted fish, and pickles. The evening meal is similar to that served in the morning. During the wheat harvesting, the noon meal is still better: more wheat bread is served; a stew of pork and green vegetables is frequently enjoyed; wheat-flour noodles are eaten every day; salted fish and pickles are continuously supplied.

After this season, however, the consumption of wheat flour is limited and the use of other cereals increased. Green vegetables, especially beans, are consumed in large quantities, because the vegetable garden is full of greens and they also grow on the edges of fields and between the rows of millet plants. The harvests of these vegetables cannot be wholly consumed, and therefore, great proportions of them are sold to the dealers in the market town or preserved for the winter and early spring. When sweet potatoes and peanuts are harvested, the busiest time of the year, the diet of a well-to-do family is better than at any time except during the New Year celebration or at special feasts. The food is both plentiful and varied—more pork and beef, more wheat flour, and cabbages are added to the menu. Everybody is well fed, even the beggars look healthy. But as soon as the fields and threshing ground are cleared up and the hired laborers are gone, the diet is again restricted until the coming of the New Year season.

For a period of about three months, that is, from the tenth month to the last part of the twelfth, the food consists of sweet potatoes, peanuts, barley, soybeans, turnips, and cabbages. These are all nutritious, but the people suffer from the lack of calories and the monotony of the diet. The villagers show an especially great longing for better food in the winter and early spring. This is temporarily relieved by the coming of the New Year celebration, when most of the families enjoy better food for ten or fifteen days. Protein consumption is high, and besides this, much more fat, and large quantities of bean curd, of wheat and other flour, of cabbage and better vegetables are consumed.

The diet of the few wealthy families is, for the most part, similar to that of the average families during the busy seasons. The only superiority lies in the fact that the wealthy family has the better food throughout the year. Their New Year feast may be especially elaborate, but there is no marked difference at other times, except when guests are entertained. During the farming season both rich and middle families have hired laborers, and if they did not offer equally ample meals, labor trouble might arise. A family may deny certain food to the children and women in order to satisfy the laborers.

Because wheat flour is the preferred food, a number of social practices center around it. When a marriage is arranged, for example, the most important gift presented by the boy's family is a number of big steamed rolls made of pure wheat flour, each weighing two catties (about three pounds). On top of the roll is pasted the Chinese word "happiness," cut from a piece of red paper. The girl's family distributes some of the rolls to relatives, friends, and neighbors, thus formally announcing the engagement, and returns the rest to the boy's family to be distributed among their relatives and friends.

At the wedding, relatives, friends, and neighbors offer gifts of wheat-flour rolls to the groom's family; about thirty or forty are the expected allotment. These rolls are smaller than those presented by the groom's family to the bride's parents, but they are beautifully decorated and unless they are made of refined wheat flour the donor is sharply criticized. The groom's family invites the wedding guests to "come to enjoy our noodles," because noodles of fine wheat flour are the food prepared for informal gatherings of familiar guests.

A group of poor villagers speaking of a Christian preacher, a school-teacher, or a businessman from the market town, will say: "He is a man who eats wheat flour every day, why should he not have a smooth face!" When a person has a run of good luck, his fellow villagers might say: "Just as meat is always served with wheat flour rolls." A successful man is compared by the villagers to winter wheat, which is superior to other cereals because it survives the severest winter weather. So a person who has achieved success and fortune through hardship and self-denial is compared to wheat and admired by all who know him.

Nien-chu, a gruel made of barley and soybean powder, is an indispensable item in the villagers' diet and the source of many common sayings. Should a person risk his family's property in some speculative venture, his friends warn him by saying, "Are you going to give up your *nien-chu kuo?*" (*Kuo* means boiler.) If a person is about to give up a job, he will say to his friends, "I'm not going to hold this poor *nien-chu wan* any longer." (*Wan* means bowl.) When a person dies, people say, "He's dead; he won't drink *nien-chu* any more!"

The people of the whole area under discussion have long been identified by outsiders as sweet-potato eaters. They find it insulting to be so addressed, since the sweet potato is the food of poor people, but they realize how dependent they are upon this crop. There are many special techniques for the processing of sweet potatoes. Although women are not often required to work in the field, the cutting of sweet potatoes is done largely by them; in fact, skill in this work is one of the special qualifications for a daughter-in-law. A particular type of cutter is used exclusively for this processing. Part of the crop is always dried and stored. In every home one will find that in several of the bedrooms there are stages or platforms suspended about four feet above the brick beds. These are used mainly for the preserving of sweet potatoes. The materials and the space needed for the construction of the platforms must be taken into account when the house is planned. Outside masons and carpenters, unused to village ways, often get into trouble over this.

Another general practice is the preserving of green vegetables. In the summer when string beans are abundant, one sees boiled string beans hung up to dry in the sunshine. They will not be eaten until the following spring when green vegetables are scarce. When turnips are abundant, or when they start rotting in storage, some of them will be sliced, boiled, and dried, and kept for the time when the food supply is low.

Considerable quantities of vegetables are salted in the autumn for winter use. Every home has two or three big jars of salted vegetables and pickles. In the late spring when swordfish are numerous in the sea, the farmers usually buy and salt them in considerable quantity. However, meat is never salted, since no families can afford much meat. Whenever it is needed, it can be bought fresh in the market town or in the butcher's shop in a neighboring village. Hogs are raised for fertilizer, rather than for meat. Even if a farmer does kill his pig at home, most of the meat is sold and only the inferior parts are consumed by his family.

The celebration of the New Year on the lunar calendar is more important to the Chinese than the celebration of Christmas to the Western people. Many kinds of special foods are prepared in advance for it. From the beginning of the twelfth month all the women in the village are busy grinding wheat and other cereals to make the holiday cakes, wheat flour rolls, vegetable balls, and bean curd. A certain kind of cake is so large that it takes two adults to lift one. The cakes are made from two kinds of glutinous millet, boiled sweet potatoes, and yeast. When these ingredients have been mixed and fermented, the dough is put into a big round container and steamed in a deep boiler. When the cake is done, it is about six inches thick and two and a half feet in diameter. It is cut into a number of square pieces and stored until the celebration. A small family makes only one such cake, a well-to-do family makes two, while a large and rich family makes three or four. The preparation of these cakes is regarded as an important undertaking, especially by the children, for it heralds the coming of the New Year. Because they are so large, much skill and experience are actually required in making them, and the outcome is a matter of great concern to the whole family. In fact, it is so important that myths have developed for insuring success. When the raw cake is fixed into the boiler and the steaming has begun, all the people in the family must remain quiet and do their work in a neat and orderly fashion. Youngsters are not allowed to go out or to come in, but must be unobtrusive. The front door is closed and locked, for visitors are not welcome at this time. The person who takes care of feeding the fire in the stove is the one who has had the most experience in this regard—usually the head of the family. A stick of incense is burned beside the boiler to check the time needed for the steaming; but, because incense burning in China, especially among the farmers, has a religious or mysterious connotation, this custom is also regarded as a way of praising the kitchen god so that he will guarantee the success of the .cooking. If the cake does not turn out well, the family will say that someone, sent by an evil god, must have come knocking at the door during the steaming. If a stranger arrives at this time, he will most certainly be accused of being a devil come to spoil their fortune, or, if he is someone from the neighborhood, the family will become suspicious of him and assume that he has evil intentions, and the intrusion may give rise to a quarrel between the two families.

A considerable quantity of bean curd is made in the New Year season. This is a complicated process requiring the cooperation of several neighbors, whose help is especially needed to operate the quern. Soybeans are broken into small pieces, soaked until soft, and then milled in a quern into a white mash. Water is added, the mixture is heated in a large boiler, and is then poured into a cloth bag. The bag is pressed on a board to extract the juice. This is poured into another boiler, cooked again, and then put into a big porcelain jar in which sea water, or some chemical acid, is added to curdle it. The addition of just the proper amount of sea water to produce curds of the right consistency requires much skill and experience. After the curds have formed, the mixture is again put into a cloth bag and pressed, after which it is ready for the final cooking. The residue from the final pressing is stored for pig food.

A special type of wheat flour rolls are made for the New Year season. Mashed sweet potatoes are mixed in the dough and boiled chestnuts and sugar are used for stuffing. The smaller rolls, made primarily for children, are decorated with sweet red dates, to symbolize happiness coming soon. *Tsao*, the word for "date" is pronounced like the word for "early." Chestnuts are called *litze*, the first syllable of which is similar to the word for "favorable," while the second syllable is the same as the word for "son." Thus chestnuts symbolize "the easy birth of sons," the greatest happiness for a Chinese family.

The most representative of the New Year foods is *chiao-tze*.* This is a kind of ravioli, and, being both expensive and difficult to make, it figures on the dining table only on rare occasions. It is made in great quantities for the New Year celebration, because this is the most important feast of all. The best parts of cabbages and pork are chopped together. To this mixture soybean sauce, sesame oil, ginger powder, chopped onions, and salt are added. The cabbage should be squeezed—not too hard—before it is mixed with the pork. The dough can be made either of pure wheat flour or of a mixture of flours, depending upon the resources of the family, but at least some pure wheat flour must be used, or the spirits of the ancestors will not be pleased when the food is offered them. The dough is rolled, cut, and pressed into small round pieces about one sixteenth of an inch thick and two and a half inches in diameter. A soupspoonful of the mixture of cabbage and pork is dropped into each piece, which is then folded into a half-moon and carefully sealed to prevent opening in the steam or boiling water. A relatively large quantity of water is boiled and the raw *chiao-tze* dropped into it, care being taken that the pieces are not broken or stuck together. After ten or fifteen minutes, when the water is boiling again, the *chiao-tze* floats on the upper part of the boiler and are gently stirred until they are done. The head of the family tastes one or two, during the cooking, and when he pronounces himself satisfied, they are done.

Housing reflects, to a marked extent, the economic status of a family. There are exceptions however. One of the Yang families, for instance, has more houses than it can use, and every house is in good condition, but the family has very little land and was, for a while, on the verge of starvation. Some decades ago, when the good houses were built, the family was well-to-do, but the income was depleted by some of its older members and almost all the land was sold. The houses were not. In the

* See pp. 75, 93, 94.

last ten years, the young generation began to work hard and live frugally, and the position improved. Now they not only can keep their houses but have begun to buy land again. On the other hand, another Yang family possesses sufficient land and produces a surplus every year, but it has only two houses, one of which is very small and in poor condition. Generally, however, houses are a very accurate index, for people are much concerned with them and build or repair as opportunity permits.

The houses of Taitou can be classified roughly into three types. Those of the wealthiest group are built of stone, burned bricks, lime, and a good grade of wood and roofing material. A stone foundation is laid underground and rises aboveground about six inches. Upon this foundation are built the walls. The lower part of the walls, about four feet high, is built of stone blocks. The blocks used on the front wall are well cut in squares or oblongs; for the back wall irregularly shaped stones are used. Above the lower part is a layer of burned brick. From here on, the wall is constructed of small stones or beaten earth with a layer of lime plastered on the outside. This is topped with an arched wooden roof covered with thatch. The inner side of the wall is set with small, unpolished stones.

The houses of the average income group are constructed in the same way except that the materials used are inferior. The stone is not as well worked, fewer bricks are used; the framework of the roof is not as strong and the wooden pieces may be crooked. The houses of the poor are small, made of inferior materials, and not regularly shaped. They are simply huts. Little stone is used in building them, bricks and lime are not used at all. The wooden pieces are merely the unfinished branches of small crooked pine trees. The walls are of beaten earth, sun-dried bricks, or *kaoliang* stalks, and the roofs are thatched with a thin layer of straw, which is not proof against the wind and rain.

The main house, or the north house, called the *cheng wu*, is usually composed of three to five rooms, while the house on the left or right side of the court generally contains two or three rooms. The width of a main house in the wealthy first group may measure about twelve feet; the length varies greatly. The floors in all kinds of houses are of beaten earth. The walls are papered. The windows are pasted over with thin white paper (sometimes oiled), which usually admits sufficient light and sunshine. The rooms are crowded by the big brick beds and wooden beds, the tables, bureaus, cabinets, and numerous personal belongings. As the kitchen is connected with the bedrooms and the stoves are attached to the tunnels inside the brick beds, the house is kept warm in the winter,

Fig. 1. The front wall of a good house

1. Stone foundation; upper part
2. Lower part of wall, large, oblong, surfaced with stones
3. Middle line, built of bricks
4. Upper part of wall, small stones surfaced with lime
5. Big front window with wooden frame
6. Top of wall, two layers of bricks

Fig. 2. End wall on the street side of a good house

1. Stone foundation; upper part
2. Main part of the wall; well-worked large stones
3. Top line, built of bricks
4. The gable, small stones surfaced with lime

Fig. 3. The back wall of a good house

1. Stone foundation; upper part
2. Lower part of the wall; large, irregularly shaped stones
3. Middle line, built of bricks
4. Upper part of wall; small unpolished stones or beaten earth surfaced with lime
5. Small window with wooden frame
6. Top of wall; two layers of bricks

Fig. 4. Thatched roof with tiled "dragon-bone," or lung-ku

a Side view   b End view

Fig. 5. Wooden framework of the roof of a good house

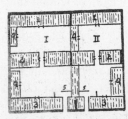

Fig. 6. I, II: Two homes of upper-class families

1. Main house, or cheng-wu, where the parents, the unmarried daughters, and the first married son live
2. Middle house, or ch'ien-wu, where the second married son or other junior members live
3. Front house, or nan-wu, where hired laborers live; also for house & farm implements
4. Small houses for keeping the domestic animals and for installing the quern
5. Spirit wall, or yung-pei

Fig. 7. Ground plan of a main house

I Reception room, dining room, and kitchen
II Parents' bedroom (also the dining room and reception room in winter)
III Married son's bedroom
IV Unmarried daughter's bedroom
1. Stove with fixed boiler
2. Dining table (also a ceremonial table at the New Year Festival)
3. Cabinets for dishes and kitchen utensils
4. The warm brick-bed, or hweh-k'ang
5. The wooden bed
6. Dressing table
7. Trunks and suitcases

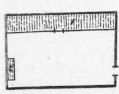

Fig. 8. The home of a poor family

1 The living quarters consisting of three (or two) rooms
2 A small hut for farm implements

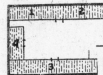

Fig. 9. The home of a middle-class family

1, 2 Bedrooms of family members
3 Rooms for hired laborer and farm implements, also granary
4 Shed for the family's animals and the quern

but in the summer it sometimes becomes insufferably hot. Temporary kitchens may then be built in the court or in an empty house.

In the house of a well-to-do family one or two rooms are specially furnished and kept for guests. An average family, however, uses the parents' bedroom as a guest room. Guests are almost always relatives so that there is no embarrassment on either side. The parents' bedroom also serves as the dining room for the whole family and their guests in the winter. The large brick bed is covered with a thick layer of straw above which a neat, smooth mat of stripped skins of *kaoliang* stalks is laid. During the winter when the nights are long and it is cold outside, the family usually gathers in the parents' bedroom to work or talk. Neighbors also come and sit on the same bed. Thus, the parents' bedroom is really the center of family life.

A married son and his young wife live in the room across from the kitchen. The door of this room is always kept closed, for the interior should not be seen by the father or by any man who is not of the family. The grown-up daughters always live in the room back of the parents' room so that no one can enter it except by first passing through the parents' room. When male guests or male neighbors are present, the daughters of the house must leave their room beforehand or remain there quietly until the guests or neighbors have gone. Grown-up children do not sleep in the same room as their parents. If the family has enough houses, there is no difficulty in assigning separate rooms to the children, but if they do not, the grown-up boys may sleep at a neighbor's or with the hired laborers. Grown-up girls may live together in one room. A married son must have his own room. The father of a family that had a two-room house went to sleep in a neighbor's barn when his son was married. Fortunately, he had but one son.

The earth floor of the houses is always dusty, and when it is swept the dust flies about the room. Sometimes water is used to moisten the floor before sweeping, and though this helps, it is not enough. Under the tables, under the wooden beds and bureaus, odds and ends accumulate and heavy layers of dust form. Mothers let their infant children urinate or soil the floor. Because the rooms are crowded, there is not enough fresh air. A pottery bucket is placed in every bedroom for night use. In the winter, when all the windows are carefully pasted over with paper and the doors closed, the air is very foul, especially in the morning. Only when the weather is fine and the doors can be left open is the odor somewhat dissipated.

The open privies are a great threat to the farmers' health. In the summer they attract flies, which then light on the food, for there is no adequate way of keeping food covered. In some families the mother insists that all the rooms be kept clean, and the father will not tolerate a dirty courtyard or a mess in the barn or storing rooms. The privy is built in a far corner of the court and is covered, thereby reducing the number of flies. The windows, all of which open to the south, are frequently repapered so that they are kept clean and light, and sunshine can permeate the rooms. The farmers of Taitou—and this is true in many other villages—insist that all beverages be boiled and all food cooked. They drink fresh water from a spring or clear stream only when they are far away from home. A few vegetables are eaten raw, but they are first carefully washed. These practices reduce the health hazards, but do not constitute adequate protection.

Most of the houses built in the last ten years are of the type formerly owned only by the wealthy. This is due not so much to increased prosperity as to the fact that the present generation like to display what they have and enjoy the comforts which they can afford, rather than save up all their money to buy additional land as their grandparents did. The new houses have framed ceilings and are papered with patterned papers bought in Tsingtao. Windows are still made of paper. Five years ago, a Yang family built a new house and had, at that time, considered the use of glass windows, but the idea was given up because of the conservatism of the eldest brother and his wife.

The farmer's work garments are made mainly of cotton. Silk trousers are worn by quite a few villagers in the summer, but this silk is raised locally and spun at home and is a coarse but very lasting material. In July and August a number of middle-aged wives of the well-to-do families wear linen jackets when working. A number of villagers also possess fur coats or jackets and wear them when they go to the market town or when no manual work has to be done. Wool is used only in winter shoes, winter caps, and winter bed sheets. A few of the well-to-do families have woolen clothes but do not wear them very often and never for work.

The dress garments of men are also made chiefly of cotton cloth. Women of the more prosperous families have dresses of good silk and fine cloth. So far, none of the men in the village have worn a silk gown or jacket on any occasion, but this does not mean they never possess one. It is quite certain that the few rich villagers must have dress garments of silk. Quite a few young wives have silk bedding. Two kinds of silk cloth are used by the rural people. The first, called *tuan-tze*, is a heavy, patterned fabric. *Tuan* is pronounced like the Chinese word for "cut," or "break," and *tze* means son or offspring; so the word is suggestive of harm to the child and has an unlucky connotation. Therefore *tuan-tze* is never used for a bride's dresses or bedding, nor is it used to clothe a dying parent. On the other hand, *chow-tze*, the name of a thinner silk, is a very lucky term. *Chow* is similar to the Chinese word "many," "crowded," and "thick," and suggests numerous children.

A farmer may have two or three suits of work garments. Cotton-padded jackets and trousers are worn in cold weather. In the spring and autumn the farmer wears a lined jacket and the cotton padding is removed from the trousers. For the summer he has two or three coats and several pairs of trousers. These coats are worn in the winter as underwear, and the same trousers are again padded with cotton. Boys and girls have practically the same wardrobe. Socks for men and boys are all made of cloth at home; the women, of course, do not wear stockings because their feet are bound with cloth. Girls who have been educated in the new schools wear homemade or factory-made stockings. The cloth shoes are mostly homemade. Formerly, shoe soles were made of pieces of old cloth pasted together and sewed with linen strings; now, however, many of them are made of pigskin. It is interesting to note that scrapped tires have come to be widely used for shoe soles in the villages. Formerly an important qualification of a prospective daughter-in-law was the ability to make shoes for her husband and his whole family, but girls no longer take this seriously, as the skill is not required. The farmer now buys his own and his family's shoes, and the homemade ones are disappearing. This change is frequently deplored by the old mothers and fathers, who object to the expense and believe that boughten shoes do not last as long. Besides, they think that the grown-up daughters and the young daughters-in-law are spoiled because they do not have to make shoes for their men.

Everyone has one or two suits of dress clothes. Young people's dress garments are usually better made and more fashionable than those of their elders. For the New Year celebration, weddings, or formal visiting, the better dress garments are worn. For ordinary occasions, work garments newly washed and pressed are worn. A man's ceremonial dress garment consists of a long gown and a jacket made of fine cloth. A woman's is a skirt and jacket made of fine cloth or silk. Ordinarily a woman wears only a pair of trousers and a jacket, and no skirt. A woman's jacket, whether it is a dress or a work garment must be five inches below her hips and must hang loosely, for if she wears short, tight jackets she will be sharply criticized and suspected of wanting to attract men.

Color is important. Girls, young women, and brides are allowed to wear bright colors—red, pink, purple, or green; the accepted color for grown-up men and middle-aged women is blue. No man under thirty should wear white shirts, and no man under fifty, white trousers. For middle-aged people, cotton-padded trousers may be white but cotton-padded jackets must not be. Dress garments are usually colored. The long gown is always blue and the jacket black. A woman never wears white unless she is in deep mourning. Men's shoes and caps are always black. Women's shoes are red, pink, or green when they are young, but black when they have passed middle age. Women do not wear hats.

Styles in clothing are changing, and with them the ways of making them. Formerly, cotton bars were bought in the market town. Girls spun the cotton into thread during the winter on old-fashioned spinning wheels. It was tiresome work indeed, and tears and complaints must have been spun into the long strands. Late in the spring a village weaver would be invited to the homes of the villagers to weave the thread into cloth. An average family might keep a weaver for fifteen days or more, not because the family had so much to weave, but because the weaving went so slowly. In midsummer an itinerant dyer would come to the village, collect the cloth for dyeing, and return it after a few days. The mother, or the family head, then divided the dyed and undyed cloth equally among the married sons and grown-up daughters. Then the sons' wives and the daughters would wash, starch, and press their share of the cloth and also that of their parents and their unmarried brothers. After this, it would all be carefully put away, for at this time of the year there was too much to be done in the field and at home to leave time for sewing. But as soon as the busy time was over, women began to make and repair the clothes and bedding of their families. By the end of September, all that was needed for the winter had to be finished. The making of special garments for the New Year celebration, however, was a task for the winter months.

Since the development of Tsingtao, this procedure has gradually changed. As a first step, young women were permitted to buy factory-made and machine-dyed cloth from itinerant cloth traders or in the market town. Later, the farmer stopped buying raw cotton and instead purchased the thread that had been made in the cotton mills of Tsingtao, thus relieving his daughters of a great deal of work. The cloth woven at home of this thread was in the old pattern, but the quality was much improved. Another change was the recent introduction of improved looms on which cloth of greater breadth can be made. The new looms are expensive and have not as yet replaced the old ones, which are still widely used in the village. Factory-made cloth is definitely on the increase; by now, almost all young women's clothes, young men's dress garments and children's dresses are made of it and only men's work garments are still made of home-woven cloth. It is doubtful that the old techniques of weaving will continue much longer, for the habit of buying ready-made goods is overcoming the old preferences for home manufacture. This applies particularly to those things that have customarily been made by the younger people. The resistance of the older generation is not proof against the young people's dislike for the laborious methods. This is to some extent a source of conflict within the household.

The Components
of a Family

5

A CHINESE family, especially in rural China, is far more than a group of related individuals. In Taitou, as well as in other villages, it is a complex organization of family members, family property, domestic animals, family reputations, family traditions, and family gods. It can be said that the family extends to the as yet unborn generations and to the long-deceased ones. The living traditionally believe that their ancestors' spirits, whether in the ancestral graves or in Heaven, are with them and are keeping watchful eyes upon them at all times. A family's fortune or misfortune is largely controlled by spirits of the ancestors. When the spirits are pleased, the family will receive blessings; but when they have been antagonized, disaster inevitably comes. They must be invited to participate in all special occasions, such as festivals, weddings, and births, and homage must be paid to them at their graves, in the ancestral halls, or before the ceremonial tables of the family. This sense of kinship is strongest at the New Year Festival, a time when the living feel their ancestors to be actually with them.

A great part of the household activities is regulated by the invisible power of the ancestors. A Chinese family, or an individual, does many things which are primarily designed to please the ancestral spirits. One studies hard, for example, to advance in the official scale in order to glorify one's ancestors; on the other hand, one does not want to be a beggar, a thief, or a prostitute, because that would bring disgrace to them. The belief in the unbroken continuity of the family is manifest in the behavior of the descendants and the bond between the generations is never broken. It is a well-known fact that the Chinese always make great efforts to protect their ancestors' graveyards, ancestral halls, and the ceremonial tables, because these things represent their ancestors' spirits, and, as such, are a real and living part of the family.

The importance of the future generations can be seen by the anxiety of the parents to see their sons married, and to accumulate property for their children. With this in mind they work hard and live thriftily so that they can save some capital for the prospective children. They feel guilty when unusually good food is eaten or extra money is spent, not because they cannot afford these things, but because they want to have something to leave to their descendants. A family may have enough houses for all its members to live in, but they keep on buying and building new ones and acquiring land for the future generations. On New Year's Eve, or on other special occasions, family members not only invite their ancestors but also observe rites to symbolize the birth of additional children. Just as the authority of the dead figures in the decisions of the living, the rights of the unborn determine the composition and well-being of the families of which they will become part.

Land is the most important form of property, for it belongs to all the generations. It means much more than a piece of earth on which crops are cultivated; it is the very foundation of the family. Without land a family can never be settled and the family members will never have a sense of security. People and land are the two pillars of the Chinese farm family. When we say a family is broken, we mean that the family's land is gone. Thus, land becomes a part of the life of the farmer and his family, and they have a very deep sense of attachment to it; their land is no less dear to them than are their children. In the village a family's status depends very much on the amount of land owned, for this indicates to others how much the family cares for its past and future obligations and how faithfully these are observed. Land ownership also gives the farm family independent personality, spiritual inspiration, and a feeling of freedom.

In the Chinese language there is no difference between the words for "family" and "home." The same word stands for both—people living under the same roof, for a group of people is not a family unless they have a permanent house, one which they own. We have mentioned before that, in the village, families of different social status have houses representative of these differences. A well-built and well-kept house always wins regard, for it is an index of the family cooperation. The roofs neatly thatched, the walls carefully repaired and protected with lime, the doors and windows properly set and continuously painted or pasted, all indicate the importance of the family to its own members. An affianced girl's parents want to know what the house of the boy's family looks like, for they judge the family from it. Though some families are really better-off than their houses may indicate, this is unusual and people feel, if this is true, that there must be something wrong with the family.

Implements and tools are also important. They were made or probably purchased by the family's ancestors and were subsequently used and handed down through several generations. Good tools are too expensive to be owned by every family so they are symbols of prosperity. Often they are lent to other village families, thereby creating or cementing friendly relationships. The tool is associated with the family in the minds of the villagers, and thus to the family who owns it, it becomes very important.

Domestic animals are an important part of the farm life. In Taitou, these are chiefly oxen, mules, donkeys, dogs, cats, pigs, and chickens. The first four are considered as part of the family and are accorded special treatment. The farmer is most attached to his ox. The feeling is so strong that he may feel worse about the loss of his ox than he would about the death of his infant child, for the loss of the animal endangers the life of the whole family. The slaughter of oxen is condemned by all. There is no law or social custom to forbid the professional butchering of oxen, it is true, but everybody looks down upon anyone who practices it. People believe that no one could become rich in such a business, that the soul of a butcher will be condemned eternally to hell, and that his offspring, if he has any at all, will always be poor and weak. A farmer usually keeps his cow or ox as long as possible. If one day, for some reason, he is forced to sell his animal, there is great sadness in the family. When the farmer turns his animal over to the buyer and sees it being led away, he may shed tears. For one or two days at least the family will maintain silence at the dinner table and the situation will not be relieved until a new cow is purchased. A farmer will not sell his animal directly to a butcher, even when he is offered a high price. Instead he will seek a good buyer for his ox with as much care as if he were looking for a good husband for his daughter. If he finds that his ox has been purchased for slaughter, he will curse himself and the buyer and the latter's ancestors.

The absence of beef in religious sacrifices, ceremonial festivals, and formal dinners is further evidence of this attitude. On market day one can find hundreds of slaughtered pigs for sale but only one or two cows. The price of beef is always lower than that of pork, and this is a direct outcome of the aversion to slaughtering the cattle. It would be insulting, or at least improper, to offer beef to a guest at an honorable dinner, and so general is this feeling that even scarcity does not raise the price.

On the hill about a mile and a half south of the village, there is a shrine known as the "Temple of the King of Cattle." In the sixth month of the lunar calendar, one day is marked as the birthday of the King of

Cattle and every family which owns an ox or a cow has a special meal in celebration of it. Simple sacrifices are prepared and offered in the shrine or at some place facing it, outside the village. The birthday of cattle is also celebrated on a day at the beginning of the year, when special feed is given them.

There is a legend about the building of the "Temple of the King of Cattle." A long time ago all the cattle of the village were pastured together on the hill and attended by one herdsman who was hired by the whole village. One day while the herd was grazing on the hill, a cow clambered up a pile of huge rocks and, when evening came, was unable to get down. All other measures having failed, the villagers made a sacrifice and prayed in front of the pile of stones. Thereupon the owners of the cattle were informed through a spiritual agent that the King of Cattle wanted a residence to be built in the district. This was immediately promised by the villagers and thereupon the sacred cow descended from the pile of stones. The local people built a shrine where the cow stood. This legend is not only an attempt to explain the beginning of the peasant cult of cattle, it also reveals the fact that the village had a common hill for pasture once, and that the cattle owned by the villagers were herded collectively. This is further verified by the name of a road leading from the village to the hill where the shrine stands. The first section of this road is named *Kan New Kou* or, literally, "Drive-Cattle-Creek," meaning a path on which cattle were driven back and forth between the village and the hill.

The quality of the ox also reflects the social status of a family. By noting the size of the ox tied to a tree before the front door, one can estimate about how many *mow* of land the family owns and to what class it belongs in the village. For this reason, a large and well-fed ox is always a source of great pride to its owner, and will be tied, for all to see, to the front door or at a place where people walk or gather. During the summer days many fine oxen can be seen standing under the big willow trees along the river bank at the southern end of the village, which is the favorite gathering place of the villagers. Recently, most of them have been either hidden in backyards or sold, because of the threat of bandits and the decline of the well-to-do families.

It is often said that when a marriage is being arranged between two families, the girl's family secretly send out people to investigate the economic condition of the boy's family. Among other things, the investigators are to see whether or not the latter's family has a cow or an ox and. if so, how large it is. It is also said that if the family are very anxious to see the marriage completed but have no cow or ox, they borrow one from a neighbor and tie it up before the front door until the matter is settled.

A mule is not indispensable on the farm or at home, but is kept primarily for the pride of the family, or for personal pleasure—not for work. In buying a mule much skill and taste are shown. The animal is always . well fed and well cared for, and its reins and saddle are elaborately decorated. It is always tended by the male members of the family—not by hired laborers or women. A mule is used in the harvesting, in the New Year season, and whenever someone pays a visit to relatives or goes to town. A well-to-do family usually has a mule and one or two donkeys for transporting the crops from the fields to the threshing ground. The mule is decorated with a chain of bells around its neck, so that its approach is heralded for a considerable distance. A little parade is formed on the country road by the mule, two donkeys, and the handsome grandsons of the family, who hold the reins of the beasts. They are regarded with great pride by the boys' family and envied by every farmer who sees them, but especially by the farmers' wives, if they are ambitious enough. Perhaps a farmer's young daughter will be bothered by many rosy dreams about the young men, for she cannot but be overcome by the sight of them with their beautiful animals.

It is rather strange that the villagers of Taitou have no sentimental associations with the donkey despite its importance for work at home and on the farm and for transportation. No customs, legends, or cults have developed around it. The poor animal doesn't even have a birthday in the family. However, it does play a significant role in local agriculture, and therefore it receives as much attention from its master as the other animals do.

Dogs are thought to be useful animals, rather than pets. A dog actually plays no significant role at home or on the farm, but as a watchdog it fills a definite function and it is also useful in announcing the approach of guests. Dogs are given a good deal of consideration. It is as reprehensible to mistreat a dog as to mistreat a child or a weak person. If one beats a dog without sufficient reason, one is insulting or attacking the family who owns the animal. A common saying goes: "When you are going to beat a dog, you had better consider the 'face' of the animal's master. If one does not punish a neighbor's child, one should not punish a neighbor's dog." If the animal is always underfed and left to wander about

the streets, the family will be sharply criticized. The dog is treated like
a member of the family. He can go into the house and even into the
bedrooms; he is permitted to lie down under the table in the kitchen
or in the dining room; he is the playmate of the children, especially the
boys. When the men go to the field, the dog always follows close behind.
At night, the family's safety depends upon the animal's watchfulness.

The intangible components of a family are also important, and the
most highly regarded of these is reputation. A family wants to be admired
and talked about by people of a neighborhood or of a considerable territory. This is a great source of pride to families of the middle and upper
classes who are generally much concerned with what people think of
them. There are five ways of achieving reputation, and the first of these
is to have members in ranking official positions. If one of the family, for
example, is a county magistrate, villagers and others will refer to the
family as the *Hsien-chang chia*, or the magistrate's family, and will
show great respect to its members. As the official position rises, the family's fame climbs with it.

Scholastic fame comes from having a member in the family who has
passed the academic examinations. In the old days, if one of the family
passed the first Imperial Examination, the family was known as a *hsiou-
ts'ai chia.** Although a *hsiou-ts'ai* was not important, nevertheless on
special occasions the family was distinguished by the title from plain
farmers. If a scholar advanced and passed the second examination, then
he was a *chiu-jen*, or a *kung-sheng*, and the family could place a pair of
flag poles before the front door to indicate that it was a family of *chiu-jen*,
or family of a *kung-sheng*, both of which were respectful terms. Since
the flag poles were the most distinctive symbols in the countryside, the
family would also be commonly called *chi-kan-ti-hsia*, or "family-beside-
the-flag-poles."

Since most of the villagers believe that farming is the most dependable
and desirable means of livelihood, a family is proud of having plenty
of land and many sons who are eagerly cultivating the land. A family
which is devoted to agriculture, and has also some scholastic attainment,
is the ideal family in the countryside, and usually referred to as a family
of farm and study.

---

* In the imperial system, *hsiou-ts'ai* was the first or lowest degree; *chiu-jen* the
second; *chin-shih*, the third; and *chuang-yuan*, the last and best. When the new educational system was first established, conservative people made equivalence between
the old and the new: graduation from a higher primary school was equal to the
degree of *hsiou-ts'ai*; from a high school equal to *chin-jen*; from a university equal
to *chin-shih*; a Ph.D. degree was equal to *chuang-yuan*.

No family of Taitou had won both of these distinctions in the past thirty years. None of the villagers occupied an official position above that of a *chwang-chang*, nor had any of them passed the first Imperial Examination. Although a member of the Yang clan graduated from a university some years ago, his family has not as yet enjoyed much fame from his academic achievement, because the villagers were unable until recently to understand the significance of the new school system. No flag poles were planted before the family's front door, and so there was nothing which differentiated the family from the others. A Yang family of a neighboring village formerly had a member who held the degree of *kung-sheng*, and, therefore, the flag poles were set up. Although the scholar died years ago and the flag poles have long been gone, the family is still referred to as Yang *kung-sheng chia*, or *chi-kan-ti-hsia*, and has been respected in the village for several generations for this distinction.

Family fame is also built on wealth. If a family is rich, it will be known over a wide area. Thus, our villagers usually say: "Don't say you are rich. If you see Pashan Wang chia [a Wang family in Pashan], or Wangtai Chuang Ho-ch'ang chia [a family named Chuang Ho-ch'ang in Wangtai], or Tsimo Lee Ping-ho chia [a family named Lee Ping-ho in Tsimo], you will then realize that your small fortune is just a drop in a great sea." In the past thirty years, there have been no Taitou families as wealthy as these. But there were some which could be considered wealthy if compared only with the rest of the village. Five of them were known by special terms indicative of status: *nan ta men*, or South Great Gate; *pei ta men*, North Great Gate; and *shih shu yuan*, or Garden of Persimmon Trees. These were all grand terms because they meant that the families had large residences. *Ta men* means a great gate; any home with a great gate must be a large residence, and any family with a large residence must be a wealthy one. The great gates were the most distinctive feature of the two families, and because they were opposite each other, facing north and south, respectively, one was called *pei ta men* and the other *nan ta men*. In a farm village no ordinary family can have a garden, except it be in addition to the small plot of land for growing vegetables, but this family who owned the *Shih Shu Yuan* had a large garden with flowers and trees. When families were known not only by clan name, but also by such descriptive terms, its members felt great pride.

A wealthy family in the village was called *Tung Yu-fang*, or East Oil Shop, because the family had an oil-pressing shop. Another wealthy family also manufactured oil, but to avoid confusion was not called *Tung Yu-*

fang but *Fu-ch'ang*, Fortune and Prosperity, after its business name. All the members of the second family had pleasant personalities and were on good terms with their fellow villagers, so *Fu-ch'ang* was for a long time a popular name in the conversation of the local people.

Wealth alone cannot build up family fame. A family may be known as a wealthy one, but not necessarily as one worthy of respect. Two additional factors are needed: first, some distinctive and gracious feature which sets it apart from its neighbors; and, second, a certain degree of socialization which makes it a pleasant topic for discussion. We have mentioned that if a rich family isolates itself from the other villagers it is regarded simply as a *tu ts'ai-chu*, meaning a person of wealth but no culture. Possessing a distinctive feature is also insufficient. Each of two families has a big sophora tree before its front door. One is wealthy and in good standing with most people of the community, while the other family is ordinary. The villagers refer to the first as *Ta Hwai-shu Chia*, or a family-beside-the-big-sophora-tree; everyone knows to which family the term applies.

Conspicuous virtue also enhances a family's reputation. A family may become well known because it has an unusually filial son or an especially good daughter-in-law, or because all its members are so good that the big household has been able to hang together for four or more generations. Filial piety and feminine loyalty are the two most treasured virtues. Although no family in Taitou is famous for such virtue as the historical Great Filial Pieties, we do have several families which are, or have been, admired by the villagers because the sons are especially filial, and we also have several who owe their development and prosperity to their loyal and capable daughters-in-law.

A family known as a good neighbor has amicable relations with most of the people in the village. If they are pleasant, mild mannered, and honest, they will be well liked, even if they are not distinguished in other ways. Such people always give way to others. Thus, all the villagers like to do business with them and will speak well of them at social gatherings. There are several families with such a reputation in Taitou. The Yang family is one of them and then there is a P'an family which has four sons, the first son being the teacher of the village school. The family with the title of *Fu-ch'ang* was also regarded as a good neighbor some years ago. A number of others are considered agreeable but not to such a degree as to merit this special designation.

Family reputation is a basic social value. Not many families have been able to achieve it, nor can it be maintained forever, or even, usually, for as long as a century. The difficulty of achieving and maintaining such prestige is that the *Taoist*-minded Chinese disapprove of it. They cite families who had proud and prosperous mansions one or two hundred years ago. "Aren't they now only piles of broken bricks and fallen walls?" they say. "Family fame or clan honor is nothing but the dew of the early morning, or a cloud on the dry sky."

Special gods, distinct from the ancestral spirits, are worshiped by the family as a whole. The kitchen god is seen in every household. In addition, some families believe in fox-spirits. Others believe, because their grain is always abundant, that there is a god in their granaries which will be their family god. Other gods, such as Buddha, the God of Earth, the God of Heaven, and Jesus Christ are believed to be gods of a village (the God of Earth), of a community (the Kwan-yin), or of all mankind (Jesus Christ), but the family gods are the special protectors of individual families who alone have the right to worship them.

Intrafamilial Relationships | 6

THE real core of family life lies in the behavior of the individual members toward one another. Marriage and descent are its foundations and determine its most important interrelationships. Within the family circle the individual develops his personal attitudes, a self-evaluation and interpretation of his place in the larger society, and a sense of the significance of his relations with people outside the family.

Since marriage in an old-fashioned Chinese family is arranged by the parents, and since the two young people do not know each other before the wedding, the problem of adjustment for the newly married couple is a difficult one. They do not have their own home, but live with the husband's family. Although the couple often achieve a genuine affection for each other after a brief period of living together, they must not let their love be apparent and the husband, if he is to be considered a filial son and a good brother, must maintain closer relations with his family than with his wife. A young husband must not mention his wife too often; he must not praise her in family gatherings or to the villagers; if she passes by when he is with other persons, he must not speak to her unless either one or the other has an urgent message. When a husband returns from a trip he must greet his parents and his brothers and his sisters before he greets his wife. Only after several hours have elapsed may he excuse himself and join his wife in their room, and that only on the pretext that he must clean up and change his clothes. Although he may be most anxious to be with his beloved one, and his family (especially his mother and sisters) understand this perfectly, he must nonetheless affect indifference.

A young wife must also keep from showing that she loves her husband. The general attitude is that a decent wife should love her husband, but must not let her love spoil his career or make him neglect his duty to his family. A good wife stays at her work with her mother-in-law or sisters-in-law during the day, and at night she must wait until all the family members have retired before she can go to her room and be with her husband. She should avoid sitting with her husband at social gatherings and should act as if she does not know him. She, too, must avoid referring frequently to him, or when it is necessary for her to do so, she should not use his name nor say "my husband," but instead use the pronoun "he." In speaking to her younger brother-in-law, or younger sister-in-law, she may refer to her husband as "your No. x brother." When her husband returns home from a prolonged trip, she does not greet him. Instead she prepares hot water and a meal for him, according to her mother-in-law's order. However, every member in the family knows that, after his mother, she is the one who is happiest at his return. The younger sister-in-law may tease her and this she will secretly enjoy.

A newly married wife cannot but feel lonesome and strange, because she is really in a strange home with strange people. The sudden separation from her mother, the stern face of her mother-in-law, the pretended dignity of the father-in-law, and above all, her sudden introduction to the continuous housework, all make her feel that she is completely at the mercy of these people. Since she cannot go back to her mother, the only one from whom she can seek protection is her husband. She will generally respond with great warmth and gratitude if she is well received by him. It is true that the husband has been hardened by the heavy work, by the rude country life, and in many cases by his never-joking father. But, on the other hand, he is just a fully grown adolescent who has not been permitted to be alone with any grown-up girl before. Now he has a wife to whom he can express his romantic ideals and reveal his love. For these reasons the young people usually become much attached to one another.

The partners of an unsuccessful marriage are in an unhappy plight. Divorce is out of the question: they must make the best of it. Outwardly they may seem no different from any other couple. They will not quarrel openly; the husband will not beat his wife; she does her work dutifully. However, it is easy to note that the loved wife is active, cheerful, and energetic, while the unhappy wife is listless and slow in her work. Although a newly married couple must put on a show of indifference in the presence of others, a keen observer can soon discern whether the indifference is pretended, as in the case of a happy couple, or real. The indifference of the ill-mated pair continues even in the privacy of their room. The husband goes to bed with a great sigh; the wife can only weep in secret and swallow her tears into her stomach. The husband will not approach her unless driven to do so, and she will be merely permissive. The two live together and have children, but their marriage is a gloomy one.

However, if an initially unhappy marriage survives at all, if the hopelessness and sorrow and burden of work do not break down the unhappy wife, the relationship between the couple improves with time. A woman who survives these hardships without committing suicide or breaking down becomes a heroine in the eyes of her relatives. She has proved that she has patience, far-sightedness, and unusual wisdom and kindness. As the couple grow older and their children reach maturity, their feelings toward each other mellow. Husband and wife can now sit together and talk more freely at family gatherings; they can walk together in public. The husband can joke at the expense of his wife in the presence of other people, even before the father-in-law, and the wife can also offer some humorous counterattack. In referring to each other in conversation, they no longer use the pronouns "he" and "she," but say "child's father" or "child's mother." If the name of their first child, for example, is Lien-pao, then the wife would say to her mother-in-law: "Lien-pao's Daddy said that."

In privacy, romantic love decreases, while the feeling of companionship grows stronger. In their bedroom the wife will tell her husband what has happened in the household during the day and what she thinks about their problems. She will also talk to him about their children. The husband tells her about the crops in the field, the work of his brothers and the hired laborers, and so on. Because of his consciousness of being a man, a filial son, a good brother, and a dignified husband, he is supposed not to listen to, or at least not to believe, his wife's complaints about other household members. In spite of this he frequently accepts her statements, and secretly acts on her suggestions and advice on other matters.

As the husband and wife mature, they come to have their own home and undivided authority over their children. The companionship ripens and is no longer kept secret but becomes the foundation of the newly independent family. The wife now becomes the undisputed head of the home. Arranging the children's marriages falls to her. The husband oversees the farm and deals with all matters pertaining to it, but since there is no clear-cut demarcation between domestic and farm affairs, and since cooperation and mutual advice between husband and wife is well-established in practice, this division occasions no real separation. According to a Confucian idea, the husband and wife relationship in this period is "Husband leads and wife follows." But in practice the wife may play the leading part while the husband follows, depending upon which is the more capable in this matter or that. The wife may become more eager to take on responsibility, but this does not mean that her respect for her husband diminishes, or that she does not acknowledge him as head of the family.

When a couple reaches the age of fifty or sixty, the wife generally becomes the dominant person in the household. She is now the mother-in-law of one, two, or even four daughters-in-law. She is the grandmother of a long line of children and is also the overseer of a large household. The middle-aged sons have almost invariably developed strong attachment to their mother but not to their father. The father's authority in the fields, now that he does not work there, is considerably lessened. He has lost his role in business transactions because he is too old to take the farm products to the market town and deal directly with the dealers. To a certain extent, his importance in relations with the neighbors is diminished, because people find that he is no longer the real authority and that his position as family head is more nominal than real, although he is still respected by all the household. His wife must see to it that he is well fed, well clothed, and well cared for. He preserves also the privilege of venting his anger upon any member of the family, except his daughters-in-law. Nevertheless, he sometimes recognizes his real position, and this may make him envy his wife. He may show this in quarrels which will elicit soothing words and apologies from her, but the real situation will remain unchanged.

After the sons and their families have departed to establish independent homes, relations between the old couple may undergo still another change. The wife now loses all her authority and is on equal terms with the husband. They may have a common feeling of neglect, and a need to look to each other for real sympathy and understanding. They thus reestablish the earlier companionship, except that where it was positive, creative, and had the achievement of a prosperous household as a mutual concern, it is now self-pitying and negative.

The relationship between father and child has none of the warmth and freedom existing between mother and child. The father's attitude is dignified, even remote; his authority is unquestioned and he expects submissiveness from his sons. Although in a farm family some informalities are permitted—as, joking in the presence of one's parents, taking a place of equal importance to that occupied by one's father, not rising when the father approaches—yet the father and son relationship is far from free or intimate. When the son is an infant, the father may on rare occasions play with him or take him out. When the boy is old enough to help in the fields, father and son walk together and work together quite often. But by the time the boy reaches the age of fifteen, the father assumes a more dignified attitude toward him and is frequently severe. The son feels uncomfortable with his father and prefers to work with other men in the fields. When father and son do work together, they have nothing to say, and even at home they speak only when there is business to discuss. At street gatherings or in places of amusement, they mutually avoid each other.

The relationship between mother and son, on the other hand, is comparatively close. Although a boy who reaches the age of ten is dependent entirely upon his father's authority and teaching, this does not interfere with his intimacy with his mother. Because of the lack of female companions and the meager possibilities for recreation, a young man spends much time talking to his mother during his formative years. After supper, when the father is absent and she is busy with the household chores, he talks with her freely of the things which concern him and even tells her if he is perhaps getting interested in his *ku-chia piao-mei*, the daughter of his father's sister. The mother may also use this opportunity to tell her son that she is arranging for his marriage and ask him if it is all right. He may make detailed inquiries about the girl, or he may insist that his *ku-chia piao-mei* is the girl he likes best and that his mother should arrange so that he can marry her. At this time the son may also complain of his father's harshness or confide that he would like to learn some trade other than farming, or that he would like to continue study. In her turn, the mother may tell him what she and his father think of him. A son at this time has no one, except his mother, to whom he can tell his thoughts freely, and this provides an unshakable foundation for the long-lasting mother-son relationship.

The affection between mother and son is threatened when the son marries. If the mother is selfish or narrow-minded, as many mothers are, she will become jealous of the young wife. Not a few of the difficulties between mother-in-law and daughter-in-law are unconsciously based on such jealousy. A common saying has it that "A son is lost when he is married." Should the marriage prove unsuccessful, the son may blame his mother because he holds her responsible for the match. A reasonable mother, who is happy to see her son and daughter-in-law getting along well, helps to preserve the original relationship between herself and her son. On the other hand, if he does not prolong his romantic indulgence but is mature enough to appreciate his parents' efforts on behalf of the household, he comes back to his mother the sooner. This does not mean that he deserts his wife, but simply that he resumes the talks with his mother that were interrupted during the early years of his marriage. If the daughter-in-law is reasonable and far-sighted, she does not oppose this intimacy, but rather attempts to strengthen the bond between herself and her mother-in-law and seeks opportunity for family talks, persuading her husband to join them. If these three cooperate, then, the mother-son relationship will resume its former intimacy after ten years or so. When the son and his wife are middle-aged parents, the mother-son relationship comes to include the son's family. In the winter, when the men are not busy in the fields and supper is usually finished earlier, sons, wives, and grandchildren will gather in the old mother's room and the grandmother will play with her youngest grandchildren, while the wives and older grandchildren and the sons talk about what they have seen and heard outside. The father may take part in this gathering if he likes, but he usually keeps himself aloof in order to maintain his patriarchal status. If he attempts to disrupt the free atmosphere, he will be chased out by his old wife.

Legally, the son is the head of the household after his father is dead, and the mother is under his authority. A woman's position is defined in a local saying, "At her parents' home she obeys her father; after marriage, her husband; when he dies, her son." When land or a house is sold, it is done in the name of the first son, the mother only being asked to vouch for it. The deed is worded as follows: "Seller, Wang Chuan-chia, with his mother's permission and through the medium of Chang Yuan-ch'ang and Ch'en Kao-fa, sells a piece of land of five *mow* [the locality and the four neighboring fields are indicated] to Lee Lien-pang at the negotiated price of fifteen hundred dollars. . . ." These legalized relations are seldom realized by the people in general and do not figure in everyday life. It is only when controversies arise regarding family property or the continuity of family line that the legal aspects are discussed by relatives and neighbors.

When a girl is born, she is cared for by her mother in much the same way a boy is. The father maintains his usual attitude of indifference. When the next baby is born, the three- or four-year-old girl has a place of her own or is temporarily taken care of by her grandmother rather than sharing her father's side of the bed as a boy does. When she is six or older, she gradually starts helping her mother to look after the younger sister or brother. By the time she is thirteen, she begins to learn to sew, cook, spin, and many other things. By fifteen, she is indispensable to her mother. Mother and daughter develop an intimate relation, and the father and daughter become more distant. He may have genuine affection for his daughter, especially if the latter conforms to the prevailing standard of a good girl, but the affection between them must be restrained. His knowledge of his daughter is gleaned indirectly through her mother. Generally, a daughter's marriage is arranged by her mother and only the mother can ask the girl's opinion in the matter. The father is consulted, of course. After the arrangement is made, the mother supervises everything the girl makes for her wedding and also persuades the father to be generous with the dowry. At the wedding both mother and daughter feel sad, which brings them even closer together than they were before. For two or three days before the ceremony, mother and daughter lie awake talking all night. The mother tells her daughter everything she knows about marriage, except the sexual details, and instructs her in the ways in which a bride should behave. Needless to say, the impending separation is difficult for both. When the girl has gone, her mother tries to learn whether or not she has been satisfactorily received by her husband and if she is kindly treated by the senior members of the household. If all goes well, the daughter appears happy when she pays her first visit home and the mother is happy too, but if the situation is not a good one, the daughter will cry at her mother's feet and the mother suffers unspeakably.

If a grown-up girl does not do her work well or does not behave properly, the person held responsible is her mother. In the same way, if a daughter-in-law is not satisfactory to her mother-in-law, the latter says that she has not been disciplined by her mother. This shows how commonly accepted the closeness of mother and daughter is. When a father hears his daughter criticized by the villagers, he does not go to the girl directly, but to her mother, and she is not permitted to say that she knows nothing of it, or is not responsible, but must apologize and then try to find the reason for her daughter's reputation. If it is based on fact, she must correct it. The villagers know that a daughter's personality is a reflection of her mother's and the mother shares in any blame directed at the former.

Relations between mother-in-law and daughter-in-law are sometimes strained, sometimes harmonious, but always less intimate than those of a daughter and her own mother. A daughter-in-law's obligations to her mother-in-law and to her husband are similar, but there are many points of friction inherent in the situation between the two women. The son's transference of affection from his mother to his wife, creates tensions between the women. The wife now takes care of mending and sewing his personal garments; to everybody else these changes seem natural, but to the mother, it is a great blow. She feels that she has been deserted by her son, that she has lost her greatest treasure. For this she cannot blame him, because she loves him so well, yet needing somebody to blame, she naturally turns to his new wife. At first, she may say that her daughter-in-law should not be so appealing to her son as to make him neglect his parents, brothers, and family duties. Later she may come to believe that the young woman purposely defames her to her son, and a bitter resent ment may grow up in her mind. Also, as a result perhaps of the traditional expectations or of the loneliness and feeling of insecurity occasioned by the new environment, a daughter-in-law is always ready to feel that she is being ill-treated by her mother-in-law. Thus suspicion and self-pity on both sides create fertile ground for the sowing of conflicts, and minor incidents assume undue importance.

It is commonly said that when a mother-in-law treats her daughter-in-law badly it is because she was herself so treated when she was a young married woman and is now trying to avenge her own past wrongs. Except for the daughter-in-law, there is no person in the household on whom the mother is able or willing to avenge herself.

In many cases, however, the mother-in-law tries to be kind to her daughter-in-law, and the latter responds favorably. There are not a few mothers who are soft-hearted and far-sighted enough to see the impor- tance of cooperation amongst the family members to the well-being of the large household. There are also not a few daughters who have been brought up in homes where broad-mindedness, obedience toward the senior generation, tolerance, filial piety, diligence, frugality, sincerity, and faithfulness have been the objectives in the training of the children. When such a mother and daughter come to live together, they will treat each other with consideration. The mother-in-law appreciates the fact that the girl has been abruptly separated from her parents and brought to an entirely new environment, and that she may be pretty miserable. She also understands that kindness and sympathy will make her loyal to the family and that her loyalty is tremendously important. Therefore, she will try to help her daughter-in-law become accustomed to her new home, and will not want her to work too much, will see that she eats enough and that she gets along well with her husband. She will on occasion look after the young children. If treated this way, the daughter-in-law will try to show her faithfulness to her husband and the whole family. If something untoward happens, the mother-in-law will assume the attitude of a mother in trying to rectify the situation and the daughter-in-law will accept the correction or blame with meekness. In this way the girl transfers her affection to the new family and accepts her position among them without continuing to long for her old home.

Relationship between a woman and her husband's father is very formal. She sees him and speaks to him, but only to a very limited extent. It is considered improper for a father-in-law to enter his son's room after that son is married. This holds true even when the daughter-in-law is not actually in the room. A father may joke with his son's wife only at a family gathering, and the joke must be free from any romantic implication. A young daughter-in-law must respect her father-in-law; she should not burst into laughter in his presence, but merely smile if a joke is told. When she is in her husband's parents' room, she must stand up when her father-in-law enters; she owes him as much deference as her husband does.

It is a breach of etiquette for a father to ask about his daughter-in-law's affairs, except when the latter has committed some wrong.

If he should behave improperly toward her he would be disgraced in the eyes of his own son and of his daughter-in-law's family. Should sexual misconduct be involved, the young members of her family confront him with the reins and feed of a mule, and do everything else they can to insult him. He loses the respect of his own family, of the villagers, and all his relatives and friends. Hereafter, everyone calls him a mule. We do not know definitely why this term is used, but we may hazard a guess. Sexual relations between a man of the older generation and a young person in the same family are considered bestial. So far as the farmers know, only mules mate with animals not of their own kind. Horses are very rare in this area and the local people are unfamiliar with them; and also a horse is rated much higher than a mule, so the condemned man is not worthy of being called a horse. This treatment is accorded a man who has any improper interest in his daughter-in-law, or who does anything to make her think he is sexually inclined toward her.

During boyhood, brothers are playmates and are on more or less equal terms. Fights between them are not frowned upon. Later, the elder brother is expected to be friendly to his younger brother, but there is some restraint in the situation. The younger one is expected to respect the

elder. Before they marry, or when only the eldest has married, they continue to get along well with each other. They work together in the field
or at home under their father's direction, and though there may be
rivalry or even occasional clashes there is also cooperation, mutual help,
and mutual confidence. After they have all married, the relationship
usually becomes less pleasant. At first, they try to maintain the original
friendliness. But gradually their efforts become less and less effective, for
they cannot but be influenced by their wives' insinuations and their
children's complaints. Quarrels or distrust rise more easily to the surface.
If the parents cannot act as arbitrators or mediators, the household is
likely to break up. A number of families in the village have held together
for a considerable period after the sons were married, and in several cases
even after the parents had died. But, for the most part, married sons set
up their own households after their children are born.

In the early years of life, a girl is usually dominated by her brother in
play or disagreements. This is due partly to the fact of male priority in a
Chinese family. The girl's bound feet may be another reason for her
"unconditional surrender." When a boy is twelve or fifteen years old, he
begins to feel that it is his duty to protect his sister, even if she is older
than he. A Chinese girl over twelve years is not allowed to associate with
any boy other than her own brother or her father's brothers' sons. Since
her desire for male company grows stronger as she gets older, she eagerly
accepts her brother's company and protection. Unmarried brother and
sister have a free and intimate relationship. He may tell her if he is interested in a certain girl or ask her about feminine psychology. A sister may
act as a go-between for her brother and a girl he is interested in. He may
confide to her his as yet unrevealed ambitions and he may ask her to
speak for him to their mother. A sister, however, would not reveal her
heart to her brother, for she is too shy and timid. A brother may admit
his own romantic aspirations, but would not like to know that his sister
is interested in a certain boy. He would feel shame at the knowledge
that she longs for love, for he must feel that she is pure. He resents
any boy's advances to her, as, unconsciously, he already hates the young
man who will be his sister's husband. Though confidences are not mutual,
a girl derives satisfaction from her brother's companionship, and since she
is not permitted to know any other boy, his friendship is very dear to her.

After his marriage, the brother's attitude is apt to change to indifference or even hostility. He now has a wife who is closer to him than his
sister ever was, and he no longer needs to turn to the latter for feminine

sympathy and help. The brother's new wife helps to widen the breach between brother and sister for she is usually jealous and suspicious of their relationship. Also, she may be unpleasant to her young sister-in-law as a means of releasing aggression against the girl's mother, for most brides suffer from their mother-in-law's domination. The brother, at the instigation of his wife, may blame the sister for minor household difficulties, thereby increasing the rift. The mother, if she is still living, protects her daughter from any open acts of hostility on the part of the young couple; this is one reason why a mother fears to die before she can see her daughter safely married. An amicable adjustment of these relationships is usually worked out eventually.

A family of the Yang clan in the village has two unmarried daughters, women already in their forties. The mother died while the girls were young, and their stepmother also died some years ago. The father is still living and there is one son who is married and has grown children. He and the father are on bad terms. The two girls have worked hard and lived frugally under their brother's authority; they have been loyal to the family's business but have never interfered with anything that was outside their jurisdiction. The brother and his wife appreciate the sisters' cooperation and treat them fairly, so the household gets along smoothly. Of course, a hired laborer can be faithful to a family's business in the same way. These two girls are pathetic, but they are shrewd in making the best of their unfortunate situation.

A daughter-in-law is inclined to believe that the trouble which she has with her mother-in-law is the result of her sister-in-law's influence and antagonism to her. On the other hand, the unmarried daughter feels that her brother's wife is her rival, and resents her because she has taken her brother away from her and her mother. It is very rarely that one sees a girl being a true friend of her brother's wife. Under ordinary conditions, the girl maintains an attitude of indifference toward the sister-in-law, and the latter is polite but quite remote. A daughter-in-law, for her mother-in-law's sake, makes concessions to her husband's sister, and she, in her turn, may look after her brother's young children when their mother is busy. She may also voluntarily, or when ordered by her mother, lend a hand when her sister-in-law needs help. On the whole, however, the relationship is not well defined; the village opinion is that it is hardly good. When a mother arranges her daughter's marriage, she always asks how many sisters the prospective husband has. Other things being equal, she probably chooses the man with the fewest sisters.

A brother's wife can have great influence on the behavior of her husband's unmarried sister. According to village opinion, when a *sao-tze* (a term by which a girl refers to her elder brother's wife) and a *hsiao-ku* (a term used by a daughter-in-law to refer to her husband's younger sister) do come together either in work or in relaxation, the conversation is very likely to be about personal affairs. The sister usually likes to listen, and she may even unconsciously incite her brother's wife to talk. This is an important source of sexual knowledge and may also furnish temptation to commit some socially condemned act. A girl can also learn from her brother's wife sewing, cooking, embroidering, taking care of a baby, taking care of a husband, dealing with a mother-in-law and sister-in-law, and so on—all very useful to her.

Relations between the wives of brothers may be harmonious but are frequently marred by rivalry. The wives form a team under the direction of their mother-in-law. They help each other by looking after each other's children, by lending each other small articles—a needle, a roll of thread, a piece of cloth, or a little money. They can generally agree as to the order of work, so as to leave time for each to visit her parents. A family with such daughters-in-law will be cited as a model and be praised by all the villagers. Unfortunately, such cases are rather rare. In many large households the rivalry outweighs the harmony, for the wives compete for the favor of the mother-in-law. One may feel that the mother-in-law favors another, and quarrels arise. The antagonism will be accentuated if children carry tales against one another. The fathers are brought into it, first to complain, then to resent, and finally to fight each other.

A woman and her husband's younger brother have a free and easy relationship. But if the brother is very young and the woman is middle-aged, the latter is supposed to play a mother's role to him, especially if the boy's mother is dead. In not a few cases motherless boys have been brought up by the wives of their eldest brothers, and these boys pay high tribute to their sisters-in-law. That the wife of one's eldest brother should be looked upon as one's mother is a proverb well known by the local people.

Between a woman and her husband's elder brother the relation is marked by respect and by a distance that borders on avoidance. Like the father, the elder brother does not enter the bedroom of the younger one after the latter is married, unless it is absolutely necessary. Even then the younger brother's wife must be informed beforehand so that she may leave the room. Only in family gatherings or in the old parents' room, when all the family members are present and talk is free, may an elder brother-in-law joke without embarrassing the wives of the younger brothers. The formality decreases when all the brothers and their wives reach middle age. In a farm home, all the family members must work and eat together, and formalities cannot be strictly observed. Sexual relations between a man and his brother's wife are forbidden, but the taboo is not as strict as it is for the father-in-law. Cases in which a woman has a love affair with her husband's younger brother have occurred in this community as well as in the neighboring villages. There was an instance in which a man married his younger brother's wife. His own clan and the whole community did nothing to interfere with the marriage, although it was bitterly condemned. Later the couple parted and the woman married a third time. Such conduct is enough to destroy one's good standing, alienate the friendship of all decent people, and even cause one to be repudiated by one's relatives.

The relationship between a man and his father's brother is almost the same as that between him and his parents when the large family is still together under one roof. The nephew is required to listen to his father's brother, and if the uncle is not married, he has as much authority over his nephew as the boy's father has. He may punish the boy without interference. After the uncle is married and has his own children, he must refrain from exercising his authority. If his nephew defies him, he should ask the boy's own father or mother to correct him. If he scolds the boy, his scolding should not be as severe as the boy's parents would administer. When a man has his own children, he should be especially nice to his brother's children because his kindness or severity will be reciprocated. Also, kind treatment to nephew or niece is a way of showing good feeling toward one's brother. Another manifestation of filial feeling is punishing one's own children unhesitatingly if they have not been sufficiently respectful to one's brother and his wife. The punishment must be purely disciplinary. Unfair treatment, actual or imaginary, of a brother's children, is a source of much misunderstanding between brothers and of family trouble in general.

The relationship between grandparents and grandchildren is a loving one, expressed with a tenderness similar to that between a mother and her child. The happiness of having a grandchild is the goal of all middle-aged parents, and the greatest pleasure of an old man or woman is to hold a grandchild in his arms.

The adjustments necessary between the members of a large family are delicate ones and it is only when they can be made with a minimum of friction that a large household can hold together. Jealousies and disagreements between certain members will throw the entire organization out of balance, and, if no immediate remedy is found for the situation, the household may break up. It is the most important duty of the head of a household to keep these relationships functioning smoothly. The task would be impossible, even for a family head of great tact and skill, were it not that so many traditions, rituals, and social sanctions operate as controls in the situation.

There are two basic relationships: that between parents and children (with the emphasis, of course, upon the sons), and that between a son and his wife. Theoretically, these two should be complementary. In practice, however, they are antagonistic to one another. It is true that when parents find a wife for their son they hope that the couple will be compatible and are pleased on the wedding day to receive such congratulations as "Harmony in one hundred years"; "A heavenly sanctioned union"; "Sincerity and love between husband and wife." However, the parents are displeased when the young couple are too devoted to each other, for this menaces the relationship between parents and son, especially that between mother and son. We have previously seen how a mother becomes bitter if her son loves his wife or his wife loves him too much. We also pointed out how a father's instruction may be neglected, rejected, or misinterpreted if his son listens too attentively to his wife's words. In case he is not satisfied with his wife, he must, if he wants to be a filial son, not quarrel too much with her lest his parents' consciences be hurt, nor must he complain too much. That is why, as we have seen, a young husband is required to assume an attitude of indifference while his parents or other family members are present, and why such mottos as, "Listening to wife's words and turning one's back to one's bone and flesh relations is not the behavior of a righteous man," are highly praised by all Chinese parents. Marriage is not primarily for the happiness of the husband and wife alone, but also for the parents—to help in their work, to wait upon them, to satisfy their desire for grandchildren while they are living, and to continue their "incense and fire" when they die.

Whether a large family can be held together or not depends very much on the congeniality of the married brothers, which, in turn, depends largely upon their wives. If the wives are on good terms, the brothers are very likely to be on good terms too—most conflicts between them are caused by their wives. There are numerous folk tales and proverbs which warn against this sort of discord. However, it is hard for any man to ignore his wife's complaints. He may be able to do so at first, but not after five or six years of marriage.

It seems that very few men, still fewer women, can escape the bias of believing their children better than other's. The relationship between two brothers can be shadowed or broken because of a child's complaint. Brothers should not quarrel for this reason, but the fact remains that a man is happy when his children are liked and admired by his brother and well treated by him, and feels uncomfortable and resentful when they are not.

Everyone who has lived in a large household knows how difficult it is to maintain harmony. There is a folk tale that aptly illustrates the point. A certain village household was so large that its members were counted in hundreds and comprised five or six generations. They had lived together amicably for a long time and because of this were famed throughout the countryside. At last even the emperor heard of them, and curious to know the real story, he summoned the family head to his palace and asked how he managed such a large family so successfully. The family head said nothing but requested a pen brush and with it wrote a character on a piece of paper. The character was *jin*, tolerance.

Relations between family members are indicated in the use of kinship terms for addressing or referring to each other. (For examples, see Appendix II.) The first important factor is age. When a boy is young he addresses his parents with affectionate terms. When he is grown, affectionate terms are replaced by the customary terms for parents. When a son is middle-aged he still speaks often with his mother and still addresses her with either affectionate or customary terms, but he seldom addresses his father at all. As a rule, when an elderly man speaks to his father it is not necessary to address him first, but he may just start to talk. To his old mother, he uses terms of address frequently, thereby expressing his deep affection. This is because, as we have mentioned previously, the sentimental relations between mother and son are usually reinforced in their old age, while that between father and son diminish very much.

Terms used by parents to their children also change according to the age of the latter. When a boy is young, or at least before he is married, his parents call him by his small name, and it is always spoken in an affectionate tone. After the son is married, especially when he has a child of his own, he is no longer called by his small name but by a number with the prefix *lao* old), or by the phrase "child's father."

This same age principle is applied to terms of address between siblings and between distant relatives. One can address a younger brother by his small name when the latter is young or before he has married, but when the brother is more than fifteen, or when he is married, he must be addressed in proper ways. The same rule is applied to a younger sister. As a rule, one should address an older brother or sister by the proper terms even while they are still young. But in some plain families a child under ten is allowed to call his older brother by his small name. But when the brother is over fifteen, or married, the improper way must be changed to the proper one.

One should always address relatives of the parents' generation by the proper terms, but if the speaker and the one addressed are both young, the proper term may be used with the prefix *hsiao* (little or junior) appended to it. When either or both of them are grown, *hsiao* is dropped. An uncle or an aunt can call a nephew or a niece with the same term the parents use, but when the nephew or niece is grown or married, the small name must be dropped. If the uncle or aunt is on the maternal side, this change should take place much earlier, out of courtesy.

The second important factor is the use of a number in addition to a proper term. Family members of the same status are always numbered according to age, for address or reference. When an older brother addresses the younger ones, the same numbers are used. In other parts of China, the number is replaced by the first name or just one character of the name. This is not true in Taitou, except in extended kinship relations.

The children of several brothers in one household are numbered together according to their ages, irrespective of their fathers' numbers. For instance, ego is the first child born to the household, which makes him No. 1. After two years, ego's uncle has a son, then this son will be No. 2. After another two years, ego's father has another son, then this son is No. 3, and so on. When these boys address each other, they use the rules given above. After the household is separated, the same custom lasts for a certain period, then each of the separated families will renumber their own boys in a new series according to the family to which the boys belong. Girls of the brothers are numbered and renumbered in the same way.

The custom of extending the use of kinship terms to distant cla members, to maternal relatives, to relatives by marriage, and to all who live in the same village is also sociologically important. First, kinship terms are applied to clan members in adjacent villages or those who come into relations with members in Taitou. A member of a Yang family, for example, should address all people of the other Yang families who are of his own generation by the terms for brother or sister, and all people who are of his father's generation by the terms for uncle or aunt. There are a number of Yang families in a neighboring village named Hsiao-chuang. When the Yangs of Taitou meet those of Hsiao-chuang, they address each other with kinship terms. Once a Yang member visited, by chance, a village sixty miles to the west. There he found some Yang families. After a brief genealogical inquiry they began to address each other with the proper kinship terms.

Kinship terms are applied to maternal relatives. But those used to address people of the mother's generation, or of the generation above the mother's, are different from those used for paternal relatives. The children of mother's brother and sister are called by the same terms ego uses for his own brothers and sisters, but with the prefix *piao* (outside). Another point regarding this extension of kinship terms is that the application does not go beyond the family of the mother's father's brother. Ego is obliged to address his mother's father's brother by the term that he uses to address his mother's father, to address the brother's children with the terms he uses to address his mother's brothers and sisters, and to address his son's children, but not his daughter's, in the same way he addresses his mother's brother's children.

When two families are related by marriage, they use kinship terms for each other. The parents of the two families use the brother-sister terms with the prefix *ts'in-chia* (maritally related family) added, or the plain farmers simply use the prefix. For example, when they meet in the market town, a married girl's father calls her father-in-law *ts'in-chia ta-ke* (elder brother of maritally related family) or *ts'in-chia*. The girl's mother calls her mother-in-law *ts'in-chia ta-sao* (elder sister of maritally related family), or *ts'in-chia*, and vice versa. Second, the couple addresses each other's relatives with kinship terms. The husband calls his wife's father and mother by the same terms he uses for his own parents, his wife's brothers and sisters as he calls his own. He also uses the terms for nephew and niece to address the children of his wife's siblings. But this extension stops horizontally with the father-in-law's brother and his children, and vertically at the third generation below the wife's. The wife addresses her husband's relatives exactly as her husband does and the extension goes as far as the husband's would go. An important point to be mentioned here is that the husband extends kinship terms to his wife's people largely for courtesy or as a formality, while the wife follows her husband's mode of address as an obligation. This is because, after marriage, a wife is a member of her husband's family, but the opposite is not true. If the husband has a brother or sister, and they all live together, then the wife's brother or sister will address the husband's by the brother-sister terms with the prefix *piao* added. This, too, is largely for courtesy. When the husband is separated from his brothers and sisters, these terms will gradually be dropped.

A local custom is to use kinship terms for addressing people living in the same village. This is, of course, not strictly observed. In daily life young people call each other by name or nicknames. Persons who are commonly considered mean are seldom addressed by fellow villagers with kinship terms. Generally, three factors make a villager address another by these terms. One is the other person's seniority. Any aged person, regardless of whether he is poor or rich, is addressed by the proper term. Only those who are not well behaved people are deprived of this honor. Another factor is an unusual circumstance. For instance, villager A usually talks to villager B without the term, but if B calls on A at home, either on business or on a social visit, B first announces his approach by shouting "Is child's third brother home?"; then A, recognizing the sound, comes to the door and greets the caller: "Oh, it is Uncle Heng-shen, come on in." There are other circumstances in which courtesy requires that one address a fellow villager with kinship terms. For instance, when one goes to ask help from a neighbor to whom one usually does not pay much respect, one begins the request by addressing the neighbor with a proper kinship term and this is done as affectionately as possible. Again, when one villager is in trouble with another and feels that he is on the losing side, he will try to pacify the other by saying: "Now look, Uncle Feng-t'ing, there could be nothing serious between you and me. I apologize. I believe you will excuse a junior like me." Also, when a villager owes another money and cannot pay it when the time comes, he goes to his creditor and says: "Second Grand Uncle, I hate to, but I have to say that I cannot pay back your money on time. I really feel sorry, but I do hope that Second Grand Uncle will excuse me and allow me to postpone it for some time."

A third factor that makes people address their fellow villagers with kinship terms is the desire to be considered a cultured person in the neighborhood. Young members of a decent family, for instance, greet every grown villager whom they meet on the street or in the field with the proper kinship terms. Gradually the whole village will come to praise the family and the young members are thought to be most promising and pleasant people. If a newly married daughter-in-law always remembers to greet everybody in the neighborhood and addresses them in the proper kinship terms, she will soon win the reputation of being a good wife.

In summary, the application of kinship terms has a great deal of social significance. Its function is primarily social. The fact that the villagers address each other, regardless of family relation, by kinship terms, contributes much to the community's sense of solidarity.

The Family as a Primary Economic Group

7

CONTINUING the family line is the main concern of a Chinese farmer, but it is easier to produce progeny than to bring them up. When a man marries, his parents and the spirits of his ancestors are made happy at the thought of the new generation, but the man himself, if he is old enough, feels that a great burden has been put on his shoulders. He is no longer a "free" man but one who has to work for his wife's and his future children's livelihood. His parents also know that the hope of having progeny requires facing the important problem of how to feed, clothe, shelter, and educate the children, and that this problem can only be solved by working hard and living frugally. His wife sees it the same way. Sometimes a young husband may forget his responsibility and be idle or spend money. Then his parents and his wife warn him by reminding him that he is going to have children to take care of. If he does not give heed, his parents will worry and his wife will talk tearfully about the livelihood of the entire family, and that of the children. On the other hand, if the husband is aware of his responsibility, all the others feel very secure.

The old parents share the responsibility, and though they can no longer work as hard as they did, they save as much as they can of what they have. The parents of many families live more frugally than their children, for they are constantly anxious lest their children face poverty or starvation.

A young wife works harder than anybody else in the family and she lives more thriftily. She does not speak of it, but to her nothing is more important than the security of the family. Her most important role is to see that her husband lives cheerfully and works well, and she advises him on the management of the farm. Further, she must see that her children are properly trained to do their share toward building up the family's economy.

When a boy, or girl, is about fifteen years old, he gradually becomes aware of his responsibility. He is frequently warned by his parents that the family may not have enough to eat if he does not work hard, and told that if he wants his family to have a big ox, a strong mule, two donkeys, three or four good houses, and many large and good pieces of land, such as a P'an family of the *tung hu-tung* has, he must learn to work hard. I have seen many sons of poor families who, though still young and unmarried, were quite mature in this respect.

All three generations have a common interest in the family's economic security. It is a source of happiness to all; when it is imperiled, all feel the disaster. This is obvious to anyone who sees a family at a time when their important crops are threatened by drought or flood. Not only the older generation manifest great concern, but the young too share the anxiety. If, on the other hand, the harvest of the year is especially abundant and there is a good possibility of having some savings at the year's end, then everybody, old and young, is happy. When a piece of land is bought, even if it be a very small piece, it occasions happiness in the heart of every member of the family. In such a year the family's New Year Festival will be celebrated with great cheer and color.

A farm family is a unit unto itself in production. The family members produce collectively and they produce for the family as a whole, not for any individual member. This holds true for everything.

The work, in the field, on the threshing ground, in the vegetable garden, and at home, is divided among persons according to experience and physical ability. For example, the father is assigned to plant the sweet potato vines, since he is the experienced one. He knows which is the upper end and which the bottom end of the vines and can put them in the right positions. He knows how deep the vines should be planted and also the proper distance between every two plants. Others may also know these things but as yet cannot put them into practice as efficiently. The elder son is asked to carry water from a distant place because he is the strongest in the family. The younger brother and sister are put to pouring water into the small holes because this does not require much experience or strength. Finally, the work of covering the vines and of accumulating earth to support the young plants needs some experience but not much physical strength, and that is why the mother and the elder sister are assigned to these tasks.

We must bear in mind that this organization is not elaborately planned beforehand, but happens very naturally. When the family arrives at the field, the members simply begin their proper tasks, neither the father nor the mother has to give any orders. Needless to say there is flexibility in the arrangement. When there is enough water for a while, the elder son may pick up his father's work for practice. At another time the second son may ask permission to carry water for at least one trip in order to show that he, also, is strong. Or, the elder daughter may insist that she exchange positions with her younger sister on the pretext that the latter should learn a grown-up's work.

This organization also depends upon cooperation. The children may sometimes quarrel, but that is a small matter. Let us still use the cultivation of sweet potatoes as an example. When all is ready in the field, the father begins work and simultaneously the elder son goes for water. By this time the two younger children are ready with their implements. When the water arrives, they immediately pour it into the holes and then the mother and the elder daughter begin their tasks. There is no gap or overlapping in the whole process. In harvesting the potatoes the cooperation shown is even more impressive. In the early morning the younger son is sent to cut and remove the vines from the field, while other members are busy putting all things in order at home and on the threshing ground. By the time the young lad has cleared up a considerable section of the field, the father and the elder son arrive and the digging begins. When all the vines have been cut, the young boy begins collecting the sweet potatoes on the ground into the baskets tied on the wheelbarrow. The elder son, the donkey, the wheelbarrow, and the boy form a team to transport the harvest to the place where it is to be processed. As this progresses, the mother and daughters arrive there and start cleaning and cutting the sweet potatoes.

The intricate cooperation and division of labor is just as evident in domestic work. When *chiao-tze* are made for the New Year, for example, all the members of the family eat an early breakfast and get the dishwashing done. Then under the mother's supervision someone is assigned to fetch the cabbages from the storage place; another is ordered to wash and chop them. One member takes out the big piece of pork and chops it while the mother herself carefully seasons the mixture. Then the whole group sits at a long desk or on the mother's warm brick bed and begin the hardest part, which is to shape the round pieces for wrapping. Since not all can do this job, the one who takes care of it is generally regarded as the most important in the group. The role he or she plays is strategic because all the others must wait for the round pieces of dough before they can themselves begin. Wrapping is also skilled work. Some merely fold the piece of dough,* while others make very fancy forms which receive a great deal of admiration. A newly married daughter-in-law who is adept at this art is very likely to win approval from her mother-in-law.

* See pp. 37, 93, 94.

Actually there is a certain amount of competition among the young people, but it is an enjoyable occupation. With the New Year just ahead, the sisters and brothers tease each other more freely than at any other time. The mother says nothing except occasionally to scold them laughingly which only makes the youngsters more mischievous. This is one reason why it is best for the father not to participate in this work, for his presence would kill all the laughter and jokes.

In an old-fashioned family, the kind which predominates in Taitou, everyone works or produces for the family as a whole, be he a farmer, a mason, a cloth weaver, a merchant or what not. It goes without saying that those who work on the family's farm work for the whole family. Any earnings made in special trades also belong to the family. If someone keeps a part of his wages, he will be condemned by the family head and suspected by all the other members of the family as being untrustworthy. A merchant who has to do his business outside may spend what he has made for his living expenses and according to his own judgment, but he must turn over all the rest and report what he has spent to the family head. If some of his expenses are found to have been unnecessary, he will be questioned about them in detail. Only when satisfactory reasons are given will his account be closed. If he is already middle-aged and has a prominent position, he may have more freedom in spending his money and the family head may not restrict him too much. But even so, he must know the limits of his freedom and must give the family the lion's share, or the others will complain and the unity of the family will be threatened. When a son goes to work on another family's farm as a hired laborer, his wages are given directly to his father or to his family. He may ask his father to give him a few dollars from his wages, or he may keep or spend the small money given to him by his employer for attending an opera or the local fair, but he is not working for himself but for the family of which he is a member.

An unmarried girl can make money for herself, if there is any work for her to do. If she gleans the peanut fields, her father will sell her gatherings and give the money to her. She might also work for the local oil-pressing shops and then the wages belong to her. Some grown-up girls gather seashells and sell them in the market town. A girl might have ten or twenty dollars saved by the time she is fifteen or seventeen. With this as capital her mother will buy her cotton and thus help her start a home industry of cloth weaving. Or she may lend it to a fellow villager and thus make it grow. By the time she marries, the girl may have accumulated thirty to fifty dollars of her own.

A family of the Yang clan has three sons, one of whom is a very popular mason in this district. The family was terribly poor two decades ago but because the sons worked very hard and saved as much as they could, the family's condition gradually improved. It was really the efforts of the eldest that contributed most to this. His trade brought in about one hundred dollars every year besides his own maintenance. A great part of this money was saved to buy land or repair houses. Recently he helped his two younger brothers to get married, though he has not married himself because he thinks he is too old and his health is not good enough. He still works as a mason and gives all he earns to the family. Their father died years ago and their mother is nominally head of the family, but it is he who manages a great part of the family's affairs.

Another family, a member of the P'ans, has four sons. They are primarily a farm family, but in addition run a small foundry in the village, and the first son teaches in the village school. One son usually works in the foundry while the others work on the farm, though when the exigencies of the season demand it, they all work together. The proceeds from work on the farm, teaching in school, and the foundry are all turned over to the family as a whole, that is to the family head. Neither the foundry worker nor the teacher would claim that a greater part of the money is earned by him. As a result of this cooperation the family is now one of the most prosperous in the village. Thus, in each of the four clans in the village there are a number of families whose recent prosperity was created or developed by the genuine cooperation and unity among brothers who were working in different fields.

Since the members of the same family work together, wear the same clothes, live in the same quarters and participate in the same social sphere, their needs are relatively the same. The family always eats together and shares what is on the table and each enjoys the same food. If the father or mother eats better food, it is not because he or she has the privilege of claiming it but because the children want to favor the parent in this way. If the younger children get more food, it is because the parents feel they need it to grow strong and the older children concur in this. It is true that women, especially young women, usually have less choice food than their men have, but the difference is by no means significant, and the women usually take it for granted. "Men's work is heavy, they must eat better; men are the family's pillars, we depend for our lives on them, so they must be fed well." It is frequently reported in other parts of the country that women as a whole are maltreated at home, that they are always overworked and underfed, and that they are almost slaves of their men. This is not true in Taitou; if it occurs at all, it is a very unusual case. When special food is served, the parents always try to gather the whole family together and are regretful if some member of the family must be absent from the feast. Special food is important to a farm family, but family spirit is most important of all. It is not simply a matter of eating good food; it is the shared enjoyment of the results of common toil. Thus, all the family members who are temporarily absent are urged to come home for the *Ching-ming, Tuan-wu, Chung-chiu* and other festivals. The New Year Festival, which is the most important, makes this almost imperative, and if someone fails to come home for it, an empty seat is kept for him and a place set at table so that the places represent the total number of family members. It is very common to hear a mother say at *Ching-ming* or *Chung-chiu* feast: "I wish Lien-erh could be home with us. Since it is impossible, I hope he enjoys the same food as we do now." One also frequently hears an absentee son saying, while he is eating a good meal on a special occasion: "This is good; I know those at home would like it too."

The joy of a good harvest is also shared with the family's ancestors. After the winter wheat is harvested, there is the festival of *Tuan-wu* at which the spirits are invited home or sacrifices are offered in the graveyard. When millet and several other kinds of cereal have been harvested there comes the *Chi Yueh Shih Wu* feast, specially designed for dead relatives, and when the most important fall harvest is in sight there is the *Chung-chiu* festival. Although this is primarily a feast for the living members, the dead are invited with the same sincerity. Finally, the New Year celebration is the most important feast at which both living and dead enjoy the total result of the year's hard work.

Except for personal belongings, everything in a farm family is owned in common, or by the family as a whole. A member who earns more for the family is honored by the others and he may even enjoy some prestige which does not accrue to them, but he cannot claim ownership of the family's property any more than they can. On the other hand, a member who produces or earns less but is doing his best is on equal terms of ownership with the others. There may be someone who produces or earns nothing, and indeed wastes money every day but, as long as he is a member of the family, he is not only entitled to his living but can also claim ownership of the family's property. Should someone work outside permanently but maintain his membership in his family, he is the owner of the family's property on the same basis with those at home and the family owns his earnings.

Personal belongings are negligible. An unmarried boy has only his own clothes, and even these can be shared by his younger brothers when the parents deem it necessary. After he is married, he has absolute ownership of his clothing. No man can have any money as his own except what he has saved from his allowance, since he is provided for out of the general fund. There are very few occasions on which a boy or an adult would need money. At the time of the New Year Festival, or when there is a fair in the market town or an opera in a neighboring village, the father or the family head will give to everyone a small sum which becomes his individual property. He can use it or save it according to his own decision. If someone has to make a trip to a distant place, the family will supply him with the needed money, but when he returns he must report his expenses to the family and return what is left to the family head. A young man may do some trading in off seasons. If he borrows money on his own credit and takes all responsibility for whatever risks are involved, the profit he makes will be his own and he can spend it as he wills. Anything like this, however, would be a most unusual occurrence.

The daughters are given a dowry at the time of their marriage, to which they add any money they may have earned and saved while in their parents' home. The young wife can either invest this sum in small home industries or lend it at interest to fellow villagers. When the sum is sufficient, she can buy land with it and this land will belong to the small family unit including herself, her husband and children, and not to the large family of her husband. Her husband's family may cultivate her land and get the harvest. Sometimes the wife may lend her money to the large family, in which case the family would pay it back with interest. This kind of property is called *hsiao hueh* and it is legally recognized but not encouraged by the family at large. When young wives manage to make money, they become selfish and, as a result, quarrels arise which threaten the unity of the large family.

Wives often think of how many *mow* of land and how many *gien* of house each unit will have when the family has separated. They are happy when a new piece of land is added to the common property but their happiness is different from the joy of the primary family group. It is not

only shallow but each of the wives secretly wishes that the land will become the property of her own group. She may think that the piece of
land is largely the result of her own husband's effort and feel it is unfair
to make it common property and have it divided equally among the
brothers. She may persuade her husband to accumulate personal property
by hiding a part of his earnings, if he has any, or by grabbing from the
family's income. Because a wife can buy land with her own money which
will not be divided among the sons, she can use her husband's secret
money to buy land for her own small unit. The small family will come to
differentiate between its own land and that of the large family, and its
members will do everything possible to increase the former at the expense
of the latter. If one unit acts this way, the others will follow without
hesitation.

The distribution of family goods may foster rivalry. Special food or
fruit must be evenly divided among the small family units, who then
retire to their own room to eat it. Thus, the household splits into several
units. A son's wife can receive gifts from her own parents or kinsmen and
keep whatever is not clearly intended for ner parents-in-law or for the
household as a whole. What she keeps will be enjoyed by herself, her
children, and her husband in their own room. This menaces the communal spirit. The covetous eyes of the children of the one brother see
that the children of another brother have cakes to eat. The depressed
ones will certainly go back to their mother and complain that they have
no cakes. If the mother is narrow-minded, and unfortunately she usually
is, she will shout, "How can you complain? You haven't got rich grandparents like they have, have you? Don't you know that you are poor
seeds?" These bitter words are shouted so that they can be heard by the
other mother, and she will certainly take it as an insult and swear to pay
it back at the first opportunity. Thus, when the other brother's children
have some special thing to eat, the same complaining and shouting will
be repeated. Of course, not all young wives act in this fashion. Many
of them divide what they have among all the children in the family
without discrimination, or, else submit the gift to the grandmother and
let her distribute it. If the other wives follow her example, it may become the general rule.

When the family is small, everyone is willing to live frugally so money
can be saved to buy more land or build a new house. Even the youngsters,
who are longing for better meals, rejoice with their parents when new

property is bought. In a large family, however, the situation is different. The brothers may still be eager to save, but this is not true for the women or the children who, though they also would like to see land or a new house added to the household, would nevertheless not raise any objection to better meals, more cloth, or to some luxury. Wives do prefer individual benefit. Their primary allegiance is to their immediate families and they look forward to the eventual division of the large household. Thus the small units are, through them, brought into comparative competition. Small households have a better chance of survival.

The continuity of a family line depends not only on having generation follow generation, but also upon the uninterrupted transmission of the family's common property. Thus, inheritance becomes an important matter in a Chinese family. As we have noted, to the Chinese mind, a family is not merely a group of related people, but also the land, the houses, the livestock, and the family reputation. A prosperous family is one which is increasing in members and in property. In a declining family both are disappearing. This idea is indicated in the common saying, *Chia pai jen wang*—"family property depleted and members perished." For this reason, when a dying father realizes that he has no property left, he feels guilty toward his ancestors and ashamed before his offspring, because he has only half accomplished the continuity of the family line. This is not only because property is the most dependable insurance for the next generation, but also because the family is an economic unit, so that family property is one of the primary interests which holds them together. As long as the property is intact the family exists. When the property is sold, the individual members may still remain, but the family is gone.

A Chinese family is made up not only of living persons but also of the dead of past generations and the prospective children of the future, and all share in the ownership of the property. If the property of the living generation is inherited from the previous one, then the present members are merely the stewards who keep it intact and hand it down to a new generation. Family ethics give a son the right to the property but also assign to him an obligation. If a man has his inherited property intact when he is old, he can die peacefully. He triumphantly summons his sons to his side and tells them that he feels no guilt toward his ancestors and no shame toward his children. Some Chinese parents have said: "Do not be oxen or horses for your children; poor or rich, they must take care of themselves," but they only say this when they have been disappointed in their sons or daughters. And even then, they only say it and do not really mean it.

If a man has inherited nothing from his parents but has accumulated all that he possesses through the efforts of himself and his wife, he will feel the same obligation toward his ancestors and his children. The need to leave property to his sons to continue the family line is just as great for him as it is for others, but he will be proud of himself. He may tell his children: "Your grandfather did not leave anything to me. What we now have is all the result of your mother's and my hard work." There is hidden bitterness in this, and it is bitterness toward his dead parents. Then the father will add: "But we want to leave this to you, children. We hope you will keep it intact forever." In these words there certainly is a feeling of pride. The fact that he did not inherit from his parents is their fault, but this does not exempt him from his obligations. It gives him no freedom to dispose of what he has, for his relations to his ancestors and to his children remain the same. Though his parents did not leave him property, they did give him life and it is from this life that he has given life to his children. There are other reasons for emphasizing inheritance.

If it is true, as the farmers believe, that after one dies one's spirit still needs things in the next world, and if it is true that these necessities must be supplied by one's own children who remain in this world, then one must leave some property to one's children, so they will have the means to care for the dead. Thus, for the fortune of one's own spirit, the transmission of property is a necessity. To the common people, leaving property is the most important way of being remembered after death. Parents who leave nothing to their children will either be blamed for a long time after or be forgotten immediately. Parents who added something to the property, or who restored the original fortune of a family, are inscribed on the family record. They are celebrated by their descendants, and are talked about with pride as long as the family exists.

In this part of the country inheritance is patrilineal, though daughters in some cases have a certain share. Sons have exclusive and definite claims on what the father has left. In spite of the new government law which gives a person the legal right to dispose of his property at will, except for a certain percent which must go to his sons and daughters, it remains true that no father, or son, had any thought but that his sons have an absolute right to their father's property.

The inheritance of the parents' movable belongings takes various forms, though the major part also goes to the sons. The equal division of movable property depends largely upon whether or not the family is well-to-do. In principle, it is supposed to be equally divided. A mother's personal belongings usually go to the unmarried daughters. A married daughter may or may not claim them. If there is no daughter, they are passed on to the daughters-in-law, or sometimes to the father's sister.

Immovable property constitutes by far the most important kind of property. It is the main item over which sharp family controversies occur. The witnesses and helpers called in to attend the division of the estate mainly concern themselves with the equal and just division of the immovable property.

The principle of division of land and houses is that an equal share goes to each son. If the division takes place while the parents are still alive, they may prefer to keep a larger share than is given to any of the sons. Whether or not they succeed depends upon their ability to exercise their authority, the opinion of the witnesses, the attitude of the sons, and the size of the total property. Daughters, if unmarried, have a certain amount of money put aside for their dowries. Unmarried sons also have an extra amount for future marriage expenses. Indebtedness is shared equally by the different parties. If one of the parents is dead, the division may be made in one of several ways. The mother or the father may have a share either larger, equal to, or smaller than that of any of the sons. The mother can choose which son she wishes to live with permanently. She can also choose to live independently, if her portion is adequate for that purpose. Or, she may live with each of the sons in turn for periods of a month or so. In such an arrangement she retains no independent property. An important feature is that the youngest son, although not expressly favored, in reality has certain advantages. The mother, or the parents usually choose to live with him, sometimes because he needs further tutelage and protection. In such instances, the parents invariably specify in the contract of division that after their death, their property must be given to the son who has served them. In this way, a further share of the inheritance is given the youngest son. But if the parent or parents live independently after the division of property, their share will be redivided equally among the sons after their death.

Adoption is closely related to inheritance. As long as the deceased has a son, the problem of adoption does not arise, but if a man has no son, the adoption of an heir is imperative. The male line must be continued. The adopted heir is always the next of kin, or the father's brother's son.

There is no definite rule as to which brother's son is to be taken in the case of several brothers. If a man dies without having provided an heir, the brother's son who is next in line and who is the first to put on a son's mourning gown, or to perform the ceremony which is designed for a proper heir, will inherit. The decision on the part of the adopting parents depends upon their personal relationship with the brother and the brother's son. They may adopt the son just before their death or long before it. They usually make known their intention by taking great interest in the prospective son's behavior. This state of suspense, if the future father is well-to-do, induces the prospective heir to be very kind, generous, and obedient to his uncle.

When a brother's son is not available, the choice falls on the next nearest kin in the patrilineal line. Adopting a member from the matrilineal line, such as a wife's brother's son, is unknown, but custom allows a son-in-law to take a real son's place in continuing the family line. In such a case, the daughter of the family will marry her husband at her parents' home. The husband and their children will take her family's name.

In discussing inheritance we must not neglect the seeming contradiction between the desire of keeping a family's property intact and the desire for more progeny. Once a Western friend told the writer that since the Chinese inheritance system is to divide the family's property equally among the sons he could not understand why Chinese parents want so many sons. Though apparently a reasonable observation, this is not the way Chinese see it. When a son is born even to a poor family, he is not looked upon as someone who will further divide the family's land, but as one who will add to it. When a second son is born, the parents do not worry that their small piece of land will be divided into two parts. Instead, they begin to hope that when their sons are grown up, one will be a hired laborer, another a mason, and they will earn not only their own living but add fifty dollars or so to the family every year. In two or three years, they can buy one more *mow* of land with their savings. Thus, when the parents are old, they will be better off than they now are. This expectation increases with each son born. A son, unlike a daughter, is always looked upon as an economic asset.

It is true that when the time comes to divide a house, a self-seeking wife may secretly wish that her husband did not have so many brothers. But at the same moment she may also proudly look at her three or four sons and say in her heart: "Why should I worry? I have four sons. Land

and houses? They will earn them." When she looks at her second sister-in-law, she secretly has pity on her: "Poor Second Sister-in-law, she has only one son but three daughters. What can those daughters do? They are only money-losers."

The Family as a Primary Ceremonial Group

IN the families of Taitou, as in families of other places, there are numerous occasions in the year on which ceremonies are held for dead ancestors, for celebrating good harvests, for worshiping the divinity, or for driving off evil spirits. It is a rule that only family members, or persons of the same family line within a certain number of generations, are allowed to participate. A ceremonial celebration, in fact, is one of the clearest indications of the family's exclusiveness, its conception of itself as a separate entity.

Of the ceremonies observed, those for lamenting and ushering a deceased parent into the long rest and those celebrating the dead ancestors are the most important. The death of a parent, especially of an old one, is taken very seriously. When the family members are convinced that the end of the parent is near, he is washed and dressed in his already prepared shroud, or *shou-i*. All his children, especially the sons, must be present if possible. When the end finally comes, the body is lifted into the decorated coffin which stands ready. The coffin is closed but not sealed. A ceremonial table is set in front of it on which are incense sticks, paper money, and a lamp. Daily offerings are placed on this table. Meanwhile, white paper is pasted on the front door announcing that the death of an old person has occurred in the family. In the evening the sons put on the white garments of heavy mourning and go to the village shrine to report the death to the God of Earth, the spiritual guardian of the village.

When a parent dies, all projected affairs are automatically suspended and signs of happiness hidden away. No wedding or rejoicing feast can be conducted during the mourning period; and all things colored red, pink, or purple are put away or covered over with white, blue, or black material. Thus, the most obvious sign of heavy mourning is white; white paper pasted on doors and windows and the wearing of white garments and shoes by the mourners. Although all mourning garments are white, there are detailed differences in accordance with the distance of the mourners' kinship relationship to the deceased. The sons wear hempen cloth garments and hats when lamenting or conducting funeral ceremonies, but plain white in their daily work. Other members wear gar-

ments of coarse white calico. Unmarried daughters follow the same dress
rules as the sons of the house; immediately after the death, their shoes
are covered with a layer of white paste, but later on shoes of white cloth
will be worn. Grandchildren wear white jackets and hats at the funeral
but are not required to do so at other times. Nephews and nieces wear
white only at the ceremonies. A brother wears a white robe and a piece
of white cloth bound around his waist, but only in the funeral procession.
For a period from nine months to a year he can wear only black or blue
cotton suits.

Wailing is the overt sign of lamenting. There is, of course, the crying
that is completely spontaneous, but in addition there is the ceremonial
wailing. When the dying person draws his last breath, the next of kin
who are standing beside the bed begin to wail. This is the signal that
death has come, and the wailing is continued until the corpse is laid in
the coffin. Then there is continuous wailing from the time that the sons
go to report the death in the village shrine until they return to the house.
Other formal wailing is in order when the coffin is finally sealed, when
the relatives and friends come to offer sacrifice, when the coffin is carried
out of the house on the funeral day, and during the funeral procession.

Immediately after the body is placed in the coffin, animal sacrifices
are made. Offerings, mostly of food, are brought to the family. After the
coffin is sealed, it is kept in the house for a period usually of from one
to three months, though some wealthy families have been known to
keep the coffin at home for nearly a year. This period varies according
to the economic and social position of the family. The richer the family,
the more elaborate the decoration of the coffin and the length of its
retention. While the coffin remains in the house, vegetable dishes are
frequently placed before it and incense sticks, candles, paper money, and
images are ceremonially offered. Money and foodstuffs are presented to
the family to help defray the expenses of the funeral, which otherwise
might seriously deplete their resources.

A parent's death must be formally reported to all relatives and friends
of the family who live in other villages or even distant places. A plain
family usually makes the report by sending a person to inform all those
concerned. In an upper-class family, however, a so-called *fu-wen*, or
written announcement, is made. The *fu-wen* is usually a folder of yellow
paper in which are printed the time of death, the date on which ceremonial lamenting will be received, and the date when the funeral will
take place. All acquaintances, friends and remote relatives are supposed

to receive the announcement and anyone who is left out will consider himself insulted.

When a family is of any significance, *feng-shui* is always seriously considered in choosing a burial place. The idea is to have a skilled geomancer choose a site for a house or a grave. It is true that in the Han Dynasty (B. C. 206–A. D. 221) people began to be concerned over a suitable spot for a burial ground, but it was in the time of Kwo-p'oh that this superstition spread throughout the country. Kwo-p'oh wrote a book in twenty chapters, setting forth the principles and arts of the selection. It is based on the assumption that the *wu-hsing*, Five Planets, and the *pah-kwa*, Eight Diagrams, have influence on a house and in turn on the prosperity or misfortune of the family owning it. If the house is built in harmony with the *wu-hsing* and *pah-kwa*, the family will be prosperous, if not there will be misfortune.

The second interpretation of *feng-shui* is based on the direction of surrounding objects and the physical configuration of the landscape. This was primarily developed as a principle for selecting burial places. According to this belief, the things to be considered are the dragon and his den, the alluvial formations, and the water courses. In their peculiar phraseology, the dragon is represented by the brink of a stream flowing round the grave and the configuration and outlines of the hills that surround the burial ground. The dragon's den is the grave pit into which the coffin is lowered. The brooks or springs near by are called water courses, and the land bordering these are called alluvial formations.

The geomancers pretend that when a family's graveyard is surrounded by water courses and hills wherein the dragon lurks, then all their ancestors buried here will draw from the bowels of the earth a mysterious fecundity which will be transmitted to their descendants. They believe that the place where ancestors are buried exerts a real influence upon the future prosperity or misfortune of the children and grandchildren. Since all families want their ancestors to be buried in a good spot and want their children to be prosperous, they all listen to the geomancer's words as if they were listening to an oracle, and, as a consequence, his directions are always followed very punctiliously.*

The funeral of a large family always forms a considerable parade. Before the procession starts, the monk of the local Buddhist temple recites

* For more detail see an article on *Fung-shui* and references in *Researches into Chinese Superstitions* by Henry Dore, S.J., trans. M. Kennelly, S.J. (Shanghai, 1922), IV, 402–16.

a prayer or reads a selection from a classic. When he finishes the chanting, the coffin is immediately moved out of the house. At this moment, all the near kin of the deceased wail loudly and sadly. The coffin is put on a heavy bier which is covered with a red cloth embroidered with dragons. Then the funeral procession begins. Heading it are neighborhood boys or men carrying banners, on which characters are written in praise of the good conduct of the dead. Next comes the brass band playing the mourning music. Then come the paper house, the paper trunks, the paper servants, and many other paper articles which are supposed to be used by the deceased in the other world. Following these is the coffin carrier, and after the carrier is the mourning group with the sons first, then the daughters, then the daughters-in-law, and finally the grandchildren. The procession proceeds very slowly and sacrifices may be offered by important friends on the way. Friends or distant relatives who come to lament may also participate in the funeral but they walk in front of the coffin. When the parade is out of the village, the women mourners leave it and return home, but the sons and grandsons follow the coffin to the grave. When the procession reaches the grave, another sacrifice is made before the coffin, which is then put into the grave while each of the mourners drops a handful or a spadeful of earth upon it. After this, they all take off their mourning garments and go home.

How elaborate or simple a funeral may be is determined by the economic situation of the family, the age of the deceased, and the number of surviving generations. If the deceased was not old, his funeral will be simpler. If there are living members of a generation older than his, the funeral also tends to be less elaborate than if the deceased was the oldest member of the household. An important point is that if the deceased is a parent, especially an old one, the surviving children must do their best to make the funeral proper. Only by doing this will they be released of guilt toward their parent. Should the sons fail in their filial duty, the villagers and the family's relatives will criticize them and will pity the deceased for having had such children. When a family is thus criticized, the reputation of all its members suffers.

After the parents are dead and buried, the descendants try to remember them, to remember their good deeds and words, their glory, and achievements. They are reluctant to believe their parents are gone and rather pretend that they are still living and still with them. Parents' deeds and words still control their children's behavior. It is easy to remember one's parents the first few years after they have died, but it is hard to do so forever. For this reason, the ancient worthies devised and developed an enormous body of ceremonies and a number of feasts by which the forgotten parents remain fresh in their descendants' minds. These ceremonies and feasts are observed by all families as a matter of course. Whether or not a family really wants to remember its dead ancestors, the ceremonies are practiced and the feasts celebrated. This ceremonial practice is called by Westerners "ancestor worship." In a strict sense, this is a mistake, because the Chinese do not worship their ancestors in the way that gods are worshiped. The Chinese do have the vague idea that their dead parents are with them in an invisible form, but this is a result of consciously trying to keep the memory alive. It should not be interpreted in a religious way; it is a consecration, but in the sense of an unbroken continuity.

In Taitou, as has been indicated before, no family or clan has an ancestral hall, and, consequently, no elaborate ceremonies of paying homage to the dead ancestors are practiced. In each of the annual feasts, however, at least some simple ceremonies must be performed for this purpose. Those of the New Year celebration are the most elaborate of the kind in this part of the country.

All festivals are fixed according to the old calendar. Although the new calendar is used in all legal documents and by the government, the villagers still use the old one in their daily life. It is too hard for the farmers to change traditions that have been followed by their ancestors for many centuries. Therefore, the New Year date on the new calendar is only observed by the public institutions in the cities. In the countryside people know nothing about it. The gayest occasion still falls on the first day of the lunar year.

Among all the ceremonials of the year, those attending the New Year Festival are easily the most important. The feast usually lasts about a month. Preparations for it are begun at the beginning of the twelfth month on the lunar calendar, and reach a climax in the last ten days. After the twenty-third day of the twelfth month there is a great house cleaning in every family, called *sao-chen* (sweeping the dust). Everything in the house is moved out, cleaned, and rearranged. Broken walls, darkened ceilings, hollow places in the floor, and old stoves are repaired. The making over is not limited to the house but embraces the people and even the gods. All who are not members of the family must leave the home before the cleaning day. A married daughter with her children, for instance, may stay at her parents' home for many months, if she is welcomed by her brothers and their wives and is not urged by her mother-in-law to return to her husband, but she must leave before this day. If the daughter has no place to go, her parents will prepare a separate house for her and she stays there for the duration. This means that she is no longer of that family. If an intimate friend has been living with the family for some time, he must also leave for the period from the twenty-third of the twelfth month to the fifteenth day of the new year's first month. If he has no place to go, he will either be adopted by the family or sent to a separate house. The kitchen god is also sent out of the home before the house cleaning. On the twenty-third day of the twelfth month a farewell sacrifice is prepared for him.

Homeless people are very miserable on this occasion. To most people, the New Year Festival is a time of great gayety, but to the lone person it is a time of heart-break. This is not due to a lack of hospitality in Chinese homes, but is the result of the fact that the New Year Festival is the great occasion of family reunion which includes not only the living members but also the dead. It is the occasion for paying homage to ancestors and, in this, only family members can take part. The celebration is also the occasion for the ceremonies relating to the family's origin, development, and future. These are absolutely the family's own affair, in which no outsiders can participate. It is believed that it would offend the ancestors or the family gods if persons outside the family attended the ceremonies. The custom makes all who are separated from their families feel that returning home on the New Year Festival is a necessity and, consequently, every family will see a reunion of its members and the wholeness of the family is reaffirmed. A guest who cannot leave will nevertheless enjoy all the good meals and amusements that the family can afford to give him.

Food is prepared in sufficient quantity to last for the fifteen days of the celebration. In addition, there is the food to be used for entertaining guests, to be given as gifts when the New Year visits are made to relatives and friends in other villages. There is also the food for ancestor worship and the religious ceremonies. Then the couplets for all the doors must be prepared. These are usually written by the teachers of the two village schools. Some poor families may buy them in the market town. The paper used for this purpose is always red or orange, decorated with golden spots. The size of a couplet is varied according to the size of the door for which it is intended. The phrases differ according to the social status of the family. If the family belongs to the upper class and emphasizes both the cultivation of land and the study of books, the couplet on the

front door, or the main entrance may read: *Chung hou ch'uan chia yuan,
shih shu chi chih ch'ang* (Sincerity and honesty make the family long
lasting; poetry and classics assure the generations) or *Kung tu chiao tze;
ch'in kien chih chia* (To teach children with farm and books; to manage
the household in diligence and thrift). If the family is of the middle
class, the phrases will be changed to: *Ch'in kien chih chia pen; hsiao ti
chiao tze fang* (Diligence and thrift are the principal virtues in managing
a household; filial piety and brotherhood are important measures for
training children) or *Yi jen ch'eng li; yu teh wei lin* (Our neighborhood
is made up of good neighbors). If the family is of the lower class, the
people usually have no idea about the meaning of any phrase; they simply
ask the schoolteacher or a neighbor to pick one for them. The phrases
might run like this: *Hwa k'ai fu kwei; chu pao p'ing an* (Blossoms bring
us prosperity; firecrackers herald peace) or *Yu t'ien chieh hwa jih; wu
ti pu ch'un feng* (The universe is brightened by the creative sun; no-
where is the earth not blessed by the spring breeze). In general, these
mottoes reflect the ideals of the family. In business houses they invite
prosperity, in official families they express the hope for official position
and promotion. In all families they exalt the virtues of filial piety and
reverence. On the inner doors the couplets concern wealth, posterity,
longevity, absence of pain and of sickness.

Pictures, firecrackers, incense sticks, candles, papers, and sweets are
bought for decorating the house and for use in the ceremonies. The
pictures generally represent flowers, historical dramas, female beauties,
cheerful children, and fairy tales. The youngsters generally buy the firecrackers, only those which are to be used in the ceremonies being purchased by the family head. The incense sticks, candles, and religious
paper must be kept and handled reverently. (A villager does not say that
he is going to buy incense sticks, but that he is going to invite them.)

Two days before New Year's Eve the doors are cleaned with water and
scrubbed with sand. The old couplets are scraped off and the new ones
pasted up. Windows are cleaned, scrubbed, and pasted over with fresh
paper to which *t'ung* oil is applied. Pictures are hung or pasted on the
walls. Everything is either put in a different place or decorated, so that
the whole house is renewed. The next day, the last day of the passing
year, sees the final stages of the preparation. Since it is a market day, all
the men go to the market town and see if there is anything that they
need but have not yet bought. The women are busy at home making the

chiao-tze. In the late afternoon, a table is set up against the north wall of the main reception room and the ceremonial articles placed on it. These articles are the incense sticks, the burner in which the sticks are planted and burned, the candles and the two candle stands, a square piece of rice cake, a bowl of cooked millet grain with some dates on top of it, a peach tree branch planted in a jar with some copper coins hung on it, several bowls of vegetables and platters covered with cakes. On a large scroll which is hung on the wall some human figures have been drawn supposedly representing the family ancestors. On the lower part of the scroll there is a picture of a prosperous home, the common goal of the family. As soon as the table is set and the scroll is hung up, the house is dignified. The adults should move carefully and formally, the youngsters are ordered to be quiet and to say nothing rude or offensive. The neighbors are not supposed to arrive until the following morning.

After supper, when it is already dark, the father and a young son go to the ancestral graveyard to invite the spirits home. Later, a ceremony is performed at the front door to welcome the god of wealth, the god of heaven, the god of earth, the kitchen god, and spirits of unknown dead relatives. The women get all the new clothes ready for the household, and, if there is still time, melon seeds, sunflower seeds, and peanuts are roasted. When all is done, the family goes to bed.

At two or three o'clock the next morning, the family wakes with a feeling in which joy, mystery, and dignity are mingled. They wash and put on their new clothes and gather before the table in the main room to pay homage to their ancestors. The father, or the head of the family, lights the candles and then the three incense sticks. He holds these reverently to his forehead and then places them in the incense burner. He kneels before the table several times and kow-tows toward the ancestor scroll. All the males of the family are asked to perform the same ritual. Simple ceremonies are also performed where the gods are located.

In Christian families, however, these ceremonies have been either completely or partly abandoned. One family, for example, substitutes a Christian ceremony for the old one. They have changed the ancestral scroll into four scrolls of flowers and landscape, a couplet of Christian verses on each side. The candles are still on the table but a Bible and hymnbooks are substituted for the other articles. Hymns are sung, a sermon is preached by the family head in which the Christian ways of remembering ancestors and celebrating the New Year Eve are related,

and a prayer is uttered for the peace of the ancestors' souls and for blessings for the living. The Christian God has replaced the former gods. In
other activities, however, the Christian families are like the rest.

When the religious ceremony is over the gayety begins. First, the family
head lets off a long string of firecrackers, and the boys follow his example.
The lanterns are lighted and hung high in different parts of the court
and in the doorways. Some people think that the object of the firecrackers
is to frighten away the demons who may be prowling about when an
offering is made. This may be true in other parts of China, but it is certainly not so in Taitou. Here the explosion of the firecrackers is traditionally a symbol of happiness. This can be verified by the fact that firecrackers are only used on joyous occasions, such as weddings, birthdays,
receiving honorable guests, or assuming official position, and have never
been used at funerals. In fact, in a Taitou family, firecrackers are not
used for three years after the death of the family head, to signify that there
can be no rejoicing while the death of father or mother is still fresh in
mind.

Women are busy preparing *chiao-tze*. Three bowls of it are put on the
ceremonial table as an offering to the ancestors. Then the whole family
gathers again, and the junior members greet their elders with the proper
terms and the phrase *kuo nien hao*, Happy New Year. For instance, a son
greets his father and mother by saying to them respectively: *Tieh* (or
Da-da), *kuo nien hao* (Father, I wish you a Happy New Year!); *Niang
kuo nien hao* (Mother, I wish you a Happy New Year)! Finally, they
all sit down to enjoy the meal. After dinner, which is usually finished
while it is still dark, the older people may go to bed again, but the
young men and boys gather into groups to make their calls (locally called
pai nien or New Year call) on the families of their own clan. At sunrise,
the men, old and young, come out into the streets and there they greet
each other in the same manner as they do at home. This is also the time
when parents and senior family members present money gifts to the
young.

In the early morning of the third day, another ancestor-remembrance
ceremony is performed; this is *sung nein*, a farewell to the ancestor's spirits
who are leaving the home. It is similar to the other but much simpler.
Only the family head and the grown-up sons take part in it. After this
ceremony, the main part of the festival is over. Clothes and meals revert
to their everyday status. Of course there are many left overs, so young
and old can still have some good food once in a while.

The last of the New Year food will be eaten at *Cheng Yueh Shih Wu*, the Lantern Festival. This falls on the fifteenth day of the first month and is really the conclusion of the New Year celebration. Its main feature is the consumption of the leftover food. In the morning, in the mill-stones at the street corners young women chop and mash the bones, ribs, and meat chips of the remaining pork. When the mash is mixed with finely chopped cabbage it looks like a kind of hash or hamburger. It is used to make soup, meat balls, and other dishes. Now, meat is a luxury to the poor farmers. The pork tasted so good to them that they are reluctant to throw away the bones, so they eat them too. Although the farmers scarcely understand the modern science of nutrition, nevertheless, they do know from experience the nutritive value of bones and marrow and have the traditionalized belief that eating the bones left from the New Year celebration is good for avoiding diseases and for the growth of young people during the coming year.

The second interesting feature of the Lantern Festival is the distributing of lamps. Formerly, this was simply an exhibition of lanterns, but it is different now. Every family makes a number of small round vessels of dough. After these are cooked by steaming, wicks and peanut oil are inserted, and when they are lighted, the vessels are called lamps. In the evening, about ten o'clock, they are placed in every corner of the house, in the court, in the backyard, in the barn, and also in the vegetable garden and on the threshing ground, to symbolize the brightness and good luck that the family hopes for and to chase out the darkness and bad luck that the family wishes to avoid. They represent, too, the hope for a good crop in the new year, and that is why lights are placed in the court, in the barn, and on the threshing ground. According to custom, the oil in the lamps should be sufficient to last through the night. In the morning, the family gathers together all the vessels and examines the burnt wicks. If most of them have a clump of kidney-like carbonate on the top, it means that the coming year will not be a lean one.

Erh Yueh Erh means the second day of the second month. It marks the birthday of the God of Soil, and is an occasion for praying for good crops. Except for a few Christian families, all make offerings to the *Tu Ti Shen*, God of Soil. In the early morning, the head of the family draws pictures of granaries and ladders before the front door, on the threshing ground and the vegetable garden, or in the backyard, by casting ashes from a basket. This expresses a wish for a good crop harvest, the wish that every inch of the family's ground shall be covered with grain and that the piles of crops shall be so high that ladders will be needed to reach the top of them. Another part of the feast is the roasting of different kinds of beans w...ch are then coated with melted brown sugar. Young people and children enjoy this a great deal. It is not easy to say what the custom really means, but it might symbolize the hope for a good harvest of beans. This day marks the beginning of the farming for the new year. It is true that work in the fields and the preparation of fertilizer, if the weather has been warm, may have already been started, but the real work is begun only after this feast.

After *Erh Yueh Erh* come the feasts of Cold Food and *Ch'ing Ming*. The first is locally called *Han Shih* (Eating Cold Food). There are two explanations of the origin of this feast. It is viewed as a religious or superstitious practice, and it is also related to an historical character. According to the *Tso Chuan* (a history of the early Chou dynasty), Wen Kung (B. c. 696–628), the prince of Tsin—the present Shansi—had a faithful follower called Chieh Chih-tui, who shared the prince's exile in B. c. 654. When the prince came back into power in B. c. 635, Chih-tui refused any reward for his services and in order to escape the prince's urging he disappeared into the forests of Mien Shan. The prince searched but could not find him; thereupon he changed to Chih Shan the name of the mountain where he vanished. Thus far the *Tso Chuan*. According to a later legend, the prince set the forest on fire in order to drive him from his hiding place; Chih-tui and his mother clasped hands about a tree and perished in the flames. Thereafter, in commemoration of their death, fires were forbidden on a certain day in the third month and food was eaten cold. This is the story related today in explanation of the feast.

In Taitou the people do not know the religious version, but they can tell both the story recorded in the *Tso Chuan* and the later legend, and have practically combined the two into one. Long ago this story was made into a drama that has been performed frequently in the villages. In it, the record from the *Tso Chuan* is only introductory; the emphasis is placed on the legend. In China, long ago a Taoistic philosophy taught people not to accept worldly compensation for a good deed. If they firmly refuse a high reward, their virtue is greatly exalted. Although it would be very hard to expect the poor farmers to act thus, nevertheless, they do admire a man of this type and esteem heroic sacrifice. Whenever the drama is performed, the old ladies shed tears, the village elders sigh, and the young people are reverently silent. The drama has been utilized as a means of reproving those who, after they have achieved success, forget the friends who shared their hardship in the early days. According to the local people, when Chieh Chih-tui shared the prince's exile, he was so faithful to his lord that he cut flesh from his leg to feed him when they were completely without food. When the prince returned to power, however, he forgot what he owed to his followers and treated them wrongfully. Knowing this, Chih-tui fled, no doubt with great bitterness, and swore that he would never see the prince again. Chih-tui's mother was so faithful to her son's ideal that she too refused to live in the prince's kingdom. So they perished heroically together. When the villagers see the drama or listen to the story, they blame the prince a great deal and say that anyone who acts like that should be condemned.

When this writer was a boy in primary school, he read an essay about Chih-tui's behavior. The author of the essay argued that all the sadness in the story was Chih-tui's fault. Chih-tui was an ambitious man; his consideration of the prince while they were in exile was motivated by the hope of great reward. Cutting his own flesh to feed his lord was inhuman, unreasonable, and unnecessary. Inhuman, because man should not be fed with human flesh; unreasonable and unnecessary, because he could have collected vegetables and fruits and hunted animals and fish. That he did not choose the easy and reasonable way must be regarded as an ambitious investment for great profit in the future. The prince doubtless understood this and purposely disappointed his follower to see what the latter would do. When Chih-tui became aware of his lord's insight he had no course but to flee and refuse to come back. This is just what any ambitious person would do after his infamy has been discovered and his hopes destroyed. Through his fault he killed not only himself but also his mother, and this was an evil thing. Whether interpretation of the essayist is right or wrong is hard to say, but at any rate, it is not the one held in the village, where Chih-tui and his mother are still admired as righteous and heroic, while the prince is regarded as a man without conscience.

Ch'ing Ming is the first great feast after the New Year Festival. It usually comes at the beginning of the third month, or at the end of the second one. The weather is usually growing warm and bright, a fact that gives to the feast its name. *Ch'ing Ming* means pure and clear; the feast therefore celebrates the fine weather and also refers to the struggle between the *yang*, the power of light, and the *yin*, or power of darkness. All living things welcome the light and dislike the darkness. The Chinese have for long seen the change from one season to another, especially that from the winter to spring, as a struggle between the *yang* and *yin*, with spring representing the victory of light. The farmer can feel the warmth of the weather, see the brightness of the day, he can witness the growing of the greens in his garden and field. During the long winter he was, for the most part, confined to his dark house and his body was imprisoned in clumsy garments. He has suffered much from the bitter cold outside and the smoky air inside. When spring comes, he regains his freedom. Thus, it is not surprising that *Ch'ing Ming* is a joyous feast.

Several interesting features are connected with it. One is the custom of *sao mu*, visiting and repairing graves. On this day, old and young go to the graves. First, an offering is spread on the ground or on the stone table before the tomb. New earth is added to the mounds and the dry grass and weeds are pulled out. Trees may be planted and the yard repaired. If there is a tombstone, the letters on it may be repainted or cleaned. Meanwhile the family members recall the deeds of their ancestors or recently deceased parents. They return home with a heightened sense of family unity.

Another practice on the day of *Ch'ing Ming* is the wearing of willow branches and evergreens. In the early morning, young members of the family cut the small branches of the willows and pines. These must be carefully prevented from touching the earth or any dirt. At home, the women and youngsters will wear a small piece hanging from the hair knot or tie a twig to their dresses. Branches are also inserted between the tiles of the roof above the doors and windows of the house. The name for the willow tree in Chinese is *yang-shu* (which sounds like the word *yang*, meaning the power of light). In North China willow trees are the first to come back to life and are regarded as a herald of the spring. The pine is a symbol of long life and expresses the wish that the family will ever grow.

The *Tuan Wu* feast, or the Dragon Boat Festival, comes on the fifth day of the fifth month. The main feature of the day is a Dragon Boat Race, but owing to the lack of waterways this is not practiced in Taitou. One of the objects of the feast is the commemoration of an historical personage. In the Chu State, located in the present Hupeh province of China, in the third century before Christ there was a great scholar named Ch'u Yuan. He was an able man who wanted to administer the State in the best possible way. He won promotion at court, but was falsely accused by rivals and lost the favor of the king. When he realized that the king was hopelessly blinded by the false accusation, Ch'u Yuan drowned himself in the river Mi-lo, hoping to open the king's eyes by his sacrifice. The king too late recognized that he had lost an able and faithful subject, and sent a searching party out to hunt for Ch'u Yuan's body, but in vain. Since Ch'u Yuan died on the fifth day of the fifth month, the king decreed that each year on that day a memorial ceremony should be celebrated. This then is the reason for the Dragon Boat Race, in which the boats race up and down the rivers in pairs as if searching for the body of the drowned man whom they hope, with the help of the all-mighty dragon, to recover.

One of the special dishes prepared for the festival is also reminiscent of this ancient worthy. It is a cake called *tsung-tze*, made of glutinous rice which is cut in triangles, wrapped in the long leaves of a particular weed, and boiled. The legend is that people threw these *tsung-tze* into the river as offerings to the tragic scholar. The custom has not been followed for many years, although the cakes are still prepared.

On the fifth day early in the morning every family fastens on each side of the main door of the house a small bouquet of sweetflag and mugwort. Their strong odor is believed to drive away disease and specters. On this day, also, children are provided with an apron on which pictures of five poisonous insects are embroidered—the snake, spider, lizard, centipede, and the green frog. Girls and youngsters wear string rings of five colors on their wrists and ankles and tie small silk bags to their clothing. Some of the bags are empty, others are filled with herb powders which give off a strong odor. Dolls and small charms are also made on this day. There is a great display of embroidery and women's handiwork. In the county seat or the market town there is usually a place set aside for the sale of these articles. The market lasts two or three days and is always held in the temple of the city guardian. The apron, the colored strings, the small bags, and the charms were originally supposed to protect children from poisonous insects and evil spirits. Today, however, except for a few old ladies, nobody thinks about this or believes in its efficacy, though all still observe the custom. Girls make the articles either for fun or to practice their embroidery. The children are delighted to wear them, and that is enough reason for making them.

A romantic legend, known by people all over China, gave origin to the *Chi Yueh Chi* feast, or the seventh day of the seventh month. The story is related to the two stars Lyra and Aquila. Lyra is the Weaving Girl who lives east of the Heavenly River (the Milky Way). Aquila is the Herd Boy who lives west of the Heavenly River. The Weaving Girl is grand-daughter of the Emperor of Heaven. She worked hard year after year weaving the cloud-embroidered heavenly dress. Her grandfather appreciated her diligence and took pity on her loneliness. As a reward, she was married to the Herd Boy. After she was married the Weaving Girl so indulged herself in love that she became less diligent in housework and gave up her weaving altogether. The Emperor of Heaven was angry, and, for punishment, the girl was recalled to her old home east of the Heavenly River. To prevent the lovers from crossing the River secretly, the Emperor ordered the bridge removed.

Only once a year, on the seventh night of the seventh month, was the Weaving Girl allowed to see her Herd Boy. But when they went to keep their tryst, the lovers found that they could not reach each other because the bridge was gone. So the Emperor of Heaven ordered all the magpies to come to a certain point of the Heavenly River, where they formed the Magpie Bridge.

Since the main points in the story are the skill of weaving and embroidering, the love between a boy and a girl, the happiness of having a good husband and the sadness of losing him, in some parts of China folkways have been developed that on earth, on the same night—the seventh night of the seventh month—girls hold parties and invite their friends to offer sacrifices to the Weaving Girl and to pray to her to grant them skill in weaving and needlework, and, especially, to send them a good husband. Hence the Festival of Wishing for Skill.

In Taitou the legend is so well known that mothers like to tell it to their young daughters in the summer evenings and point to the sky where are the two stars. But later the story has been extended with a consequent important change in significance. Our young girls are also told that there is great sadness in the meeting of the Weaving Girl and the Herd Boy on the seventh day of the seventh month, for the meeting is only once a year. When it takes place, they are so happy that their joy makes them cry. When they realize that their happiness will soon be over, they weep again, and this time with sadness. The rainy season in this part of the country always comes in the seventh month of the year and nine times out of ten it rains on the seventh day of the month, so the tears have been added to the local version of the story. This tale fosters the idea that only girls who are diligent in weaving and housework can win favor from the Emperor of Heaven so that he will marry them to good husbands. This of course helps the parents in disciplining their daughters. But more important is the idea that boys should marry girls equal in rank to them. A young farm boy should not covet a young lady of a city family, nor a farm girl dream of a college boy or a businessman. A weaving girl and a herdboy can be a happy pair. When a girl is married, she should continue to be diligent in her housework and must not indulge herself in romance or 'worldly pleasure, or the Emperor of Heaven will punish her by making her marriage unhappy. There is another reason for the appeal of this tale. It is customary in the first few years of marriage for a young wife to be frequently called back to stay with her parents, and she may stay for two or three months at a time. Though these may be welcome interludes to the bride because they end the strain of adjusting to a new family, they may at the same time be a great hardship to both husband and wife, if the marriage is a happy one.

The Harvest Festival, or *Chung Ch'iu Chieh*, is celebrated on the fifteenth day of the eighth month. It is one of the most joyous occasions of the year, for the harvest is assured and a part of it is already gathered in. The harvest moon rises large and especially bright. As thanksgiving is the background of this occasion, the enjoyment of Heaven's bounty is shared with gods and men. Most of the farmers do not know the term *Chung Chiu*, but call it *Pa Yueh Shih Wu*, meaning the fifteenth day of the eighth month. This is because in Taitou the feast is always celebrated on that day. No religious significance attaches to it, it is simply a holiday. The local people usually say that a former feast, the *Chi Yueh Shih Wu*, was for ghosts while this one is for men. In other parts of the country, especially in the cities, the ceremony performed on this occasion center about the moon. In the middle of the eighth month the weather is usually fine and the air extraordinarily clear. At night the moonlight seems brighter than usual. The poetic expression *shang yueh*, enjoying the moonlight, has therefore been the subject of hundreds of thousands of literary works. The moon is the subject of many folk tales too.

The meal prepared for this feast is the best one of the year, superior even to the New Year Festival. The mooncake is served at this time. This is a perfectly round cake made of wheat flour and brown sugar and stuffed with sweets. The villagers do not make the cake, but buy it in the market-town bakeries.

The Winter Solstice is an important festival in many parts of China, but not so in Taitou. There is a special meal at this time, but that is all. The end of the year is near and the winter solstice comes when preparations for the New Year celebration should begin. Family members who are in business outside are preparing to come home, outstanding accounts are approaching the time for final settlement, and the bitter cold of winter is close to its peak.

The *La Pa Chieh* comes on the eighth day of the twelfth month. The origin and meaning of the feast is not well known. It is a combination of the festivals of the Eight Ch'a and the Hunters' Festival. The first festival was the offering at the end of harvest to the eight *Ch'a*, the spirits who assisted the husbandman in his work. It was inaugurated by Shen Nung (B. C. 2737–2697), the divine husbandman, who invented the plow and taught the people to cultivate the soil. These eight spirits were Shen Nung, Hou Chi, who was the director of husbandry, the tutelary god of cultivator, of watchtowers, of the wild animals, of the deities of ponds and dikes, of the water courses, and of the insect tribe. The Hunters' Festival had its origin in the hunting period of Chinese civilization. Thus, the *La Pa Chien* probably commemorated the gods of husbandry and the gods of hunting. The food made specially for this day is a gruel of eight different cereals which is locally called *la pa chu*, or *la pa fan*, and symbolizes the variety of the harvest. To the youngsters, this feast's main function is that it marks the begining of the preparation for the New Year Festival.

The *Ts'e Zao*, or the farewell offering to the Kitchen God, is the occasion when the Kitchen God and Goddess are happily sent off to report the conduct of the family to the supreme ruler of Heaven. The offering comes on the twenty-third day of the twelfth month. In the evening of this day the God and Goddess are offered four dry dishes, one of which is a sweet made of sticky millet or rice. The ceremony takes place either before or after supper and the family head or one of the sons conducts it. Paper money and incense sticks are burnt. A few firecrackers are exploded. Fodder is placed in the courtyard as a token of feeding the horses of the God and Goddess, and the sweet set for them in the kitchen is supposed to sweeten their reports to the God of Heaven so that he will speak only of the good deeds of the family. The sweet is made of glutinous rice to glue their lips together and prevent them from speaking any bad of the people.

Marriage 9

THE Chinese believe that their lives are continued in the lives of their children and that, so long as generation succeeds generation, the predecessors are perpetuated. The maintenance of family continuity is one's greatest responsibility to one's ancestors, for failure to produce offspring means not only the end of the family line but the death of all the ancestors as well. Mencius has said: "There are three things that are unfilial, and to have no children is the greatest of these." The illiterate farmers may not be familiar with the literature, but they are fully aware of their duty in keeping the family tree alive.

The assumption of the responsibilities attendant upon having a wife and anticipating children is the mark of adulthood. An unmarried man of twenty-five is regarded as a boy, whereas a youth of twenty, who is married, is considered a man. Before marriage the son exercises considerable choice in the disposal of his time. He is expected to obey his parents and work on the land, but he has no definite status and is never asked to represent the family in any social matter. His parents take the responsibility if he gets into any difficulties in the village, and, though his father may be severe, his mother and his grandparents usually condone his indulgences on the ground that he is still a child.

After marriage, however, the situation is completely altered. The young man may not feel any change in himself, but the parents and the villagers have new expectations with regard to him. He no longer works for himself but for the economy of the family as a whole. His parents and other members of the family are ready to give him "face" before others, but his failures and weaknesses will not be easily excused as they were before his marriage. He now has the status of a married man: the villagers no longer address him by his "small name"; and he may now represent his family at public affairs, if he is invited to do so. When the elders of a family say to a young man: "You are already more than twenty years old; it is time for you to marry and establish a career," the words are not spoken carelessly and the young man knows it is a warning. The injunctions as to marriage and career always occur together, for marriage is considered as primary to a career of any sort.

If a man dies unmarried, he is buried without any ceremony. His spirit will not be admitted to the ancestral halls. But when a married man dies, he is mourned and buried ceremonially. Before his death, a married man may adopt a son, if he has none of his own, so that the line may be continued. A tablet bearing his name will be placed in the ancestral hall and worshiped by the descendants.

A girl has no status whatsoever in the family of her own parents. Her father and mother and brothers may love her very much, but it is recognized that she is not a permanent member of the family and can add nothing to the family fortunes. She is destined to become a wife and a daughter-in-law in another family for whom she will work and bear children.

The marriage of a son adds another working member to the family. A mother of grown sons is greatly burdened with domestic tasks unless she has daughters-in-law to help her. Only very wealthy families ever have hired help in the house. Therefore it is urgent that the eldest son marry as soon as possible. It is not unusual for a boy of fifteen, particularly if he is the eldest son, to marry a woman of twenty-five. Such marriages are undesirable from the point of view of the two parties to the union, but only a mature daughter-in-law is able to take over the work which is necessary for the family.

The sons of a wealthy family are married off as a matter of course. In a poor family, however, marriage of sons is an economic problem. Poor parents like to have a number of sons because grown sons are a great asset, but securing wives for them presents difficulties because marriage demands the means to support the additions to the family. But it is also a source of great shame to the parents, especially to the mother, to have a number of grown-up unmarried sons. This will be the subject of gossip and though the boys may not worry about it, their parents will feel greatly humiliated and the situation must be remedied before they can walk on the street with their heads erect.

Let us assume that the family works hard and begins to buy land. They accumulate some surplus and pay their debts. The mother will certainly not hesitate to inform her neighbors of the improvement and simultaneously lets her wish for a daughter-in-law be known. At first, the women of the neighborhood may ridicule her, but as the family's economic condition grows better and better, some of the matchmakers will change their attitude and start suggesting girls. Of course, the mother will not risk her chances by making the standard too high, and a match is soon arranged. Great news! Everybody in the neighborhood is surprised, and in no time the whole village is informed. Street corner conversations change.

"So, that woman will also have a daughter-in-law."

"Can you imagine, that poor family can also marry their sons."

"Why, it is a decent family. Both old and young work hard and honestly. I cannot see why their sons should not be married."

"Yes, Uncle Sheng is right, if a boy like that cannot marry, I don't see which one of us would deserve a wife."

"Poor family? Who said they were poor? Have not they bought land every year and had their houses repaired? It doesn't matter how much land you have, all that matters is whether a family is rising or declining. I would rather marry my daughter to a plain but growing family than to one which is going down."

After the marriage, the family's social status is raised and, when the daughter-in-law has been seen by all the neighbors, many congratulations are heard from the very women who had made fun of the mother's ambition.

"Well, well, I said you were a lady of great fortune. Just see what a wonderful daughter-in-law you have! Your son really deserves such a beautiful one. By the way, is your second son already engaged? If not, I should like by all means to tell my sister to give you her daughter. As I have said time and again, I don't see where we can find as decent a family as yours."

"Ah, ya-ya, isn't that the Second Aunt? I've just heard that you've married a wonderful daughter-in-law. I have always said that a family like yours should have had a daughter-in-law long ago. But just because your standard is so high that very few girls would suit your sons, so it has been delayed. But any way you got what you wanted. You must be very happy, indeed. Your fate is really a lady's. We are proud of being your neighbors. We should like to come and see your beautiful one. Please do drop in to see us when you are not too busy."

Marriage of a son raises a mother's position in a large family. Her position depends upon her children. It is true that she is a wife and a daughter-in-law to a large family. But this is not significant until she has children. The children have full kinship status in the family and the mother acquires hers through them. In a large family, all the daughters-in-law with children are supposed to occupy equal positions of respect in the eyes of the family. In fact, however, one of them may outrank the others. The ability or personality of one of them may differentiate the attitude of the family members, but the most important arbiter of a woman's prestige is married sons. A mother-in-law is the most respected female in a Chinese family: her status not only carries with it authority over a number of women but it also denotes that the mother has served the family ancestors well and deserves their consideration. Although she herself may still be a daughter-in-law under the old family head, she enjoys a certain amount of honor among the young mothers in the household. Though nominally equal, the other daughters-in-law recognize her position and this is appreciated by a young mother in a large family. Therefore, she is generally eager to have her son married early.

Marriages are arranged by the parents, more specifically by the mother. When a family has a boy of fifteen or so, the matchmaking woman, a female relative, or a friend of the parents, inquires if the boy is engaged. The mother is usually glad to answer, for if the boy is engaged she is proud of it, and if he is not she will be anxious for the inquirer to help. Such an inquiry is often merely a prelude to conversation, but if the woman asks this intentionally and says that she knows of a girl, then the talk takes a serious turn and proposal is started. The matchmaker visits the other family and poses the same question. If she happens to be related to the family, the question is unnecessary and she may begin the talk right away. The girl's mother may have a different attitude. If the girl is still young, say twelve or thirteen years old, and her physical appearance is not bad and if the description of the boy's family is not particularly appealing, the mother may say to the matchmaker: "Thanks for your concern for us, but I feel that our little maid is not in a hurry. Let us leave the matter for the time being." This means that the offer has been refused. If, however, the girl is already twenty years old, and the mother realizes that she has no reason for a standard which would exclude ordinary boys, then she would probably say: "By all means, please help us to make this match. Day and night her father and I worry about finding her a p'o-chia (a family to which a daughter will be married). After all we cannot keep daughters at home for ever, can we? If the boy is good-natured and the family has enough to eat, I would say the match is perfect. Anyway, I shall talk this matter over with her father."

At this, the matchmaker informs each family of the birth dates of the girl and the boy. They are written on paper with eight characters defining the year, month, date, and hour of the birth, or they are memorized. To determine the girl's compatibility with the boy and the members of his family, the girl's mother does the same with the boy's eight characters. The boy's mother consults some old ladies in the neighborhood who know a system of calculation based on the eight characters. If there is no one in the neighborhood who can read the characters, a professional fortune teller is invited. As far as this writer knows, the people of Taitou do not have great faith in the fortune tellers and do not take the reading of the eight characters very seriously. Nevertheless, when both mothers are satisfied that the eight characters of both children are compatible, the formal proposal is started.

Generally, the selection of a daughter-in-law is simpler than that of a son-in-law. The economic condition of the family is more important than the boy's personal qualities, provided he has no particular physical or mental defects, but in the girl's case her family is not subjected to the same scrutiny. The chief requisit s for a daughter-in-law are physical health to insure progeny, efficiency in domestic work, a good reputation—which means that the girl is not known for love affairs or disobedience to parents—and, lastly, freedom from physical or mental defects. Unusual attractiveness is not desirable. The economic or social status of the girl's family is not important, but it must be of good name, or at least not have a bad name. The well-known idea of "equality of gates and doors," or the proviso that the two families be of equal or comparable social status, is not general in the rural communities, though it might hold in an urban community or among a few prominent families. Frequently the girl's family is of poorer social and economic status than the boy's. The prevailing opinion is that one should not select a daughter-in-law from a family that is much more prosperous than one's own, otherwise the bride may compare the new household unfavorably with the home she has left, complain about the deprivations, and feel superior to the other daughters-in-law.

In choosing a family for one's daughter the situation is reversed. The parents' first consideration is the economic condition of the family—how much land and how many houses the family owns. The girl's mother finds out how many sons the family has and calculates how much each one of the brothers will have when the property is finally divided. It makes a great difference when one compares a family that has twenty *mow* of land but only one son, with one that has thirty *mow* but three sons. If the economic condition is satisfactory, the mother will take the boy's personal qualifications into consideration, but will not make too much fuss about this. It is a strong rather than a handsome body that matters. A pockmarked face will not matter if everything else is all right. Careful mothers also pay attention to the boy's personality. The moral standard for a man is different from that for a woman. He is not strictly subjected to sexual morality, to conventional manners, to domestic regulations as a woman is, but if he is known to be hot-tempered, or to have unpopular habits, such as drinking, smoking, or gambling, the chances for marriage will be lessened.

When the two families are satisfied, a formal letter is sent by the boy's family in which the engagement of the girl to the boy is requested. This is accompanied by presents to the girl's parents. Generally, these consist of forty big steamed rolls made of refined wheat flour, a large piece of pork (about 15 pounds, or less), and several kinds of cakes. The girl receives jewelry, dress material, money, and other articles useful to a bride, the amount and quality varying according to the economic condition of the boy's family. In some cases a sum of money, from one to two hundred dollars, is also given to the girl's parents. Sometimes part of the money is changed into cloth or cotton yarn. Generally, when a girl is to be engaged to a boy who has a lot of brothers, or whose family is not well-to-do, the girl's parents will drive a hard bargain and demand as much money or goods as possible for the girl. Or, should the girl's parents be too poor to prepare their daughter's marriage even according to the minimum requirements, a certain amount of money and goods will be asked for the trousseau. The money thus secured will for the most part be spent on the girl. Occasionally, however, some of it will be spent by her father for the family's livelihood. This would make the parents unpopular, and fellow villagers would say that they are selling their daughter. The daughter herself may complain that her parents have taken advantage of her. For this reason, decent families never mention money in arranging marriage for their daughters. But, unfortunately, it makes it rather hard for a poor boy to get a wife, and this may explain the fact that the size of economically lower class families is generally small.

The engagement ceremony takes place at the girl's home. In most cases, the boy's father, or a person who can act in the father's place, presents the letter and gifts. The girl's parents formally entertain the guest. Senior members among the close relatives are invited to the party. If the families are orthodox enough, the letter will be formally presented. From this time on, the two families are relatives and address each other with the proper terms. At this time the boy's father can see the girl personally, and she pays her respects to him. Both families announce the engagement by distributing the big rolls to relatives, friends, and neighbors.

About a half year to three or five years elapses before the wedding. Children of rich families are usually engaged when they are very young and the period may last three years or more, but if a family is poor and it is hard for a son to find a wife, so that he is not young when he is engaged, the wedding takes place immediately after the engagement, with only enough intervening time for the girl to make her wedding dresses.

The wedding outfit includes a number of jackets, shirts, trousers, gowns, underwear, shoes, and bedding. A girl should have at least twelve suits for winter weather and twelve suits for warm weather. All of them should be made of either silk or fine cloth. About ten or twelve pieces of bedding are prepared. All this takes time and the wedding of a well-to-do girl requires a very long period for preparation. In addition, things like trunks, suitcases, boxes, bureaus, cabinets, and toilet articles must be either bought or made. Of course the boy's family supplies some of these things, but the girl's parents must do their best if they do not want themselves and their daughter shamed. The girl, if she is still young, will learn under her mother's direction many kinds of domestic work, such as cooking, sewing, grinding, and embroidery. Naturally, she also secretly learns how to be a good bride and how to get along with a strange man. If her engagement takes place when she is about twenty years old, she dresses her hair in the fashion which indicates that she is betrothed and ready to marry.

In this period of waiting, the members of the two families are not supposed to see each other often, and even avoid each other except for necessary meetings. In spite of this pattern they remain extremely attentive to each other's affairs. Because the engagement is not as final as marriage, it is not immutable. Although no decent family likes to see the engagement broken, nevertheless, such cases have happened and, if the two families are intimate with each other, a broken engagement will be the occasion of great embarrassment for all. The meeting of the engaged boy and girl before marriage is definitely improper. The boy is not allowed to visit the girl's family and it remains impossible for him to see his fiancée, unless she is seriously ill. Since all but a few of the engagements are between families of different villages or communities, any meeting of the two parties is difficult at best.

When the period of preparation is over, the boy's family pays a formal visit to the family of the girl for the purpose of setting the date of the wedding. The father or a senior member of the boy's family must attend this meeting. A formal dinner is prepared for the guest and arrangements for the wedding are discussed by the representatives of the two families. Gifts are presented at this time to the girl's family, mostly gifts for the family as a whole, with a few minor presents for the prospective bride. The wedding usually takes place a month or two after this occasion.

Several days before the wedding, the family of the groom begin preparing food, collecting extra utensils, and decorating the *hsi-fang*, the room in which the young couple will live. Presents and congratulations are received, and invitations are sent out to relatives who live in distant villages. Paternal and maternal aunts come with their children and stay several days.

In the bride's home, mother and daughter are also busy with preparations, but the atmosphere is one of sadness. The mother is grieved over the impending separation; in the heart of the girl there is a mixture of hope, fear, anxiety, and shyness. The father and brothers are also depressed over their loss but they say nothing. The family does not entertain guests at this time and the bride's relatives are not invited to the wedding.

On the morning of the wedding day, the boy's family sends a decorated bridal chair born by four able-bodied men to the girl's home. The four carriers are either the boy's cousins or young men of the village. In other places, a brass band is hired to play for the occasion, but this is not done in Taitou nor in the villages of the surrounding area. When the chair arrives at the girl's home, the bride, who has been waiting for it, is immediately carried into the chair by one of her elder brothers or by an uncle, while the mother weeps and the father stands silent. The bride wears a formal wedding dress or bridal robe of red or deep pink and her face is covered with a piece of red satin. The bridal chair is closed with a curtain so that nobody can see her on the road. Two brothers, close cousins, or perhaps her uncle, accompany her. On the road, the bridal procession proceeds slowly so that the bride will not get seasick, and also so that the enormous and extravagant dowry can be seen and admired by the people in the villages on the way. Meanwhile, the groom, attired in formal wedding gown of blue and jacket of black, waits in the wedding room.

When the bride arrives at the bridegroom's front door, two elderly women come out to meet her, while the men take care of the dowry and welcome the guests who have accompanied the bride. The women's duty is to transport the small boxes in which the bride's toilet articles are contained from the bridal chair to the *hsi-fang*, and then to take the bride to the place where the wedding ceremony will be performed. This is usually the front court of the home, if the weather is good. In the center of the court is set a table on which are offerings to the gods of Heaven and Earth, a pair of red candles and three sticks of incense. The bride and groom stand side by side in front of the table and pay homage to the gods. Then, facing each other, the bride bows to the bridegroom and he returns the gesture. After this, they are led into the house and to the *hsi-fang*, the bridegroom walking ahead of the bride. She is helped by the two elderly women because her head is still covered. Meanwhile, a square piece of sweet cake, wrapped with red cloth, is given to her by a sister of the bridegroom. A saddle, supposed to represent an evil spirit trying to block the union of the two, is placed in her path. Passing over it means the obstacles are overcome, the success of the marriage is assured. In the house both the bride and groom make ritual homage to the ancestors, if the family is orthodox enough—otherwise, the ceremony performed in the court is assumed to have been shared by the ancestors. In the *hsi-fang*, the bride is seated on a wooden bed, while the groom takes his place on the brick bed. He is asked to take the red cloth off the bride's head. This is a very important moment to both bride and groom because they are to see each other face to face for the first time. The bride is fed with food which has been brought with her from her home and this is shared by the groom and his parents. After this, the bride is led to pay her respects to her parents-in-law and the groom accompanies her. When they return to their own room both of them will sit on the brick bed and the formal dresses are taken off. The young members of the family and of the neighborhood can now come to see the bride and look at the dowry. The bride is expected to sit on the bed quietly without speaking. The bridegroom also sits there looking very much embarrassed.

The whole family is busy entertaining guests. The two people who have accompanied the bride are the most honored guests and are entertained by senior members of the clan or village leaders, or by the schoolteacher. The feast is the best that the family can afford. The presents given by the relatives before the wedding day are used to help the family prepare for this occasion. Friends who come on the wedding day or before also bring gifts of money, a piece of satin bearing words of blessing or congratulation on golden paper, or perhaps merely a pair of paper scrolls with lucky words written on them. Popular phrases for this purpose are, "Give birth to a son early"; "Marriage that will last a hundred years"; and the like.

On all the doors of the home new couplets are posted. A large character for happiness is painted on the spirit wall (a wall built behind the front door in the court), or written on red paper and then pasted on. The house, if the family can afford it, is painted and the walls in the rooms newly papered.

The family and all the guests are in their best clothes as on New Year's Eve. The bride's dress must be cotton-padded, even if it is summer, because cotton-padded clothes symbolize riches or the continuation of the family. In Chinese, the character for cotton is pronounced *mien*. The word which denotes the continuance of progeny is also pronounced *mien*. Clothes that are not cotton-padded are called *tan yih*, or clothes not lined. The word *tan* means thin, single. or lonesome; therefore, it is not proper for an occasion like this. Chestnuts and dates are sewn between the layers of cloth at two ends of the bride's dress; they are also sewed into the cotton-padded bedding, and are placed in the bureaus, cabinets, and in all the small and large boxes in the *hsi-fang*. The words for these two nuts are similar in sound to the terms for good fortune and the early birth of sons. In the classic families, or families with imperial honors, the bride should wear an official bridal robe during the ceremony, but an ordinary family does not require this.

On the evening of the wedding day, the room of the bride and groom is well illuminated with candles and lamps. The room is fully packed with young relatives and intimate friends, who have come to make fun of the bride and the groom. Sometimes the joking gets out of bounds, but usually it takes the form of jibes at the expense of the groom. The groom's male cousins, friends of more or less equal age, wives of the groom's elder brothers, and cousins are all present. They insist that the new couple do amusing things. In all instances the idea of the fun-making is to stay in the room talking and acting nonsensically as long as possible, so that the bride and groom cannot retire too early. After they have all gone, though it may be midnight or still later, the bride and groom perform the last ceremony of the wedding before they retire. This is called toasting each other for the union. A small tray with a bottle of wine and two dishes of vegetables is brought to the room. The door is closed and the couple are alone. They are supposed to drink the wine and eat the food, but in most cases they are unable to do more than pretend to drink and eat after the day's mental and physical strain. Only after this ceremony are the two really united and the titles of husband and wife assumed.

The three things which sanction the marriage are the bridal chair which brings the bride, the parade from the bride's home to that of her husband, and the ritual homage to the gods of Heaven and Earth and to the ancestors of the husband's family. It is well known that in rural China marriage is not recognized through a formal contract signed by the two parties, although the *mei-chi*, marriage-requesting-letter, has been written by the boy's parents and consented to by the girl's. It is not registered in any kind of civil agency. The bridal chair has for long been socially recognized as the only proper vehicle for carrying the bride to her husband. If she is brought in anything else, she will not be regarded as a proper wife and will perhaps have a shameful position in the family and in the eyes of the relatives. This chair can only be used in a first marriage. It is not used in a woman's second marriage, for a second marriage is a matter of shame. If any serious dispute or legal controversy arises between husband and wife or between the wife and members of the husband's family, the wife may say to her husband or to the others involved, "Whatever you may do, remember that I did not walk to your home by myself, but I was carried in a bridal chair sent by you," thus indicating that she is a properly married wife and protected by social sanction and law.

The parade of the bridal chair and the dowry is for the purpose of showing that the marriage is being properly performed and also to let people see the dowry. The homage to the gods of Heaven and Earth assures that the marriage has been sanctioned by gods and not merely by men. The ceremony performed before the table of ancestors is a way of informing them that the woman has been properly introduced into the family and that hereafter she is one of them. She will assume full responsibility toward the living members and the spirits of the dead. Thus, a Chinese marriage is recognized first by the two parties, second, by the two families and their relatives, third, by the society in which the couple is living, fourth, by the divinities. It is not surprising that a broken marriage in rural China is rarely seen.

In other parts of the country, marriages between girls of fifteen and of boys of seventeen years old have been reported, but in Taitou the average age is about twenty years. No bride under seventeen, or groom under nineteen, is known. The sons of poor families marry even later. A daughter-in-law is needed to help with work, not for the satisfaction of the boy's desires. Since a girl of fifteen or seventeen is still too young to be useful, it is better for her to stay home a few years more to learn the necessary skills. It is economically disadvantageous to take a daughter-in-law as an apprentice, for she serves her apprenticeship, so to speak, in her own home. Of course, the younger the bride, the longer her period of fertility, and a woman's child-bearing function is very important to a Chinese family. But it is questionable if a girl of fifteen or seventeen is capable of having children. At least the local people firmly believe that a girl of this age is too young to be a mother. It is interesting to note that, until very recently, most young couples had their first child after about two years of marriage. This gave further weight to the belief that boys and girls under the age of twenty are not mature enough to have children.

Unmarried people are not given information about sex. When a daughter is ready for marriage a mother may tell her everything about being a wife except the sexual aspect. A girl may learn something from her brother's wife, but this is unusual and is strictly forbidden in a decent family. A boy is similarly handicapped. As a matter of fact he has less chance to learn, for a mother, or any female relative, is more embarrassed to discuss this with a son than with a daughter. His father, brothers, or uncles do not speak to him of such things, nor would his married cousins enlighten him. He cannot learn from fellow villagers of his own age because most of the young married men are too shy to tell of their experiences. Information gathered haphazardly is likely to be vague and misleading. In general, every couple has to go through a period of trial and error. A married girl is told about raising a child only after she has become pregnant. At this point, our villagers strictly follow Mencius' teaching, "No woman learns to raise children first and then marries."

The situation has recently begun to change. It is said that unmarried young people, especially boys, now know more about sexual affairs. They also talk about it more freely and are no longer so embarrassed when they are asked if they want to marry. Young couples now have their first child in the first year of marriage. A young father is not too shy to carry his baby in the street, nor does he feel uneasy when he accompanies his young wife on a visit to her family. Many mothers complain that their married sons are too ready to side with their wives when family controversies arise. It is obvious that the social attitude toward sexual affairs has more or less changed and this may result from the importation of ideas from Tsingtao.

Marriage is absolutely monogamous, though until recently the possession of two women by one man simultaneously was not illegal. A few years ago, a man of a neighboring village became rich and after he came home to settle down he married a concubine on the ground that his first wife, who was then forty-five, had failed to bear a child. This was frowned upon generally, though it was permitted by the old civil law. Recently, the National Government promulgated a series of marriage laws according to which no husband is permitted to marry a second time unless the first marriage has been dissolved by death or divorce. Thus, concubinage has been abolished. The law has not changed the situation fundamentally; or, to put it another way, the absence of polygamy in our village, as well as in most of the rural areas, is due not to the legal prohibition but to other factors, chiefly the economic one. It is hard enough for poor families to find one wife for each of their sons; to support additional wives, if they could be found, would be impossible. But even families who could meet the additional expense have not done so. There must be a reason besides the economic one, and this writer assumes it to be a deep-seated antagonism to plural marriage that constitutes a social tradition of the locality. For generations no family has had a concubine in the household, with the single exception noted. Adoption, rather than concubinage, solves the problem of childless wives. Anyone who married a concubine would be subject to severe criticism not only from his own brothers and cousins but from the whole community. The man mentioned above was on bad terms with his brothers and had to move to Tsingtao after he had taken the concubine. His brothers argued that he could have adopted a boy of theirs and by not doing so indicated that he preferred to separate himself from the family.

Marriage in Taitou, as well as in most parts of China, is patrilocal and patrilineal. The woman is taken to the husband's family and his clan name is added to hers. Although four different clans are represented in Taitou, marriage between a boy and girl of the same village is discouraged, and no case of intravillage marriage is known to this writer. Some villages are all of one clan and, in such cases, village exogamy is necessary. Another possible reason for the absence of intravillage marriage may be that families related by marriage do not like to live near each other. The engaged couple would be likely to see each other and be tempted into a love affair. Families related by marriage should always be reserved with each other and if they lived in the same village, they would see or visit each other very often. Families in the same village can also very easily become involved in the same village or neighborhood controversies. It would be extremely embarrassing for affinal relatives to find themselves on opposite sides in such a dispute. On the whole, intravillage relations are more intimate than is considered proper for affinal relatives.

There is a tendency for a family to marry several of its members to families in one or two neighboring villages. In one Yang family, for instance, a daughter was married into a family in a village five miles south of Taitou, and the son and grandson married girls from the same village. Several P'an families have found husbands and wives for their children in another locality which includes a number of near-by villages. Most of the families, especially those better off, do not use professional match-makers but ask their relatives or friends to act for them. It is very common for a daughter-in-law to suggest a cousin, or a girl from her own parents' neighborhood, as a wife for her younger brother-in-law. A married daughter may enjoy acting as matchmaker between her own brother and a girl from her husband's neighborhood.

In the last thirty or forty years, there has been only one case of divorce. The wife had become pregnant before her marriage. After she was married, she stayed only a few days at her husband's home. When she was paying her formal visit to her mother after marriage, she refused to return to her husband and took refuge with her lover. Neither her family nor her husband's could find her, so her husband could do nothing except to announce a divorce. Since there was no newspaper to publish the announcement, nor a legal agency at which to register it, it was written on paper, witnessed by several village elders, and communicated to the woman's family. The rarity of this incident caused it to be told and re-told for a long time afterward. Later it was said that the divorced woman had not been happy with her unlawful husband, and had regretted her action. If she had not been pregnant, she would not have refused to return to her real husband and might have expected forgiveness if she had confessed her guilt. This account of the affair shows how reluctant the local people are to recognize the reality of divorce.

This attitude has changed in the last ten or fifteen years, although the change has not as yet been felt in Taitou. Divorces in farm families have been reported in increasing numbers. Most of these recent divorces are results of discrepancy in education. Many young sons and young daughters of well-to-do families now go to the new schools. After graduation, they find jobs in the cities and do not return to farm villages. Away from home, modern boys meet modern girls. They fall in love and want to marry, even though many of them already have wives in their farm homes. In these cases divorce is the only solution. These young men are beyond the ties of the old communities and the family rules cannot reach them; the new government has legalized divorce and the families are financially able to support the wives at home, so that no great difficulty arises. In such cases the young men simply dictate a divorce to their ignorant and old-fashioned wives and then marry and establish new homes in the cities, relinquishing their right to inherit their share of land. These divorces have been bitterly criticized by all the relatives and friends of the young men, but the criticism is ineffectual since the object of it is out of reach. Even when the divorce is illegal, as it sometimes is, the family does not take action. The rural people still regard this kind of affair as their own business and would feel it a great shame or embarrassment if the case were brought to public view or dealt with in court. Second, the divorced wives are ignorant of any legal procedure and afraid of strangers. They are heartbroken, to be sure, but they also realize that there is no use in fighting—their husbands are already lost to them. They accept it as their fate, and without too much antagonism, since they have children to depend upon and parents-in-law to support them.

The most common criticism of divorce is that it is unfair to the wives, for they are unable to remarry. On the other hand, men who have fallen in love cannot be expected to remain married to their former wives. Their careers take educated men to the cities and they need wives for companionship, for participating in social activities. Country wives cannot satisfy these needs, particularly since the city women are also educated, and country wives would not know how to cope with them in social situations.

No social inequality between men and women is so apparent as the discrimination in the matter of remarriage. When a man's wife dies, he is perfectly free to marry again, and he can marry a virgin. The ceremonies, the congratulations, the parade, the happiness of his relatives, occur just as at his first marriage. The dead wife is forgotten altogether, unless she left a child. A widow, however, must not remarry. If she is the wife of a family of status, or if she has a child, especially if the child is a son, she is supposed to remain in widowhood for the rest of her life. Public opinion is that a decent woman should be the wife of only one man. When a widow of a poor family or of a family that has not much social prestige does remarry, she is not carried in a bridal chair, nor accompanied by her brothers or uncles, and no parade or ceremony is held for her. Her husband will simply take her to his home on the back of a beast or on a wheelbarrow, usually in the early morning or late afternoon when they will not be seen by many people. The family of the new husband will treat her like a maid rather than a wife. Women in the neighborhood will not speak to her, nor come to visit her. A widow can find as a husband only a very poor man, or an old man whose grandchildren or kinsmen would not permit a formal remarriage.

In Taitou there have been only two cases in which men married, or simply took, widows. The first was a woman left childless and propertyless after being married four or five years to a very poor man, the youngest of four brothers. Soon after his death the widow married one of the elder brothers. He had been married and had a son but his wife had been dead for many years. The four brothers had separated years earlier, after their parents died. The widow's husband was the poorest of the brothers and also one of the meanest persons in the village. The woman came from a distant village. Nobody spoke to the couple at all after the marriage. Social relations with all fellow villagers and kinsmen were broken. People talked about the marriage and criticized it severely. The couple had a child, but they lived together only three or four years and then separated. (This was also the only case of separation in the village.) The woman took her child and went to live with a third man, a fellow villager, but with a much better standing than the other. He worked for the gentry and the clan leaders. Gradually he showed his ability and became a village officer. His marriage was criticized but not as severely as in the former case. This was because he had never married before and was not previously related to the wife.

Regarding the woman, people just got tired of gossiping about her. They still held aloof, but, after the husband became a village officer and established a family with child and house, the villagers gradually assumed friendly relations with the family and no longer discussed the marriage. The woman was greeted by neighbors in the street and received at homes when she occasionally went to visit someone.

Another case was that of an old man of a decent family who took a widow home to attend him at night and to take care of him. He was too old to have a formal marriage and his sons and daughters-in-law would not permit it.

A daughter of a Ch'en family in Taitou was married into a distant village. A few years after her husband's death, she remarried. Her action was considered very regrettable because both her family and her husband's were people of good social standing. Besides, she already had a son and she had some land-property to live on. When she came back to the village to visit her relatives after the second marriage, she was given a cold reception and never returned again. The son by her first husband was given to one of her brothers.

Local custom permits a man to marry his dead wife's sister, and sometimes the marriage is encouraged by both the already related families. It is favorably talked about in the neighborhood gossip. But this depends much on the desirability of the man. If he has been considered a good husband by his wife's people and has a sound economic standing, the so-called "continued marriage," or *hsiu-ts'in*, is very apt to take place. If the girl has had deep affection for her dead sister and has great sympathy for the motherless children, she will signify a wish to fill the vacant position even if the man is not a very desirable husband.

It is also permissible for a boy to marry the daughter of his father's sister or his mother's sister. If the boy's mother and the girl's get along well, they will encourage the marriage in every way. However, public opinion holds that this kind of marriage is far from satisfactory. It is frequently observed that the relationship between an aunt mother-in-law and a niece daughter-in-law can be worse than bad. For this reason, far-sighted people disapprove marriages between cousins.

Sexual relations without formal marriage are morally forbidden. Adultery between persons of the same clan or family is severely condemned. The male suffers permanent loss of social and family position. The woman, if unmarried, will probably commit suicide, for she has lost her chance of being properly married. If a young man has an affair with a girl of a different clan, his punishment may be light—sometimes no more than the laughter of the villagers; but the girl will suffer. There are three or four families in the village whose social standing is so low that the villagers do not think of them in comparison with other families. Sexual immorality in these families is taken for granted and nobody cares unless in some way it shames the community as a whole. If one swears at a fellow villager with such words as "I attack your ancestors," "I sleep with your mother (or sister)," "Your mother's (or sister's) vagina," this is a serious matter and causes great shame to all the on-lookers. If the person invoked is one's wife, the case is not so serious, but rather a kind of joke.

Marriage usually relates individual families of different villages. If two important families intermarry, all the people of the two villages may treat each other more cordially than they do outsiders, for the eminence of the families creates a link between them. On the other hand, if the marriage is unsuccessful, if the daughter of an important family, for example, is ill-treated by her mother-in-law and this is known, then antagonism springs up between the two villages and relations between them will be uniformly distant. In average marriages, the relations are limited to the two families concerned. They do not involve other vill gers unless numerous marriages cement the tie.

The introduction of a young man to his wife's family is the most significant acknowledgment of affinal unity. This always takes place in the first New Year season after marriage. Several days before the visit, the young wife tells her husband about her family, especially about her brothers, brothers' wives, and her sisters. This is to help her husband meet the situation. The young man's parents will also instruct him on the proper manners or customs to observe when he will be treated as an honorable guest by his new relatives. The presents prepared for the visit vary according to the resources of the family, but they must meet certain requirements. They may consist of forty big steamed rolls of refined wheat flour, ten or twelve catties of vermicelli made of pea flour, ten or twelve catties of pork cut in one piece, a pair of dressed hog legs, one or two live cocks, and innumerable cakes and sweets.

On the morning of the visit, the young man puts on his best clothes, a mule is cleaned and decorated with a chain of bells and other ornaments, and the gifts are loaded on its back. The young husband's heart is beating fast, for he is teased by his brothers' wives and by his sisters. When he nears his wife's village, he finds one of his brothers-in-law waiting to meet him. They greet each other and walk together into the village. Almost at the same time the other brothers-in-law run home to announce the arrival of the guest and the whole family come to the front door to wait. All the girls and young wives of the neighborhood also rush to the street to see the young husband of their married cousin. As the guest passes through the neighborhood, all the eyes of the women are upon him. Whistling, laughter, shouting, and remarks accompany him, so that it is hard for him not to become nervous and embarrassed, but this is just what the spectators are waiting for. At the first sign of discomfiture, they will increase their jibes. If the groom does not remain impervious to the taunts, he will be thought ill-mannered by the entire village.

This particular ordeal ends when his parents-in-law come out to greet him, but as soon as he becomes conscious of the fact that he is standing amidst a group of people to whom he must make obeisances, his embarrassment returns. His face is red, his tongue unmanageable, and he cannot say the proper words of greeting. As he lifts his head he sees new female eyes looking at him. The wives of his brothers-in-law are making mischievous gestures behind their elders' backs. Relief comes again from his parents-in-law who try to ease the situation by asking him about his parents and his trip. Meanwhile, his beast and the gifts are taken care of by his brothers-in-law and their wives. As he walks toward the main reception room, he has to pass another barrage—the eyes of his grown-up sisters-in-law. According to local custom, it is not proper for grown-up but unmarried girls to meet their sister's young husband. But they, too, want to see what he looks like, so they hide in their rooms or some secret places and peep through the windows as he passes by.

Finally, the young man is ushered into the main reception room, or into the guest room, or the room of his parents-in-law. He is now the most honored guest of the family. He is entertained with the best dishes that the family can possibly afford. Important clan leaders or the village gentry are present at the first dinner in his honor. If the young man is handsome, well-built, and has the reputation of a scholar, the parents-in-law will be pleased, and the occasion will be very gay. The dinner is rather formal; the father-in-law and the distinguished visitors act as hosts, the eating and drinking is curtailed, the conversation is larded with expressions of praise and flattery. After the father-in-law and the dignitaries have excused themselves and left, their places are taken by the brothers-in-law and their cousins. The duty of young hosts is to make the entertainment gay and to see that their guest drinks enough. Each one attempts to persuade him to drink more and more, by playing the so-called finger game, toasting innumerable relatives and friends, and making speeches, in the hope of getting him drunk. The original purpose of all this was to permit the guest and the younger people to have a good time and to show the family's sincerity. Since a new son-in-law will feel uneasy before his parents-in-law and other elders, he is permitted this drinking bout in their absence, but he is expected to be moderate and well-behaved, to drink without getting drunk. His brothers-in-law, feeling that they are testing the young man, urge him incessantly to drink. If he carries his liquor well, he will be praised after he is gone; if not, he may well have some apprehension as to the impression he left behind.

When the entertainment is over, the young man is ushered into his mother-in-law's presence. She, on her side, is very anxious to see and talk to him. Sometimes a woman will be more fond of her son-in-law than of

her own sons. She is very strongly attached to her daughter and this
sentiment extends to the daughter's husband and children. On this occasion, the mother-in-law treats her son-in-law with great tenderness and
affection, much as she has treated her daughter. She talks to him about
all kinds of domestic affairs and praises her daughter's good nature, all
the time trying to find out whether the young man really loves her
daughter or not. She takes care of all his needs while he remains with
the family. This excessive attention sometimes displeases her sons and
their wives, who may wish the guest to leave them as soon as possible. In
the first New Year call, a son-in-law should stay at least one night, but
after this time he is free to go.

After some years, when children have been born to the young couple,
the visit becomes much more ordinary. Formalities disappear, the guests
are greeted casually, and the sisters-in-law may joke with the couple.
These visits generally occur once a year, though the wife may visit her
mother frequently. When she goes without her husband, a male relative
will escort her on her return to her husband's family, and in this way becomes acquainted with them. The women of the two families, however,
see each other rarely, for the husband's family does not visit his wife's
family. The affinal bond remains weak.

<table>
<tr><td>## Child Training</td><td>## 10</td></tr>
</table>

WHEN a child is about to be born, all the men, unmarried girls, and children are sent away, or, if the house has many rooms, they may merely be banished to some of the empty rooms and told to keep quiet. Some of the neighbor women may be asked to help, but, unless specifically invited, guests and neighbors are not welcome. The necessary articles for the confinement are made ready in the mother's room and the midwife is called. She is usually one of the old women of the neighborhood whose only qualification is the fact that she has delivered other babies; she may also be a witch doctor, and this is considered an added recommendation. In some poor families, the husband assists at the confinement without the aid of a midwife. The midwife is not held responsible for the safety of the mother or the child and receives no specific fee, but is rewarded at the discretion of the family.

After the child is delivered, its mouth is "opened" with a few drops of water, a ceremonial feeding which is called *kai kou*. The soiled articles and the afterbirth are carried out to the backyard and buried. The mother is fed with a gruel made of glutinous millet and brown sugar, the only food allowed her on the first day. The child is wrapped in pieces of cloth and allowed to nurse at the mother's breast.

The third day after the birth is called *kuo-san-jih* and is ceremonially celebrated. The child is bathed and clothed in its first garment, a little jacket made of a single piece of red cloth. He is then presented to his grandparents. The family has a feast on this day, but not an elaborate one. The main dish on this occasion is a special kind of noodles made of flour, eggs, and the powder of sesame seeds, and cooked without salt or sauce. It is believed that these noodles are good for the mother's milk and speed her recovery. Food is also distributed to neighbors and clan members so that they may share the family's joy in the newborn child. Upper-class families take this occasion to thank their ancestors for the birth of the child and to pray for the safety of the new life. Congratulations and gifts from neighbors and clán membe are received. Neighboring families usually offer glutinous millet, twenty or thirty eggs, and some brown sugar, since these foods are thought to be the most nourishing for the mother. The gifts come in a fine basket covered with a piece of red cloth and are presented by the mother of the donor's family. She sees the child when presenting her family's gift and praises it and the mother. All gifts must be recorded or at least the givers' names must be remembered, so that similar congratulatory offerings may be made on the birth of a child in the donor's family. These reciprocal presentations go on for many generations.

Also on the third day the baby is given its small name by the head of the family. If there are no grandparents, this duty falls upon the baby's parents. Generally a male child's small name directly or indirectly refers to the family's prosperity or continuity. This is because a boy is expected to be a breadwinner and one who will bring fortune to the family. These expectations create great joy when a boy is born and a high value is placed upon the child. Both the celebration of the birth and an appropriate name reflect the parents' wishes for his health, longevity, and expected talents. Names like *Hsi* (joy) and *Lo* (happiness) indicate the parents' feelings on the occasion. Words like *Pao* (precious), *Kwei* (highness), *Kin* (gold), *Yu* (jade) are often used as names. If the parents feel that the child is a token of the coming of good fortune to the family, they will name him *Fu* (fortune), *Jui-hsiang* (blessing), *Fa* (prosperity), or *P'ing-an* (peace). They may also choose from among words like *Ch'in* (diligent), *Hsiao* (filial piety), *Shun* (obedience), *Hsueh* (learning), *Ts'ung* (intelligent), *Ch'iang* (strong), *Hu* (tiger), to express their hopes for his being blessed with special gifts. Since a boy is so important, his parents and other relatives wish him a healthy and a long life, so some parents like to call their boy *Ch'ang-sheng* (long life), *Ho-ch'ang* (monk)—which means he has been dedicated to Buddha so that the demons will fear to attack him. *Hsiao-mair* (little maiden) is a general name for all girls; a boy may be called this to fool the evil spirits into thinking he is only a girl so that they will not covet his life. *Wu-shih-i* (fifty-one) indicates that when the child was born the grandfather or grandmother was fifty-one years old, while *Hsiao-pa* (little eight) is an abbreviation for eighty; naming the child in this way expresses the gratitude of the grandparents that he is the means of continuing their lives. Sometimes a boy is named in remembrance of the time or the date when he is born, as *Cheng-yueh* (first month), *La-yueh* (twelfth month), or *Shih-wu* (fifteenth).

When a girl is born, her parents and other relatives do not expect her to earn property or to bring fortune to the family. Since a girl must marry and her important prerequisites are beauty, talent, and other virtues, her name is generally chosen from among words descriptive of these. The names of flowers, beautiful insects, or pretty birds are chosen, or those of musical instruments (organ or flute), of jewels (pearl, jade, or gold), or of natural beauties. *Ch'in* (diligence), *Sheng* (thrift), *Cheng* (chastity), *Chieh* (purity), and the like are also common names for girls.

Parents who do not know any of these rules select a name at random, one which may be altogether meaningless. If the baby is a girl and not desired because there are already too many in the family, she may be called either by the general term for all girls (*Hsiao mair*), or by a name that expresses the parents' dislike, such as *Hsia To* (Little Too-Many), *Hsiao Chou* (Little Unpleasantness), *Hsiao Tsueh* (Little Mistake), and so on. A boy baby is never named with any derogatory term.

A formal message of the birth of the first-born child is sent to the mother's parents. A messenger is dispatched with some gift within the first three days after the birth of the child. When the mother's parents receive the good news, they get together a great many presents, and the father, sometimes with the mother, goes to congratulate the child's family. The reception is more elaborate if the child is a boy. Since a young wife's mother or other relatives are not expected to assist at the birth of the child unless specifically asked to do so, their unexpected arrival would be taken to mean that the mother is afraid her daughter may not be cared for properly. Therefore the parents must wait at home until the news is sent them and only then go with great formality to see their daughter and the grandchild. If, however, the wife has no mother-in-law, her own mother will be invited to come. Poor families often have need of this outside help.

A daughter-in-law should try to leave her bed on the third day after her delivery. Of course her mother-in-law does not allow her to get up, but she is expected to make the attempt. After five or six days she should insist upon getting up to work, and her mother-in-law may still say that she is not strong enough yet. Generally, the young mother can stay in bed, or keep to her own room, for about ten days. Her parents call to take her and the child home with them when the baby is about a month old, and there the young mother has a leisurely recovery.

Usually the first birthday of a son is marked by a big celebration. Sometimes, if the family is well-to-do, a tray bearing a number of articles is placed before the child. The tray may hold a seal of some kind, a writing brush, a book, a cart, a floor sweeper, a coin, or a bottle of woman's face-powder. The child is induced to grasp for one of them while relatives and guests watch. If he takes hold of the seal, he will be an official; if he chooses the writing brush, he may become a writer, but if he takes the face powder, it is assumed that he will care only for women and this is deplored. If the boy is the first son in a large and rich family, an opera performance and an offering to the ancestors are important parts of the occasion. The child's maternal relatives come to the celebration with presents including jewelry made of silver and gold, dresses of wool or silk, or some other luxury.

The birth of a child, especially a boy, is tremendously important to a mother. When the young wife finds that she is pregnant, her thoughts, her interests, her activities, in short her whole personality begins to change. She thinks more and more of the coming of the child and asks her sisters-in-law to tell her what kind of child it will be. She is most interested in ascertaining its sex. She fears the birth pains, but she also looks forward to the honor which will be given to her as the mother of a child. Since she has been taught by her mother and mother-in-law that a child must be protected from evil spirits, certain foods, adverse emotions, ill-omened words, she carefully avoids looking at abhorrent things, she becomes quiet, is often silent, and frequently falls into revery. She watches herself carefully. When her husband comes upon her unexpectedly, her face reddens and she smiles at him with embarrassment. Occasionally her behavior may impress him, but usually he mocks her and belittles her seriousness.

The period of pregnancy is usually a time of sexual abstinence, in the common belief that intercourse between husband and wife will prove harmful to the growing foetus. Intercourse is not specifically forbidden, but a husband is supposed to abstain, and the young wife can call upon her mother-in-law for assistance in keeping the husband away. Quite often, an expectant mother will live with her own parents until the delivery is near.

After the birth of the child, the mother is in constant attendance and generally wants very little assistance. She feeds him at her breast (later he will have liquid and soft foods) day and night. She changes his wet clothes and washes him frequently. She is the only one who attends the child in case of sickness, and it is she who worries most if the illness is serious. The young father shows no interest in his child; on the contrary, he is angry if it disturbs him by crying at night. Occasionally a father hates the very existence of his child. He will not touch it for any reason.

He is embarrassed when a relative asks him about it, and to be seen actually holding the baby is a disgrace. He believes that he has helped in "making" the child, and that this in itself was shameful to him. He won't do anything to help because he believes that baby-tending is entirely a woman's job.

When the child is three or four years old, he stays close to his mother most of the time. Unless the grandmother is available to take care of him, he follows his mother around even when she is at work. One always sees a young wife with her child playing beside her as she washes her clothes on the river bank, grinds grain on a street corner, or works in the vegetable garden or on the threshing ground. By this time, however, she is usually pregnant again When the second child is born, the mother will have to shift her attention from the first one. From this time on, the older child begins to sleep with his father instead of with his mother. The small family sleeps in the same bed, it is true, but it is a very broad one and the parents sleep at opposite ends of it. The baby sleeps beside the mother and the older child then moves to the father's side. When this change occurs, the father begins to dress the child, too. When the father is busy in the field, the boy is taken care of by his grandmother or by an older sibling, either his own, or the older child of one of his father's brothers. The only chance he now has for being with his mother is on the rare occasions when the new baby is sleeping. If the first child has been weaned before the new one arrives, he will adjust more easily to the separation from his mother; the separation is not too keenly felt, for his mother is still much in evidence, even though she is not directing her attention to him, and his new companions are people to whom he is already accustomed.

Boys under ten years or so may go around entirely naked in the hot summer, but girls of the same age must cover the lower part of the body. Boys over ten must wear shorts or trousers, but may leave the upper part of the body naked. Girls of the richer families start to wear dresses when they are still very young, but daughters of poor families may wear nothing above the waist until they are seven or eight years old. A man may be stripped to the waist when the weather is hot, but a woman must always wear a dress that covers her entire body.

At the age of six or seven, a boy will either be sent to the village school, if the family is well-to-do, or be taken to the farm. If he goes to school, his duties at home will be light—sweeping the courtyard or carrying food to the field. During the harvesting seasons, he learns by trying to work within sight of his father. Sometimes he steals away from work or school, and enjoys for the first time the excitement of running wild with his playmates along the river bank or in the fields, free from the surveillance of an adult. If he does this too often, or if he injures himself or damages his clothing, he will certainly be punished by his father. He must be careful to avoid damaging any crops in his escapades or the punishment will be even more severe. In the absence of his father, his mother may punish him, but she will probably only threaten to do so. A mother usually punishes her son by scolding him or perhaps slapping his buttocks, if he is under ten years of age. When he is older she will seldom scold him directly and is even less likely to administer any physical punishment, which then becomes the sole duty of the father. A boy often seeks refuge from his father's anger by going to his mother. Since a mother's heart is too soft to see her son beaten by an angry father, she often fails to report his misbehavior. Even a mother who believes in the necessity of discipline will tell only those deeds which she deems serious and then she tries to check the father lest the punishment be too severe.

Boys and girls under ten years may play together but from that time until they are fifteen, they may play together only in groups and remain in places where they can easily be seen by adults. Girls over fifteen are not allowed to talk privately with boys of their own age. Conversation between adolescent boys and girls in the same neighborhood or between cousins is permitted if others are present but bodily contact is strictly forbidden. They may joke with each other, but strictly without reference to sex. Grown-up boys and girls of different neighborhoods do not see each other often and consequently do not talk much. A grown-up girl should not do any favor directly or privately for any young man who is not a member of her family, except with the knowledge and assistance of an adult.

In case a son who is over ten years of age must be punished, he will be beaten in privacy and his mother is the only person permitted to watch. The younger children are frightened and stay away without being told to do so. The other older members of the family may console the child afterward but must not in any way interfere during the chastisement. The other children will look at the sufferer in silent sympathy but will generally say nothing nor go near him. Should one of them tease him about the beating, he will be severely scolded by the boy's parents. It may occasionally happen that a man in a sudden fit of anger will strike his son in public. Such an act is sharply censored by all who see or hear of it. Should a neighbor see a father beating his son, he would himself take offense, and feel that the father was directing his anger at him. This might lead to actual avoidance between the neighbors, or at least some interruption in the warmth of their relationship.

A father is not expected to beat a boy over fifteen years of age. If he does so, the son resents it fiercely and the father himself is severely criticized by his fellow villagers. In addition, his own family condemns him—not only his wife but also his wife's brothers will protest, and the boy's grandparents and uncles will warn the father to stop. A decent father with an unmanageable son can only use persuasion, warnings, or explanations and, if these fail to correct the bad behavior, then father, mother, and all the senior members of the household hold a conference to talk the matter over.

A father should not only keep his hands off a married son but also should refrain from scolding him. When a son is married, he is supposed to be an adult, and the former discipline no longer applies to him. If the son does not behave properly, then his father must talk over any matters that seem to require correction with his family members, including the son's wife, when they are sitting together after supper. The father addresses himself to the whole group and not to any particular person. The son is present at the time. The father may start by saying something which seems remote from, but is really related to, the subject in his mind. Then he comes to the condition of the household and reiterates the common hopes and problems of the family. He may also talk about his own parents and grandparents, how hard they worked, with what self-denial they lived, and how they trained their children with such unremitting care that they had little time left in which to enjoy the fruits of their hard work. He may then go on to compare the present household with things as they used to be, commenting at length on the difficulties that beset parents who are trying to build up and maintain a prosperous household. He concludes his talk with encouragements, interspersed with warnings to his sons and their wives. He might, for instance, say: "I believe that a family with two or three sons like you should be more prosperous. I believe that young people with bodies as strong as yours should accomplish much more than we have so far accomplished. If we were all willing to work harder, to live more thriftily, and to follow more strictly what your grandparents have done, I believe we should be able to buy more land and build more houses."

By this time, the father has come to the main point of the evening's address and he adopts a more serious tone as he warns: "Listen, children, there is nothing in this world that can be won easily. A piece of bread must be earned by one day's sweat. You cannot buy any piece of land unless you save all that you can spare through two or three years. The desire for better food, better dress, a good time, or the easy way, will lead but to the ruin of our family. If any one of you has such desires or has already slipped into these bad practices, he had better look at Wong Hsiao Erh of East Street, or at Lee Tao Laor (Beggar Lee) of Lee Chia Chuang, and see what has happened to them. Your mother and I have done and are doing our best to keep this family as well as possible. It is not because we fear we will starve that we save, but because we want to see each one of you with a prosperous family of his own. Should you fail to behave yourselves, and consequently bring yourselves and your children to poverty and shame, remember, it will be your own responsibility. And remember that it would be a great disgrace to your ancestors."

After this speech, the father puts his pipe in his mouth and the whole group is silent. But in a moment or two, the mother makes some comment of her own in a soft tone. Her words serve to relieve the momentary tension and create an opening for the sons, should they want to say something. An elder son may say a few words to indicate his general agreement with his father's views: to say nothing would imply disagreement, to say much would indicate that the son had thought the lecture directed primarily at himself. When the group falls silent again, the mother disperses them by sending them away on forgotten errands or back to some task or other, and the father rises and walks off by himself.

It is hard to judge the efficacy of these family meetings in changing the conduc of an erring or stupid son. Much depends upon the attitude of his wife: she may persaude him to accept the warning, mend his ways, or she may make matters worse by telling him that all the father has said is nonsense and an insult to a married son, thus encouraging the idea of separation from the family group.

Young men and women of the same neighborhood should greet each other when they meet on the street or in the field. If they are not of the same neighborhood and do not know each other well, the greeting is usually avoided. When a man of a neighboring family comes to call, the women, both old and young greet him in the same fashion as the men of the household do. They can talk and laugh together, but if the guest is a man from a distant family, the young women should avoid him except for a brief greeting.

When a stranger comes to the village he must not stare at any young woman. If he wants to ask the way, he should go to a man or to an old lady for the information. It is not proper for a young woman to speak to a man she does not know.

Occasionally romantic attachments spring up between boys and girls of the same village, but these are unrelated to the idea of marriage because the tradition of exogamy is so strong that it is never violated.

The Rise and Fall of a Family | II

A FARM family's rise is largely accomplished by the buying of land, its fall occasioned by the emergencies that force the sale of land. It is interesting to note that no family in our village has been able to hold the same amount of land for as long as three or four generations. Usually a family works hard and lives frugally until they can begin to buy land. Members of the second generation continue in the same pattern so that more land is added to the family holdings and it becomes well-to-do. Those of the third generation merely enjoy themselves, spending much but earning little. No new land is bought and gradually it becomes necessary to begin to sell. In the fourth generation more land is sold until ultimately the family sinks into poverty. This cycle takes even less than a hundred years to run its course. The extravagant members die out, and their children begin again to accumulate property. Having suffered, and being fully acquainted with want, they realize the necessity of hard work and self-denial to repair the family fortune. By this time the original big family is gone and in its place there are several small, poor families. Some of these begin to buy land. Thus the same cycle is started again.

Families can be divided into three groups, those at the beginning of the climb, those in the middle and those who are the victims of the evolution. This explains why there are no permanently fixed social classes in our village and no large landlords in the whole area. Because the cycle of change is common to all, no family regards another as significantly different from itself, and each family takes pride in its own possessions. The emphasis is, therefore, not on quantitative comparison at any given time, and the inequality of income does not seriously threaten the sense of village solidarity.

Since the rise and fall of the various families is constantly in process, land transactions are also continually going on. Every winter sees the transference of some pieces of land from the jurisdiction of one family to another. The amount of money needed for buying one *mow* of crop land varies according to the quality and location of the land. Each year the price may be different. When a family needs a fairly large amount of money urgently, they usually get it together by mortgaging some of their land. The family which has the money and wants to lend it gives some to the needy family and receives the right of using the land for a certain length of time, with full rights to whatever it produces during that period. A written certificate is issued by the landowner to the money lender, for perhaps three years or longer, and the land cannot be redeemed before the stipulated time has expired. No mortgages are foreclosed. The time may be indefinitely extended, for the money lender can use the land until his money is repaid. The land tax is paid under the name of the owner but it is in fact paid by the person using the land. A family that has to secure money by mortgaging land will feel sad on the New Year and ashamed to walk on the street. The family which has authority to use the land will feel happy, their happiness second only to what it would have been had they actually bought a piece of land.

When the members of a family feel that their land is insufficient for their needs and cannot support them, they will, if they have saved a little money, lease one or two *mow* of land from a family which has more land than it can cultivate. The lease usually lasts only one year; the rent is low but is not less than thirty percent of the land's net return in the year. The rent is paid in cash and in advance. The transaction requires no written certificate but depends upon mutual understanding. It is usually made between two families, one of which is small but is rising economically, while the other is well-to-do. After the small farmer pays the rent he is entitled to use the land entirely according to his own choice, and has no other obligation to the landowner. There is no feeling such as exists between a tenant and a landlord, probably because the family that leases the land has other land of its own. To lease one or two *mow* is only to make full use of all the family so that more food can be secured for all. Besides, the family's economic condition is rising, all its members are respectable farmers. Nobody in the village would look down on such people. On the other hand, the family that has one or two *mow* to lease is not relying upon rent for income. Its members are also farmers. They may not work as hard as the members of the little family, to be sure, but they do not pretend that their economic status is much higher than that of the other's. No family can say that it may not at some time be without enough land to cultivate. Each family head often warns his family not to shame others lest they themselves be shamed.

The direction in which a family is tending can also be seen in its position in the clan, and the general strength, or lack of it, of clan consciousness among its members. When a family has developed into a number of separate households, most of which live in proximity and maintain close relations with each other, it is called a clan. A clan is a group of families connected not only through kinship but also, and more importantly, by means of mutual obligations and privileges. Each family, as well as each individual in it, has duties to perform for the benefit of the others and at the same time has the right to benefit by their efforts. The bond that holds these families together is informal but powerful. Authority is vested not in a particular family or individual but in the group as a whole. The manipulation of this force is the basic function of the clan. When the clan's influence is far-reaching, it indicates that the clan as a whole is strong and has good morale. A clan is the extension of the family and therefore when a clan is prosperous, the families in it are strong; when it is decadent, its families are probably approaching poverty and disruption. A well-functioning clan is really an indication that most of the basic families of that group are developing, not declining.

A clan provides its members with a sense of social orientation and acts as a transitional grouping between the family and the village, uniting them in some ways and bringing them into conflict in others. In South China many fairly large villages are composed entirely of families belonging to one clan. There are villages composed of only one clan in North China also, but for the most part villages contain two, three, or four clans. In some villages the kinship is heterogeneous. Taitou includes four clans as well as three or four isolated families. Of these the P'an clan is the largest, with the Ch'en, Yang, and Liu following in that order. The P'an clan is divided into five or six branches; some groups of families maintain close relations while others have drifted away and have made their homes in the territories of other clans. However, the clan association is recognized by all the villagers. In ordinary social occasions, clan members who live outside the P'an group may associate more freely with their neighbors who belong to different clans than with their own clan members, but if a controversy arises to involve the clan, or if families within it have special cause for rejoicing or sorrow, the clan members seek each other out and proffer help.

The Ch'en clan has altogether a dozen families. All of them live in the same neighborhood, so that their association is obviously close. This does not mean that they are all on good terms with one another or form a well-organized body, but people of other clans refer to them as a Ch'en section—*Ch'en Chia Hu Tung*. The Yang clan also has about a dozen families, two or three of which live away from the clan center. Nine or ten Yang families live in the same neighborhood and form a Yang section—*Yang Chia Hu Tung*. Recently, three leading families of the clan having risen economically and socially, the clan decided to have a copy of the clan book brought from their kinsmen in a neighboring village. This action stirred up a great deal of clan consciousness among the younger members and as a consequence quite a few of them advocated the strengthening of the interrelationship among the clan's families. However, one of the leading families has shown a rivalrous attitude toward the others, and the organization has not been too good. In many cases this family prefers to associate with some of the P'an families, and sometimes the association may be against the interests of its own clan. The Liu clan is declining. There are only three or four families left, all of them poor. Two of them associate frequently with the Yang families and do not attempt to form a close group of their own.

In the past the clan had numerous functions. Until very recently, there was in China no kind of public social security for the provision of the needy. The clan took care of its members and was supposed to provide for the destitute. Religious organizations or private philanthropy might serve this function in the cities and the market towns, but in the villages the clan was the most important agency. Indeed, one of its chief duties was to see that none of the members should starve or suffer. A poor and childless old couple unable to earn a livelihood would be assisted more or less regularly by the clan. If a child was left without parents or near kin to care for him before he was able to take care of himself, the clan would be responsible for bringing him up and seeing to it that he was enabled to make an independent living. If these responsibilities were neglected, it was either because the clan was too poor or because they did not mind the criticism directed at them by others. Beggars, paupers, or suffering people are mostly members of declining clans. In a poor clan, families do not associate very much and they lack the spirit to help each other. In a flourishing clan, the situation is different. The members have both the mind and the means to take care of their poor, old, and suffering people. They would feel ashamed if one of their old men had to beg for a living. They would either give him food or supply him with the means of earning a livelihood. However, we must not assume that the clan responds to all appeals with alacrity. Help is often reluctantly given and, to receive it, one must be on good terms with his kinsmen. If a poor man had formerly refused advice from his kinsmen or did not try to do his best after receiving help, he would be deserted and his further pleas for aid ignored.

In our village, the P'an clan usually took care of its poor and old. It was not a program of the clan as a whole, but each branch took care of its own closest relations. There were no beggars among them. Recently, however, the clan has declined. Morale has been broken because of general poverty. The Ch'en clan too had no beggars or paupers. Each family could make an independent living. There were two beggars in the Yang clan about five or six years ago. One was a man who had completely failed to correct his bad behavior though many chances had been given to him by his kinsmen. Later, he became a professional pickpocket and made his living that way. Knowing that there was no hope for his reform, his clan members and the villagers left him alone. As time passed, the Yang clan's reputation no longer suffered on his account, because everybody knew that he was unchangeable and not worth much attention. Another case was that of a man who, although he had two grown-up sons and property, had to beg for a living in his old age. The sons were both married. One went to Manchuria after his wife died. There, he was idle and accumulated nothing that he could bring back with him. The other son, when his wife died, had remarried a widow and adopted her boy. This man was not at all a filial son. Goaded by his second wife, he left his father alone and helpless, too old to cultivate the land and with no recourse but to become a beggar. The clan felt that it was a great shame and tried to effect a reconciliation. When this failed, they did not offer to help, because they felt that if father and son had been reasonable and had accepted the arbitration, everything would have been all right, but, since they were in the wrong, it was not incumbent upon the clan to help either of them.

Years ago a family of the Yang clan moved to the market town and opened a small business there. They did not prosper and after a while found themselves unable to make a living. The daughter was married, but the son had no work and was restless. Their situation went from bad to worse. They had moved to town because of a series of quarrels between the family's head and his brother, and therefore returning to their native village was impossible for them. Still their kinsmen did not like to bear the shame that this poor family had brought on them, so some of them who had the means gave them food, grain, clothing, wine, and sometimes a little money for the New Year season. This help continued until the old couple died. Then the son disappeared and severed all relations with his clan.

Because of the difficulty of making a livelihood in a Chinese village, the care of the infirm and needy is often neglected. To provide for emergencies, a clan has to be relatively well-to-do and there must be generous and capable leaders among them. Strong clan consciousness is also a necessary factor, for only in that case are all members interested in their clan's good reputation and concerned about the fate of any one of their members. Even if all these things are true, not everyone receives aid, but only those whose poverty has not been brought on through any fault of their own. A person who has been idle or who has gambled away his money cannot expect help from his clan. If the needy person has a near relative who has the means to help him, the clan acts only if this relative has refused any assistance. The duty of taking care of infirm members is not compulsory nor is there any definite or agreed way in which it should be done. It depends upon a number of things and so is uneven and unpredictable. In Taitou none of the clans is really large and the care of suffering people is far from satisfactory. Clan consciousness is weakening on the whole and clan organization is declining every day throughout the country.

Diverse functions of the clan include supporting a school, maintaining a hall for ancestor worship and for disciplining the unfilial or misbehaving members, keeping a clan book and teaching young members the clan's history including the good deeds of their ancestors, and collecting funds to support a brilliant but poor clan member in obtaining advanced education. The P'an clan had a school in Taitou. The schoolhouse changed locations frequently, but the teacher was always a member of the P'an clan. It was established primarily for P'an children, but children of other clans were also allowed to attend. Because some members of the other clans felt that their children were not treated like the P'an children, the Ch'en and Yang families established a bi-clan school where children of the Lius and P'ans were also received. Recently the P'an clan school has been recognized by the county government as a public school and is now subsidized by public funds. The bi-clan school has changed into the present Christian school, under a council composed of members of the Yang and Ch'en families, its pupils are for the most part children of these two clans.

So far none of the clans of our village has built an ancestral hall. It

seems that the villagers do not have much interest in the elaborate ceremonies of ancestor worship. The P'an clan did discipline their young
members when the clan was still prosperous. The other two clans, Yang
and Ch'en, were generally poor and small. They have been members of
the Christian church for a long time and since ancestor worship is regarded as unchristian, it has not been practiced by them. In other villages, however, one frequently sees the ancestral halls of a large clan.
It serves rather as a symbol of a clan's unity than as a functioning institution. Clan consciousness is not active in everyday life, but it can be
refreshed when the members see or enter the ancestral hall. On the New
Year Festival and other similar occasions the members are summoned
to the hall, where they go through some of the ceremonies, listen to the
preaching and lectures of the leaders, and discuss clan affairs. This re-
vives the feeling of unity among the kinsmen, and consequently the
association of the clan's families becomes stronger than before.

No doubt the P'an clan keeps a clan book because it has been large
and wealthy for many centuries. The Ch'ens may also have one. Until
recently the Yang clan did not. When some families grow rich and there
are educated members among them, the status of the clan rises as a
result and a leading member may suggest a clan book. The Yangs acquired their book in this way. Someone went to a neighboring village
where the Yangs are a large clan and made a copy of the book, adding to
it the names of the Yangs in Taitou, including both the living and dead
members.

Like many of the national histories, clan books generally do not recount the questionable deeds of the ancestors. They tell of the origin and
development of the clan and of the creditable actions of its departed
members, and are a source of self-esteem to all the living descendants,
who feel that their ancestors were, and that they themselves are, decent
people.

When a grandfather summons his family to see their clan book and
to listen to the stories about their ancestors, he speaks in the following
fashion. "Now, let me see. The history of our family covers three hundred
years. From our first ancestor down to you young children, we have
fifteen generations. Our first generation ancestors were poor people but
they worked hard, lived thriftily and had good relations with their neighbors. As a result, the succeeding generation was much better off. In the
fifth generation our family became quite large. Four sons passed the
Imperial Examinations and received Chiu-jen and Kung-sheng degrees.

One of them was a *hsien* magistrate and later became a prefect of Chi-chow, Honan. In the tenth generation our clan became a very large group; it included more than twenty families. These families comprised four separate branches which started with the four sons of the fifth generation. Our family is one of those of the third branch. My great-grandfather was unfortunate, because in his time our family suffered from a great hardship. My grandfather and his brothers and their wives were extremely good people. They all worked hard and lived thriftily. They never quarreled among themselves nor with their neighbors and by their efforts our family gradually became well-to-do again. My father was a businessman. It was he who started our oil-pressing business. I remember how hard he worked in order to make the business a prosperous one. Although he was a businessman he never forgot that farming and studying were the two important and safe roads through which a family may come to prosperity and glory. His children all believed in his words and that is why we kept our farm and continued sending our children to school. You children have been taught farming and studying. So, remember our ancestors' words and follow their good deeds. Yes, our family is a great family—we have wonderful ancestors!"

In most of the preaching on the occasion of a clan gathering, three main points are made. First, there is a description of the merits of the ancestors in creating the family or the clan; second, emphasis is laid upon the rules established by the past generations, and a general request is made that clan members behave in accordance with these rules of benevolence, righteousness, sincerity, and endurance; and third, the present generations are enjoined to remember the fine repute of their ancestors and to avoid any acts that would tarnish it. These points are all contained in the three famous works on family education, the *Yen Shih Chia Hsun* (Teachings on the Family), *Chu-tze Che Chia Ko Yen* (Mottoes on the Government of the Family), and *Tseng Kuo Fan Chia Shu* (Collections of Family Letters, by Tseng Kuo Fan).

Some years ago a certain large clan, not far from Taitou, raised funds for the education of a poor but promising student. At that time the clan was prosperous and well organized. Some of its leading members held official positions. The clan as a whole enjoyed a good reputation and had a high social position over a considerable area. A young boy who had just graduated from high school in the county seat showed talent and interest in further study. Because of his merit and his family's fame among the kinsmen, the boy was soon recognized by the clan as a most promising member who would add to their common glory. He was helped at school in a foreign country for several years. Later, when he showed an inclination to study in the United States, the necessary money was contributed by all the richer families of the clan, and even by one family which really did not belong to the clan but was merely of the same name. Thus the young man realized his ambition. Later, however, as it was told to the writer the case became very unpleasant. When he returned from the United States with his Ph.D. degree, every one of his clansmen and friends who had contributed toward his expenses was delighted because the harvest of their investment was in sight. This young man was a person who liked to boast; it was his practice to make promises, without feeling that they must be kept. He must have told his kinsmen while he was still in school that he would have a high position when he returned home. But when he did return, he refused to visit them. He forgot all his promises and did not even thank his benefactors. He also showed indifference to his brothers, cousins, or nephews when they came to visit him. Gradually people realized that he would not have a prosperous career in officialdom nor would he repay what he owed. His kinsmen grew bitter and some severed all relations with him; others were not on speaking terms with him.

In Taitou no clan has actually given financial support to any of their young members for education, though they have taken interest in similar cases. A member of the Yang clan, for example, had a very good reputation as a student when he was in the market-town school. He was praised by the teachers, the community leaders of the whole market-town area, and also by the senior members of the P'an clan, so that great hope was roused among all the people of the clan. This was the first time that one of their number had a chance to win an academic position, something that until then had occurred only in the P'an clan. They all hoped that the boy would pass several government examinations and would finally get an official post. After his graduation from the primary school, the boy went to a Christian high school, and then to a Christian university. This not only disappointed his kinsmen but also the villagers, because Christian schools at that time were not known to many Chinese and they were not, to them, the "door" through which contacts with the government could be made. There was a further disappointment in store for them. The young man was very unconventional. Even after he became a college student, he still came home to work on his father's farm during the summer vacations. He dressed like an ordinary farmer. This gave the kinsmen and the villagers the impression that he was not going to be a scholar or a gentleman or an official and they became indifferent toward him. He was also forgotten by the community leaders because he did not visit them when he was at home, nor did he dine or drink with them in the market town. After he was graduated from college, the young man did not become a government official but went to the field of Christian education and then into the rural reconstruction movement. These did not offer him a good salary, and he could not send his father and brothers much money. In ten years he was able to help his family buy only a few pieces of land and to build one new house. So far, he has done nothing to help his clan as a whole. Even his own brothers lost faith in him.

This illustrates an important point regarding a clan's interest in supporting someone for the purposes of advanced education. The interest is not based solely on an interest in the development of the young man but primarily on the prospective benefits that will accrue to the clan if he turns out to be a success. In the past, the Imperial Examinations were so important that a person who passed even the first one was qualified for some sort of Imperial Honor and was certain to secure a position, albeit a minor one, in the government. The honor and the benefits accruing therefrom were shared by the whole clan. After the establishment of the Republic, the old system was abolished. The number of students in the country has increased greatly and graduation from primary or high schools has become an ordinary event. Even graduation from a university no longer assures one of a government post. These changes have no doubt greatly disappointed the orthodox, both in the country and in the cities, who no longer see the point of expensive training and long years in school. They may continue to send their children to school because the latter insist upon going, but they certainly have lost interest in helping their poor relations go to college.

A clan still disciplines its errant members, though there is no formal procedure for this. If the clan is well organized, if relations among the different branches and individual families are good and there is capable leadership among the senior members, the clan head will advise, warn, and finally punish a misbehaving member with the consent of his own parents and the approval of the whole clan. Otherwise the matter will be kept within the confines of the household and the clansmen will not interfere. If a clan is growing, most of its members will be very interested in seeing that its reputation is not damaged. One member's misbehavior would be condemned by all. When a clan is declining, all its families are poor, the morale is low, and the members do not have the same interest in reputation. We can see this in the attitude of the Liu clan and also the P'an clan. Formerly the P'ans were very conscious of their reputation. Recently, however, young members of many of the rich families have destroyed their property by gambling or opium-smoking and some of them have even joined the local bandits. None of the senior members have dared to protest. The decent families have all learned to say nothing lest they be condemned by their own rebellious children.

The new social trend helps to break the clan's control over individual members. In the last fifteen or twenty years most young people have learned to disobey their families and the seniors of their clans. They depend more and more on themselves and show less and less trust in the older generation. The political chaos and the general social disorder have helped to disrupt the old unquestioning reliance upon traditional ways of living. Moreover, under the new system the households of a village are organized into numerous small units. Families and individuals are directly under the authority of the leaders of these units, a fact which has contributed markedly to the decline of the influence of the clan.

Village Organization | 12

FROM a survey of the surrounding crop land one receives a strong impression of the unity of the village. The fields belonging to village families lie side by side in a circle around the cluster of houses. Although the area overlaps at many points, the boundary line is quite recognizable and there is never any doubt as to which village any piece of land belongs to.

Village solidarity can be seen in many things. Methods of cultivating crops, of threshing, storing, or preparing foodstuffs, of cooking or preparing feasts for the New Year celebration are exactly the same for every family within a single village. In a neighboring village, even though the activities are the same, there will be slight variations in technique. One often hears farm laborers who hire out to different villages tell each other that this village's food is superior (or inferior) to that village's.

Organizations in the village can be roughly divided into three categories: those which cover the whole village, those limited to a single neighborhood, and those based on family associations.

The first village-wide organization is the village defense program, in which every family is required to take part. The families are divided roughly into three or four classes according to the number of men in the family and to its economic status. Wealthy families are expected to equip themselves with rifles, pistols, old-fashioned tube-guns, and the necessary ammunition; other families need to have only a rifle and ammunition. Families that cannot afford to buy rifles are asked to contribute other materials useful in defense. The very poor are asked for nothing except that they behave themselves and obey the defense regulations. The able-bodied men of all the families are registered and organized into a number of teams. The recruiting system is based on the family unit, each family supplying one grown-up son for duty each night.

Two defense lines were built around the village, the outer one consisting of removable mines—iron tubes filled with powder and scrap iron and connected by wire. The villagers knew where they were and how to pass through the line safely, but a stranger could not enter the village without being trapped by the wires which exploded the mines. The defenses were removed in the daytime for the safety of the villagers. The second line, built within the limits of the village, consisted of a number of fortifications, lane gates. and gun placements on the backyard walls. At night, the young men were assigned, first, to lay the explosive mines and wires for the outer line, and then to patrol the streets, lanes, and strategic points. Meanwhile, several other teams were on guard in two or three places in different parts of the village. When an alarm was sounded or a signal given by the leader or patrolman, the men on guard went immediately to the fortifications or gun placements with their guns ready. The teams alternated with each other nightly. It was estimated that at one time the villagers owned a total of fifty rifles, ten or more pistols, five or six big tube-guns, a great number of explosive mines and some ammunition. It was also reported that some of the young villagers could fire the modern weapons remarkably well. The village had not been attacked since the organization of the defense. It was rumored that bandits feared to come near it. Later, this organization was weakened, due to the bad conduct of several young men of the P'an families and also due to the gradual restoration of government control.

The village school, though it had been built by the P'an clan and was mainly supported by them, was attended by boys from the entire village. Until the establishment of the Christian school, this was the only general educational establishment in the village. Girls were not sent to school but trained in the domestic arts at home by their mothers. A few girls now go to the Christian school. At school, boys made contacts that were not dependent on the neighborhood or the clan. The school council was made up of the heads of families and this cooperation in managing and supporting the school brought families together; families too poor to send their children to school did not, of course, participate, but nonetheless the council was a village-wide organization.

The villagers regard education as a means by which a family can raise its position. Children are taught to read names, to understand the content of land deeds, and to recognize the different kinds of paper money orders so that they will not be cheated in business transactions. The sons not needed for farm work are trained for a career, for business or a trade. Calligraphy, account keeping, the use of the abacus, and the learning of the terms for farm products, farm implements, domestic utensils and manufactured commodities also held an important place in the curriculum, and there were some who regarded the school as the place where one learned good manners and absorbed the teachings of the ancient worthies.

In the past, most boys were not in the least interested in their school-work. The school itself was a one-room affair with a dirt floor. The walls were dark and the windows were pasted over with grimy old paper so that the lighting was very bad. The tables, benches, and stools were brought by the pupils from their homes. Boys ranging in age from six to twenty years were herded together in one room. The teachers' quarters were partitioned off from the schoolroom and here the teacher sat all day, except when he had calls to make, went to the market town, or was invited out to entertain a guest or to write documents for a village family. At school, his chief function was to maintain order.

The students were sent to school before the sun was up in the morning, about an hour before the teacher arrived. Each boy was expected to use this time in reading his assignment at the top of his voice and to memorize what he was reading. When the teacher appeared, another hour was spent in reviewing the textbooks. Then the boys were called upon to recite one by one. Each boy, as his turn came, placed his books on the teacher's desk, turned his back, and recited all or part of his assignment. All of this took place before breakfast. Both pupils and teachers went home to eat. When they returned from the morning meal, they practiced calligraphy and tried their skill at filling in couplets and composing poems. Occasionally there were lectures on good manners and on the ethical doctrines of Confucius. The teacher gave out the new assignments to each pupil individually, as there was no class system.

At noon the school closed again for luncheon. After luncheon the teacher took a nap and the boys were ordered to sleep at their tables. The teacher usually woke about three o'clock and gave a cough or some other signal to rouse the boys, who were pretending to be asleep. The teacher then heard the lessons of those who had not been reached in the morning session, and corrected the calligraphy with a pen brush dipped in red ink. Calligraphy was very important under the old system and the teacher devoted a great deal of time to it. Then there followed another period of recitation and until the close of the day the school resounded with chanting.

In summer the school day ended around eight o'clock, when supper was served. In the winter, however, when supper was served much earlier, it was followed by another two-hour period of school. These evening sessions were usually spent in reading advanced textbooks or in writing short essays and poems. The local people regarded these winter evening classes as the most important part of the school term. Those parents who wanted their boys to prepare for the Imperial Examinations made sure that their sons did their best in the evenings. There was a common saying that any degree won from the Examination was the result of a great deal of oil and fire.

There was no systematic curriculum in the old-fashioned village school; each student advanced at his own speed. In his first year, a boy would usually be taught to read the *San Tze Ching*, a reader containing the rudiments of national history, politics, economy, literature, philosophy, geography, and ethical principles. It was written in short and rhythmic sentences, each sentence composed of three characters; hence the title. The other reader was the *Pei Chia Hsing* which contained one hundred family names. The first-year boy was required to read these two books, but he did not have to understand the contents. It is doubtful that the teacher understood them.

The second-year textbooks were the first and second parts of Confucius' Dialogues. Supplementing these were the *Jih Yung Za Tze*, a dictionary of everyday words and terms, and the *Sze Yen Za Tze*, a collection of rudimentary biology, chemistry, geology, and physics, which was somewhat Taoistic. To the teacher, the two parts of the Dialogues were most important, because they contained the essence of Confucian doctrine and were the main source from which the standards of morality were derived. Practice in calligraphy was continued throughout the second year.

In the third year the boy read the first and second parts of Mencius' Dialogues, the Great Learning and the Principles of Mean (Chung Yung). If the teacher was capable, he might begin to interpret some parts of the Confucian Dialogues to the boy at this time. In the third year the pupil also started to learn how to use the abacus.

In the fourth year the regular textbooks were the *Tso Chuan*, Annals of the Chou dynasty, the Book of Poetry, the Book of Rites, and the *Shu Ching*, China's earliest history. These were never interpreted; the boys simply read them without knowing what they meant. Ordinarily, a fourth-year student was a senior in the school. He was supposed to learn how to make couplets and to compose poems and short essays. But in the country school this was neglected, since very few of the boys were expected to take part in the Imperial Examination. Therefore, most of the boys in the fourth year learned more of the abacus and calligraphy instead. Intelligent students sometimes finished in three years. If their parents were not ambitious for them, they left school and either returned to the farm

or learned a trade. The few boys who excelled and who were able to continue at school prepared for the Imperial Examination as soon as they
finished the regular courses. They studied the poems and essays written
by the early scholars and also wrote some of their own.

We have said before that most of the boys did not like the school.
They learned their lessons by rote without understanding the meaning
of what they were required to read. Except for the *Jih Yung Za Tze*, all
the textbooks were completely incomprehensible to them, but they were
compelled to read and to remember what they had read. It was painful
work. Unfortunately, neither the teacher nor the boy's parents had any
interest in remedying the situation, and the boys were forced into endless
memorizing and were punished severely if they failed in this dull task.
Fear of punishment also made school hateful. Once a six-year-old boy,
who was reading his *San Tze Ching*, fell asleep at his table. The teacher
woke him with a thunderous call, scolded him harshly, and then asked
him to recite his lesson. The boy was too frightened to do it well, and for
this failure he was beaten. This sort of thing used to occur very frequently.

The old-fashioned school offered no recreation. As a rule, a schoolboy
had to sit on his seat and keep quiet all the time. When he heard the
noise, the laughter, and the wild running of the boys out on the street, he
and all the other pupils felt a great longing to join them but did not
dare. The only chance for fun was when the teacher was not in school.
On these rare occasions the boys' energy, imagination, and joy broke
forth immediately and simultaneously. They overturned tables and piled
up benches as a stage for an impromptu "show." They threw paper balls
and water holders in a game of "war." They stole into the vegetable garden near the schoolhouse to pick fruits, cucumbers, or radishes. The
shouting, swearing, and laughing could be heard even by distant neighbors. One or two small boys stood guard at a far corner to watch for the
teacher's coming. As soon as he was sighted and the signal was given, all
the boys ran wildly back into the schoolhouse and put everything in
order. Occasionally they were discovered and punished.

Thirty years ago, the first modern school was established in Iisinanchen
by the county government. Following this, several semimodern schools
were opened in different villages. The school in Taitou was also
modernized to a certain extent. In these new schools life was interesting to
the pupils and, as a result, the attitude toward going to school changed.
The textbooks were fascinating; they were written in the contemporary
idioms familiar to the pupils and were beautifully illustrated. Above all,

they contained interesting stories about children's daily life, which were entirely comprehensible and opened new vistas to the young minds. The arithmetic was new and interesting. Learning the symbols of numbers and new methods of counting was most fascinating. The chalk, the blackboard, the clay stick and the clay plate were all delightful things which had never been seen before. In the old school, singing had been absolutely forbidden, but now the young teachers cheerfully taught the boys to sing as part of the curriculum. They sang the songs of the coming and going of the swallows, the joy of study, of patriots, and of the flowers and the stars. The boys also learned the symbols of music. Few had any musical talent, but they liked to sing and imitated the teacher with great gusto. Physical education was a regular part of the school day. This was most exciting. In the old days they were punished for making noise or for having fun, now they were taught and led by the teachers in exercises and games. They also had some military instruction. The teacher sometimes made a short address before the lesson was over. "Do you know that our nation is in danger? Do you know that we have been attacked and disgraced many times by foreign countries? The Japanese devils looted our grain and animals. They attacked our sisters and beat our brothers. We hate them, we want to fight them to death. It is well for you to remember these things. We will some day avenge our national disgrace, but now we must know what has made it possible. It is because we are weak. Our people are weak, so our nation is weak. Our body is weak and our knowledge is weak too. Our people do not know how to work together, therefore, the foreigners can attack us one by one. We have no good soldiers, so we cannot defend our nation. Therefore, the first thing we must do is to make ourselves strong—strong in body and strong in knowledge. Our young people must become good soldiers because only good soldiers can defend our nation and protect our people. Do you all understand? Physical education is to train our body and to teach us how to march together. The other lessons are to give you knowledge so that you will know our nation and other nations. Do you all agree with me?"

Another village-wide organization is the collective protection of crops. A crop-watcher is hired by the village every year. His duty is to see that the crops are not damaged by animals nor stolen by thieves. He receives a yearly wage and while he is on duty is supplied with meals by families who have more land than the average. A schedule, arranging his stays, is worked out beforehand by the village council. The watcher boards three consecutive days with one family and then changes to another

family for another three days. With one family he may stay only two
days, with another one day. When he has had a turn with each of the
families who were appointed to supply meals, he starts the process again.
When the year is over, a wage is paid to him and a certain amount of
grain or other foodstuff is collected for him from the families which have
land to cultivate. The watcher's position is rather low in the eyes of the
villagers. They think of him as a servant of the village. When he comes
to a home to eat, no special food is prepared for him as is always done
for the artisans; he eats what the family members and the hired laborers
have.

Punishment of theft is a common concern of the village. Petty theft
is dealt with summarily. Sometimes a boy or girl of a poor family may
steal some heads of the millet crop, or some string beans, or other crops.
If the culprit is caught on the spot by the owner of the field. he may be
scolded and forced to give up what he has stolen, or he may get a beating.
If he is caught by the crop-watcher, however, the punishment is more
severe. His basket or other belongings may be seized and held until his
parents come to redeem them. The punishment depends upon the boy's
age and on the seriousness of the theft. An adult thief is merely shamed
and derided if the theft is a minor one. A professional beggar of the
village had often stolen beans, vegetables, and other things during the
growing season, and this delinquency was well known to all the villagers.
The heads of the rich families sometimes said to him: "You should be
ashamed of yourself. Why don't you make a living by work? But if you
only take for your own needs and not for sale, we will not bother you." If
a woman steals, nothing is done, but she is looked down upon.

There were two professional thieves in Taitou some years ago. They
seldom stole from the people of Taitou but concentrated on the market
town. They had been caught time and again and had been frequently
punished. The villagers considered them contemptible but did not bother
to do anything about them.

Burglary, however, is regarded as a crime. When a home is robbed at
night, the owner may use weapons to defend his property, and if the
burglar is killed no action will be taken against the man who kills him.
If the thief is caught he will either be punished according to village
custom or sent to the county government. A man who steals a considerable
quantity of the crops, or who breaks open the doors of homes to steal
grain, animals, or other useful things at night, is considered a criminal;
he is fined or punished by the local leaders according to the local regula-

tions, and though he loses his social position, he may continue to live in the village and eventually to redeem his reputation. Those who break into houses to steal money, threatening the family with weapons, are unforgivable criminals and must be tal en before the government authorities if they are caught. If they escape, the case must be reported. This is true of highway robbers, arsonists, and kidnapers, all of whom must be punished outside the village.

Social control is a village-wide affair; its chief instrument is public opinion. For the kind of behavior that is approved by most of the villagers, a person is everywhere honored and praised. Disapproval, therefore, is a powerful check. For instance, though the villagers do not interfere with or harm a promiscuous woman, they sever their relations with her family and ignore the greetings of any of its members. Social isolation is a terrible punishment. Only the three or four families whose social position is so low that they are in a sense immune from public opinion are indifferent to disapproval and fear only physical punishment.

The government has recently initiated the *Pao-chia* system (see p. 244), but the villagers do not, except very rarely, comply with it. They would not report that a son of their neighbor was involved in anything wrong. This reluctance is largely due to the traditional relations between neighbors which make it very hard for one villager to report another's bad behavior to a government authority or an outsider. It is also due to the fact that the system was primarily adopted for eliminating politically undesirable persons, especially those who have been accused of being communists, and often a person in disfavor with the political authorities may be on good terms with his fellow villagers.

Witchcraft or magic may also be considered a means of social control. There was once a very poor family, a mother and her young son, which practiced witchcraft in the village. The mother was a beggar and a delinquent; the son was often hired by other families as a cow-boy. In the winter they used to open their house to villagers for gambling. One day the mother found that her money had been stolen. She suspected two or three persons but since there was no definite evidence, she decided to determine the guilt by witchcraft. She made some small figures with dough, one for each person who was accustomed to come to the house. She saw to it that this act was made known to the whole group. Then she heated peanut oil in a boiler and dropped the figures into the boiling oil. It was believed that when the figures were suffering in the oil, the persons who were not guilty would feel nothing, but the person who was guilty would suffer great pain. Since all the people believed in this, the person who had really stolen the money could not but show great uneasiness and admit his guilt.

When a family has great hatred for another family and desires desperately to harm them but either is not brave enough or has no reason for open attack or public denouncement, resort to witchcraft is made. (The writer suspects that these cases are village tales rather than actual practices.) It is said that if a family knows of an intended wedding in an enemy's family, two small charms may be made and pinned together to represent a newly married couple. On the wedding day a member of the family will go to the enemy's home as a guest and hide the charms somewhere in the bride's room. It is believed that the new couple will then embrace each other like a pair of infant children, thereby bringing great embarrassment upon their relatives. To make the marriage an unhappy one, the two charms are pinned back to back, so that the couple will quarrel all the time.

Close neighborhood associations in many cases supersede the village feeling or the clan consciousness. A family of the P'an clan, for example, may have closer relations with some Yang families than with their own clansmen, simply because the Yangs live in the same neighborhood. Frequent contact in daily life brings families together, and consequently the whole village is divided into a number of neighborhoods, or *hu-tung*, which have no reference to the clan. There are nine neighborhoods within the village limits. To be sure, there is no clear-cut demarcation between the different neighborhoods, and the same family may belong to two neighborhoods simultaneously or two adjacent neighborhoods may sometimes be considered as one.

People living near by recognize certain social obligations to each other. When there is a marriage, the bridegroom's family distributes steamed rolls made of wheat flour among the neighbors to announce the wedding and extends an invitation to the party. In return, the neighbors offer presents, mostly of food needed for the occasion. Some members of the neighboring families may also come to help in many ways on the wedding day and participate in the feast of celebration. In case of a funeral, the neighbors help to build the tomb. They may carry the coffin, or take care of the domestic work while the relatives of the deceased are mourning. This aid is offered voluntarily. When a family has a funeral for a senior member, relatives and friends come to lament and offer gifts. In return, the family of the deceased must entertain the guests. In this they are helped by the neighbors who divide the guests into a number of groups, each family entertaining one group at its own expense. This assistance is absolutely reciprocal and forms a particular relationship between two families.

When a baby is born, all the families of a neighborhood present gifts, which are remembered or recorded by the baby's parents, so that they will be able to reciprocate properly should the occasion present itself. When a family needs extra labor in housework, neighbors will come to help. In transporting, plowing, sowing, harvesting or threshing, neighbors lend each other assistance. In time of emergency, such as fire, theft, or sudden illness, neighbors are far more helpful than relatives or friends who live at a distance. A common saying runs: "Distant relatives are not as dependable as near-by neighbors."

Families of the same neighborhood who are on good terms with each other may on occasion borrow small sums without any interest. But this is rare; borrowing with interest is the usual practice. The money comes from a small family or from individual members of several large families. It is interesting to note that a small and seemingly poor family may have savings of thirty or fifty dollars; this is insufficient for buying land, but if lent to a needy person or family at a rather high rate of interest, it may bring in some profit. A young wife or the daughter of a big family may have a private sum of money which will be lent to the fellow villagers, usually for 2 or 3 percent. When a person needs money to pay debts incurred by gambling, opium-smoking, or drinking, he can borrow the sum from his neighbors, but the rate of interest will be exceedingly high and a contract is drawn up. Two men of good credit are required as guarantors and a certain amount of land or a house is demanded as security. These loans extend for short periods and if the payment is postponed twice, the creditor is permitted to cultivate the land of the debtor. This indicates how difficult it is for a person or a family without a good reputation to borrow any money. In Taitou there are no professional money lenders, probably because no family is a really big landlord. There has been very little borrowing and lending between the richer families and the needy ones, for the money changes hands between individuals who know each other. A person of a well-to-do family who needs money may go to the sources we have mentioned—a woman with a little savings or a small family. Usually, however, he will sell his land or other property rather than borrow. Borrowing or lending is a rather embarrassing thing to do. Both parties prefer to hide the fact if possible. No organized credit society, such as the old *yao-hui* or the new credit cooperative society, exists in this village.

Women of neighboring families gather before their front doors to talk and gossip. Especially in the summertime, when the men are eating at home, the women come out to have a breath of fresh air under the trees. A spontaneous and informal group is formed and the talk ranges from discussion of the daily work to gossip about the marriage of a family at the other end of the village. This continues until the men come out and it is the women's turn to eat. After dinner when the weather is hot and the people don't feel like working, the men and boys go to sleep or play on the main street, on the river bank, or in the groves. The old women go to their bedrooms to take a nap. But the young women and little girls come out again to sit under the trees or in their doorways, bringing with them some piece of work. All of them are members of the same *hu-tung.* They sit about for one or two hours, then return to their homes and resume their important work—sewing, mending, ironing, embroidering, and the like. The men and boys go to the fields. The grandmothers also get up; they go to visit neighbors or stay home to help their daughters-in-law by watching the young children. Little girls and little boys gather and play the whole afternoon in the neighborhood.

After sunset, the men and boys come home and supper is served immediately. After supper, men go to the hard and clean threshing grounds at the outskirts of the village. Large groups gather and community life is at its height. At home, the women rush through their washing as quickly as possible because they also want to have a neighborhood gathering. Since they are women, they do not meet on the threshing grounds, but in the little open spaces in the small lanes between their homes. Men never participate in the women's gatherings, nor is a woman allowed to join the men. The men feel free to talk of anything they like, perhaps gossiping at the expense of young women, telling dirty stories, or exchanging rumors of love affairs between a boy and a girl of certain families. In the women's groups, freedom of speech and freedom from convention are also enjoyed, but to a lesser degree. Older women lie down on a mattress and swing their fans without embarrassment. Younger married women can joke at the expense of each other's husbands, or tease the grown-up girls by saying that they are dreaming of handsome young men. The daughters can laugh and talk much more freely than in any other circumstances. The women return to their homes before their men come back, so that the latter cann·t see their gathering, nor hear what they say.

In the wintertime, these social gatherings are rarer, because it is too cold to sit outside the house and it is not proper for many women to gather in one home. Two or three grown-up girls who are friendly with each other may sew or embroider together. Children play together as usual before the walls or in the enclosed backyards. In the evenings, men who are intimate with each other may meet at one home or another alternatively to spend their extra time in talk. Young men play cards or chess, or one of them may read aloud the more popular stories.

These neighborhood gatherings are very influential in the development of the young people, a fact recognized from ancient times. The story of Mother Meng's selecting a neighborhood for her son is so well known in China that every man and woman can tell it. When Mencius was a boy, his mother moved their residence three times in order to select a decent neighborhood for the boy. In one place most of the neighbors were employed in playing in a brass band for funerals, so Mencius learned to play too. Since this was a low career, Mother Meng had to move away lest her son become a brass-band player. The people of the next place were butchers, so Mencius and the other boys started to play at slaughtering. This was considered by the mother even worse than the first, so she had to move again. Whether or not the new place encouraged the boy to become a sage is not known, but it is undeniable that the neighborhood exerts great influence upon the young.

Because of the need for children's labor in the field and at home and also because there is no surplus money for frivolity, recreation for children is not encouraged and almost no toys are provided for them. Children of the same neighborhood, however, play group games which require little equipment. One of these is *Ta-wa*, a game played with two teams, which requires only some small stones. Each child has a stone, and another stone is used as a goal for shooting. Five parallel lines, about five feet long, are drawn on the ground about three feet apart. The first player stands on the line at one end of the playground and tries to hit the goal with his stone. If the goal is hit, he hops on one foot over the lines to the other end and picks up his stone and hops back to his original place. The next player does the same. There are about a dozen different ways of throwing the stone and hopping over the lines. Members of one team can help each other in any part of the action.

Ta-ke is a bowling game that can be played by ten or more children. Each player has a bundle of pins made of *kaoliang* stalk and a small polished roller of brick or stone. At one end of a long narrow lane the boys set up two bricks with a horizontal stick across them to form a frame. Each boy puts one of his pins against the frame so that one end touches the horizontal stick and the other end rests on the ground. The boys first throw their rollers toward the opposite end of the lane. The one whose throw is the longest has the first chance to bowl with his roller at the pins. The one who knocks off all the pins is the winner.

Ts'ang-more, a girl's game, is somewhat like blindman's buff. The girl (occasionally a boy) who plays the "blindman" leans against one of the walls and covers her eyes, pretending not to see anything. Then she runs here and there searching, and when she finds and catches another player, he captive becomes the "blindman." Another game, played by two big girls and a group of young children, is locally called "eagle catches chickens." One of the big girls is the old hen and the other is an eagle, while the young children are the pullets. The pullets and the hen form a line by clasping hands; the eagle tries to catch the pullets one by one while the hen tries to protect her "children."

"Catch a thief" is a rough game, usually played by boys over twelve. One boy is a magistrate, another a thief, and the rest are policemen. All the boys who want to play stand in a row against a wall, their feet close together. The feet are counted from one end of the line to the other in time to a chant of rhythmic but meaningless sounds. The boy who chants uses his right foot to touch the left foot of every boy in the row. Each word of the chant should fall upon one foot. The foot upon which the last word of the chant falls is drawn back a little, and the boy who withdraws both feet first becomes the magistrate, the next is the thief, and the third one is captain of the policemen. The thief attempts to escape and the policemen try to catch him. When the thief is caught, he is brought before the magistrate and a trial is conducted, the magistrate sentences him to a beating and appoints two boys to carry out the order. Another game played by boys is *Ti-Chien-tze*. A group of older boys or young men play with a shuttlecock made by tying some poultry feathers on a coin. This *Chien-tze* is thrown up in the air, and the players try to keep it from touching the ground, kicking or butting it but not touching it with their hands. The game is popular in winter since it is very active and helps the boys to keep warm.

Usually in the backyards or enclosed courts, swings are set up for the girls. While the girls are playing, no young men except their own brothers, cousins, or boys of the same neighborhood are allowed to be present. The schoolboys are very fond of flying kites. They must be careful not to let the kite land in the court of any home. The local people believe that this brings bad luck to the family, and the kite will certainly be destroyed and the boys cursed. A kite is usually made of paper secured to a bamboo framework and is painted like a human figure or a bird or butterfly. In many cases it looks like the images used at funerals, or for witchcraft, and suggests death.

It is easy to draw a checkerboard on the ground and to use stones as checkers. For this reason, checkers is a very popular game in the summer. Younger girls and boys play quietly under the trees on the riverbank with a number of others sitting beside as on-lookers. Sometimes the players get into a serious argument and the spectators take sides with them. While the cows are grazing, the boys sit down and play the game, sometimes letting their animals wander far away over the fields. In the winter a group of young people may gather to learn Chinese boxing or to sing songs in the houses where social gatherings usually take place. During the New Year Festival some active young people may also organize country dramas.

Village Conflicts	13

IN addition to the clan and neighborhood organizations, there are other kinds of intravillage groupings. Families of similar social and economic status, families which support a certain school, and the families which have become Christianized all tend to divide off into special groups.

Families of the same neighborhood may not be as close as families of different neighborhoods, because of status differences. Two or three Liu families, for example, live in the neighborhood where most of the Yang families live. The Lius are very poor and do not have much to do with the Yangs because they feel inferior to them, and the Yangs do not make overtures to them, either. But another Liu family, which has recently become prosperous, has gradually become intimate with the Yangs. Their children were asked to attend the Christian school. The mother of another Liu family had tried desperately to achieve these social relations without success. To this end, she sent one of her two sons to the Christian school, but failed in her purpose because her husband and sons had a bad reputation in the village.

A Yang family which lives in the northwestern part of the village had gradually built up their relations with a P'an family who lived in the eastern end. Each family had four sons. Most of the sons and grandchildren of the two families were graduated from modern schools. Consequently, they are regarded as learned families. Some of them have traveled a good deal, and members of the two families are familiar with the new currents of thought. In addition, each family owns about the same amount of land. For these reasons, members of the two families consider themselves equals and meet frequently. Both families have attracted others which are either equal in status or have educated members. Formerly, the ten or twelve wealthy families of the village had more intimate relations with each other than they had with their neighbors. There was also a group of middle-class families. Their association was not strong but recognizable. The poor families also constituted an informal group. In the past decades, distinctions based upon wealth have broken up because of the decline of the rich families and the general disruption caused by the war. In general, this kind of stratification is rather superficial, for, as we have seen, the status of a family may change in a few generations. The shifting certainly counteracts the building up of permanent social classes. Another point to be mentioned is that a family with wealth but no culture is usually the most isolated; the rich cultured farmers look down upon it, and yet it does not want to associate with the poor people. Thus, wealth alone does not give a family high position in the community.

For several years the village school and the Christian school divided the village into two groups. Families who sent their children to the village school were drawn together by numerous activities, such as organizing the school council, discussing the finances, making plans for entertaining the teacher, and so on. In the same way, the families who sent their children to the Christian school also came together.

The introduction of Christianity brought about new groupings of families. Ten or twelve families belong to the Protestant church, and five or six families belong to the Catholic church. The Protestant families include the Yangs and Ch'ens and, formerly, also one of the P'an families. The Catholic group is composed of four or five P'an families and two of the Ch'ens. Because Christianity is a new religion and is contradictory in some ways to the traditions and customs of the local society, the two groups of families which identified themselves with this belief are sharply differentiated from other families. This differentiation caused a kind of "we-group" consciousness in each of the two groups. The dozen Yang and Ch'en families have maintained closer relations than would have been likely under other circumstances. The several P'an families which belong to the Catholic church are poor and of very low social status, and are considered by their kinsmen as a group of outcasts. As a result, they have developed a feeling of unity among themselves. Both the Protestant and the Catholic groups regard themselves as "chosen people," thinking that they belong to Heaven while the rest of the villagers are sinners, or people of this world. The preachers of the churches have taught their members to distinguish themselves from the other people. Needless to say, this has tremendously widened the gap between the Christian groups and the rest of the families in the village. But the distinction does not stop here. Protestant-Catholic antagonism has split the two Christian groups. All the non-Christian families practice ancestor worship. They have the Kitchen God in their kitchens, burn incense sticks and kow-tow in the shrine of the God of Earth on the New Year Festival, and patronize the Buddhist temple in the district. For these reasons, we may consider them as another religious group, though they are by no means organized

When a village is thus partitioned, it is natural that conflicts between different groups should occur now and then. Here are some important village conflicts which actually took place in Taitou in the last few decades. One was a conflict between Protestants and Catholics. The first converts were members of the Ch'en and Yang families and included a Ch'en scholar and his second brother. They were all ambitious men, and their primary purpose in conversion was to get positions as country preachers, and then to establish a church-subsidized village school, to use foreign influence through the church to deal with their opponents, and to sell food to the missionaries. As a result, resentment was fostered in the minds of the other villagers and the whole Christian group became a target for attack. Later, for some unknown reason, a top member of the P'an clan also joined the group. His action stirred up a great controversy in his own clan. It was regarded by some of his kinsmen as a great shame to the clan and their ancestors, and measures against him were secretly planned. Since he was a rich man and a member of the important clan, the few Christian members and the church authorities honored him as their top man in every case. This created jealousy among the Christian Ch'ens, one of whom felt so badly that he refused to stay in the group.

A few years later, the Catholic church in a distant village also secured members among the villagers. The Catholics wanted converts and did not care what kind of people they were. They hinted that those who came to the church would have financial help and the protection of a foreign power if they were ever involved in any legal disputes. This attracted many restless, propertyless, and oppressed people. Before long, a group of several dozen poor people of the village declared their affiliation with the Catholic church. The priest and headman imitated the Western church fathers in assuming a belligerent attitude toward the Protestant group. This situation was immediately seized upon by the villagers, who hated the foreign religion and its believers, and by the ambitious and discontented Ch'en scholar, as well as by the P'an clan heads, who resented the affiliation of some P'ans with the Protestant group. The anti-Christian villagers wanted the two groups to destroy each other; the Ch'en scholar wanted to defeat the P'an who had defeated him among the Protestants; and the clan heads of the P'ans wanted to punish their rebellious member. They all set to work. The villagers and the P'an heads incited members of the Catholic group to quarrel with the Protestant group, while the Ch'en scholar joined forces with the Catholics. One day a rumor reached the Catholics to the effect that the Protestant members had insulted their

God and their priest. The young Catholics immediately seized the P'an member and did the most shameful things to insult him. Then they threatened and abused the other members. They also insulted the brother of the Ch'en scholar. The Yang members had been threatened but not actually insulted. The clash did not develop into a real row because the Protestant group decided not to oppose the Catholics. After the P'an member and the Ch'en scholar's brother had been insulted, the main purpose of the fight was accomplished and the village leaders mediated the conflict, which ended with the Protestants' promise to entertain the important Catholic members at a formal dinner.

The Christian groups and the other villagers came into difficulty over the question of sharing expenses for practicing opera in the village. The opera was a most important amusement and it was an annual occasion. All the families contributed to it according to their means, except the Christian groups who refused to pay their share. They held that the opera was a kind of thanksgiving to the Dragon God and therefore contradictory to Christianity, and Christians could not give money to it; but that did not prevent the Christian families and their relatives from attending the performance and enjoying the entertainment as much as anyone else. This greatly annoyed the other villagers and the Christian groups were regarded as no longer properly belonging to the village. The villagers' resentment grew when they were told that the Christians were protected by foreign power.

This was not the only friction that occurred between the Christian groups and the other villagers. The Christians were taught that they were God's chosen people, that they no longer belonged to this world but to God's world, and that they must organize themselves into one body against all who were not Christians, and who, therefore, were "sinners." The poor Christians who felt that they had been oppressed or ill-treated by the wealthy people, wanted to avenge themselves and to express their feeling of injustice. The ambitious members assumed that they were as good as, or even superior to, those who held leadership in the village, the village gentry. They considered it an injustice that they did not have the opportunities to demonstrate their leadership. Besides, the Christians had the attitude that the non-Christians were pitiful because they resisted the "true God" and were, therefore, committing the sin of worshiping false gods. On their side, the non-Christian villagers regarded both the Protestant and the Catholic groups as mean people—people who refused to pay homage to their ancestors, who betrayed their countrymen but made friends with foreigners. Since both sides had prejudices like these, conflicts could hardly be avoided. It was only after people had had time to become more familiar with the religion, and the excitement at the strange things had abated, that the hostile attitude of the non-Christians was lessened. The reconciliation was also attributed to the enlightenment of many of the Christians. In recent years, many well-trained leaders grew up among the Chinese Christians who understand Christianity much better than their predecessors, the first converts, did. These men take a liberal attitude and cooperate in many collective activities with other groups, and refrain from condemning other beliefs.

A conflict between school factions also made village history. Years ago, an ambitious and self-made scholar of a Ch'en family wanted to become a schoolteacher. He fostered the idea among the families of the Yang, Ch'en, and Liu clans that their children were not treated as well as the P'ans by the teacher in the P'an clan's school. Since all three clans felt subordinate to the P'an clan, indignation was not difficult to arouse. In addition, a number of families of the Ch'en and Yang clans had accepted Christianity, and this new religious belief had brought the families into close relationship. The scholar vigorously advocated the establishment of a new school for their own children so that they could be independent of the P'an school. He finally succeeded, and a second school was opened in the house of a Yang family. All the pupils were boys of the Ch'en and Yang clans. The teacher of the "orthodox" school and important members of the P'an clan resented this new move. Rumors were spread by them about the Ch'en teacher, attacking his scholarship, and also warning the minor clans that they could expect retaliation in one form or another. The Yangs and Ch'ens called a meeting at which they resolved to uphold their rights and support their teacher in every way. The antagonism between this group and the P'an clan lasted for several years. Since the second school was primarily a result of the ambition of the Ch'en scholar, the bitterness of the P'ans was largely directed to the Ch'ens rather than to the Yangs and Lius. Besides, most of the Yang families had fairly good relations with many individual P'an families as well as with the clan as a whole. The Yangs, understanding that they were in a minor position in the village, never tried to compete with the P'ans in any of the village affairs, and the P'ans treated them frankly and generously.

An interesting point in this conflict was that, in both the Yang and Ch'en clans there was a leading family which did not take sides with its own kinsmen. The head of the Ch'en family, a younger brother of the Ch'en scholar, believed that good relations with all the clans in the village should be maintained by all means. As a result, he was not on speaking terms with his own brothers, but later was supported by the P'ans when he held the office of village head. The head of the Yang family was a very ambitious person, who kept aloof from the conflict because he himself was antagonistic toward the Ch'en leaders as well as the important members of his own clan. Had the Ch'ens and Yangs asked him to lead the fight, however, he would certainly have taken part, for he loved to dominate.

The two schools had both undergone some change, as we have seen. The one supported by the P'an clan became a public school, receiving recognition and subsidies from the county government, while the one sponsored by the Ch'en and Yang clans became an institution of the village Protestant church. Conflict between them was considerably eased because of the automatic division of territories from which each school recruited its pupils. The territory of the Christian school was the western section of the village, while that of the village school was the eastern section. Further improvement was brought about by the good relations between the young teacher of the Christian school and the younger generations of the P'an families. When the teacher of the village school realized that his school could not take care of all the boys and that his training was really inferior to that of the teacher of the Christian school, the antagonism was lessened. The seeming harmony between the two schools and the friendly attitude of the P'an leaders encouraged two brothers of a Yang family to hope that the schools could be united. One day they invited the village head and the teacher of the village school to talk over this idea. The brothers made it clear that their suggestion was entirely for the good of the two schools and for the children of the whole village; that they themselves did not have any personal interest in the affair because their careers lay outside the village; that one school would be much stronger than two, separated in both finance and teaching; and that the present teachers would have charge of the new school, where they would have the advantage of dividing the courses among themselves in accordance with their specialized training. The response from the teacher and the village head was favorable. The next day the two brothers left the village to attend to their own businesses. After several months, news came to them that dissention had again arisen between the two school factions. In the first place, the village schoolteacher and other P'an leaders had misunderstood the proposition. They thought that it was a trap, a trap set up by the Yangs and Ch'ens, or by the council of the Christian school, to absorb the village school for the purpose of upsetting the position of the P'ans. Second, the members of the Christian council were unable to convince the others of their sincerity and unselfish motives as the two Yang brothers had done. Because of this the teacher of the village school and all the leaders of the P'an clan resumed their unfriendly attitude toward the Christian school and the Protestant group. A son of the village head was studying in the Christian school and the village head himself came to the school to talk with the teacher and members of the school's council almost every day. But both the father and son ceased their visits and were embarrassed when they met persons of the Christian group. This was because the village head was also a member of the P'an clan, so he had to act on the side of the village schoolteacher. The originators of the plan were greatly disappointed. They had a deep fear that the good relations between the leaders of the Yang clan and the leaders of the P'an clan might be undermined. The situation has now been remedied to a considerable extent, but the idea of consolidating the two schools must wait for a long time to come.

Clan feuds were a not uncommon source of village conflict. Such a feud existed between some families of the P'an and the Ch'en clans. In the course of it, a Ch'en family was attacked one night by gangsters whose faces were either painted or covered by masks. The family and their relatives all suspected some of the P'ans, but since they could not produce any evidence for their suspicions, the P'ans pronounced the accusation a great insult. Although the case did not develop into a serious clan fight, the bad feeling between the two clans was heightened and another incident occurred. On the main road north of the village, the Ch'en clan had erected a stone monument to honor a faithful widow among their ancestors. It had stood there for several decades when one day it was found lying on the ground. The Ch'ens discovered that the damage had been done by some young people of the P'an clan, and they immediately took this as a challenge. They were ready to undertake a lawsuit but, fortunately, the P'ans realized that the mischief they had done could not be justified or excused in the court. Therefore, they sought the aid of the village leaders to arbitrate the case. The Ch'ens finally accepted the P'ans' offer to erect the monument again and build a brick frame to protect it, and the case was settled.

It is clear that the causes of such feuds are complicated and refer back to a number of things. Clan prejudice is an important factor, for upon it depend most of the associations or divisions among families. Religious prejudice has intensified these divisions, though this is an unfamiliar and a recent thing in China. There is suspicion in relations between a strong clan and a minor one. The Ch'en families, for instance, had in the past thirty years always thought that they were unfairly treated by the village officers (who happened to be members of the P'an clan), in regard to the sharing of the expenses of village administration. For this reason they were considered troublemakers, and the important P'an families could not but come into conflict with the Ch'ens.

Insult to a family's or a clan's ancestors will always bring repercussions. Damage to an ancestor's graveyard, speaking of an ancestor's less worthy deeds, making derisive signs or gestures at an ancestral hall or at anything related to ancestors cause serious ill-feeling between families or clans. When a family or a clan is prosperous and clan consciousness is strong, its members vigorously defend their ancestors and all that pertains to them. Children of poor families may swear at each other at the expense of their ancestors without causing serious clashes between their parents, but this is not true of richer families. The *fung-shui* (graveyard site) is sometimes an important factor in conflicts between clans. Since a clan's most important function is to make sure that their ancestors' spirits are happy in the other world and their progeny numerous, rich, and honorable in this world, finding and defending a place of good *fung-shui* is a very important task. Any damage to the place endangers the happiness of the family, and such an offense could not be tolerated. This belief has become so strong in Chinese minds that a deep-rooted sentiment has developed around ancestral halls and ancestral graveyards. Lawsuits over ancestral property are all too common in the Chinese countryside. Because of their agricultural occupation and their peace-loving tradition, the Chinese masses are comparatively hard to arouse against a national enemy. But once convinced that the enemy would destroy their ancestors' residence and turn over their ancestors' graveyards, they will fight to the last ditch. In Chinese history one can find numerous war slogans referring to the "protecting our ancestors' graveyards."

Quarrels between neighboring families are often caused by children's squabbles. The children of the upper-class families are usually taken care of by their siblings when they are young and by a schoolteacher when they are above six or seven years old. They have few chances to get into trouble with other children. Their parents are afraid of being criticized for spoiling them and therefore refrain from siding with their own children when quarrels arise. When upper-class families are involved in such a quarrel, it is a more serious matter than a noisy dispute between women or a street fight between men. It may lead to a lawsuit or a long lasting hatred.

Through many generations the Chinese village gentry have learned an interesting way to end certain kinds of village conflicts. This is to do nothing about it. When two lower-class families get into a dispute, the mothers scold each other on the street, their husbands may have a fist fight, and then it all suddenly stops. The next day their children play together as usual, the adults may not speak to each other for ten days or more, but they conduct their own business as usual and gradually forget the matter. Disturbances of this kind are usually ignored by the village leaders. To be sure, this is not always the case. Occasionally, small matters develop into something extremely serious. For instance, two poor families quarrel one morning. Every one of the neighbors think it is just another quarrel, but the next day the head of one of the families is found murdered. This lies beyond the power of the village leaders, because the case is no longer a village conflict but a criminal act, and can only be settled by law. Or, a family may find one night that their home, or a heap of straw, has been set on fire. This must also be dealt with by law.

When two leading families, or two village dignitaries, or two clans, come into conflict, the case will not be ignored but must be mediated by the village leaders. Pacification has been for long the measure usually employed to end important village disputes. Usually this is done through the good offices of the village leaders, but when the gentry or the chief clans are involved, the ordinary village leaders do not have sufficient prestige to intervene. In these cases, leaders from other villages are called in. These may be no more capable than the local leaders, but because they are from a different village their presence means more to the conflicting parties, and, therefore, they have a greater "face." Many disputes are thus settled by outside intervention.

The general procedure is as follows: First, the invited or self-appointed village leaders come to the involved parties to find out the real issues at stake, and also to collect opinions from other villagers concerning the background of the matter. Then they evaluate the case according to their past experience and propose a solution. In bringing the two parties to accept the proposal, the peacemakers have to go back and forth until the opponents are willing to meet halfway. Then a formal party is held either in the village or in the market town, to which are invited the mediators, the village leaders, clan heads, and the heads of the two disputing families. The main feature of such a party is a feast. While it is in progress, the talk may concern anything except the conflict. The expenses of the feast will either be equally shared by the disputing parties or borne entirely by one of them. If the controversy is settled in a form of "negotiated peace," that is, if both parties admit their mistakes, the expenses will be equally shared. If the settlement reached shows that only one party was at fault, the expenses are paid by the guilty family. If one party chooses voluntarily, or is forced, to concede to the other (as in the case of the Protestant-Catholic dispute), it will assume the entire cost. When the heads or representatives of the disputing families are ushered to the feast, they greet each other and exchange a few words. After a little while they will ask to be excused and depart. Thus, the conflict is settled; but sometimes the settlement may not be conclusive.

Generally, when the two conflicting parties both belong to the middle or upper class, no compensation is paid when the settlement is made. Receiving money or other material compensation from a losing opponent causes great shame. The victory lies in the general opinion of the public that one is right and the opponent wrong. When this is won, any damages suffered can be overlooked. The important thing is that your opponent has to admit that he has been wrong, and this is very hard for a man of equal status to do. A feast provides the ideal situation for such an enforced acknowledgment. Overtly the feast is given to the mediators, actually it is an admission of defeat. The person who pays for it apologizes by this means.

Very few—perhaps none—of the disputes in this village have been solved by a lawsuit. Even the case in which a Ch'en family was attacked at night by their neighbors was settled out of court. Villagers forced into a legal case must go to the county seat and hire lawyers, and the ensuing costs are prohibitive for any of the farm families. Nine out of ten families who have sought recourse to the law have had to sacrifice a great part of their small property. Countless stories and proverbs have discouraged farmers from referring their cases to the government. Private mediation has been and is now the most important legal mechanism in rural districts throughout the country. Social justice has been in the past much more important than legal power in protecting the weak against violence of any sort. It is a fact that no matter how small or weak a family may be, if its members behave fairly to the other villagers, both the strong and the lawless will either help it or leave it alone. If it is unreasonably attacked, the attacker would sooner or later be discovered and the whole village would punish him. In the last twenty years, when bandits have been numerous in the countryside, the families that were attacked were those who had bad relations with most of the villagers, especially the poor ones. A number of rich families who seemed logical targets for the bandits were unmolested throughout the chaotic period because the members of these families had always behaved well in dealing with their fellow villagers, rich or poor. The bandits refrained from attacking them because the deed would be condemned by both men and gods.

Since a number of village conflicts are caused by hurting somebody's "face," it is necessary to discuss the losing or gaining of "face." "Face" is a literal translation of the Chinese character *lien* or *mien*. Although *lien* or *mien* means just what the English word face does, the Chinese expression *tiou lien* (losing face) or *yao mien-tze* (wishing a face) has nothing to do with face in our usual understanding of the term. It does not mean a certain expression on, or the physical appearance of, the face, such as implied by "a funny face" or "a sad face." When we say in Chinese that one loses face, we mean that he loses prestige, he has been insulted or has been made to feel embarrassment before a group. When we say that a man wants a face, we mean that he wants to be given honor, prestige, praise, flattery, or concession, whether or not these are merited. Face is really a personal psychological satisfaction, a social esteem accorded by others.

Perhaps this can be better understood by analyzing the factors involved in losing or gaining face. The first factor is the status of social or other equality between the persons involved. For instance, if a village dignitary asks another to make a social call with him or to grant some other favor and is refused, he will feel that he has lost face. If, on the other hand, a peasant is similarly refused by one of his own rank, he will not have this feeling. As another illustration, when one of two equally popular professors is refused by the other in some request, the former will have lost face, but if a student is similarly treated by a professor, the student does not suffer loss of face.

The second factor is the inequality between the social status of the two persons. When a boxer is defeated by an opponent as strong as he is, he will feel sorry but will not lose face. But if the victor is known to be inferior to him, then he will consider his defeat a great loss of face.

Likewise, a village gentry's embarrassment at being defeated by a man of his own class would not be as serious as if he were defeated by a junior village officer. However, this principle cannot be extended indefinitely. It would not be true to say that the lower the opponent's status, the greater the loss of face. If the insulting person is only a plain peasant or one who has been considered ignorant or mean, a cultured man does not lose face at all, because people will say that the trouble is caused by the peasant's ignorance and is not the other's fault, and if the latter remains impervious to the taunt, he will win great praise from the villagers for being too great to quarrel with a mean person, or so kind that he can forgive another's ignorance. Inequality of social status can nullify the feeling of loss of face in another way. When a plain villager is scolded or injured by a gentleman, he may resent it but he will not lose face. Similarly, a junior village officer can be insulted by a government commissioner, by a powerful village leader, or by an influential clan head without much loss of face. In the academic world, a junior writer who is scolded or insulted by a well-known scholar is proud of it rather than ashamed.

A third factor is the presence of a witness. In fact, the question of losing or not losing face is based on anticipation of the effect upon a third person or party. If the indignity has not been witnessed or is certain to remain unknown to anyone else, then bitterness may be roused but not the sense of losing face. When one does something socially wrong but keeps it secret, he does not feel embarrassed before other people. Whenever the secrecy is violated, he will lose face. Therefore, the village streets or public gatherings are places where one is in danger of losing face. The restoration of face must also be accomplished at a party presented by mediators, village or community leaders, and the two parties involved. But the effectiveness of the presence or knowledge of a third party varies with the degree of intimacy between the third party and the persons involved.

Thus, social relationship is a fourth factor. If the third person is intimate with one or both of the opposing parties, the defeated or insulted party does not feel that he has lost face, or at least the feeling will be negligible. But if the third person is not an intimate, the situation is quite different. In the family, for instance, there is no problem of losing or gaining face in relations between husband and wife, parents and children, or between siblings, but there is such a problem between the in-laws. The problem becomes more serious when the social distance extends outside the family to the neighborhood, to the village, and even beyond. Beyond a certain distance, however, this factor becomes ineffective. When a man lives in a completely strange society there is no problem of face, no matter what kind of mistakes he may make, because nobody knows him. He can visit disreputable places or commit an immoral act without uneasiness as long as he can keep it from reaching the attention of his friends or home folks. That is why a person who always behaves well in his local community may act very differently in a big city.

A fifth factor is social value or social sanction. One may commit different and numerous mistakes, but not all of them entail loss of face. In a society where agriculture is the main occupation, one loses face if his farm is not cared for. People pay much attention to filial piety and ancestor reverence, and a family loses face if its members do not hold together as long as their parents are alive or do not conduct a proper funeral for them when they die. On the other hand, a person of such a society can come back to live as usual after having failed to be a good apprentice in a market-town store or a successful student in the high school in the county seat. A father-in-law would be greatly shamed to be caught joking with his daughter-in-law when no third person was present, as would a girl discovered in a love affair with a neighbor's boy, for these actions violate deep-rooted traditions.

The consciousness of one's own social prestige is a sixth factor. The more conscious one is of his status, the stronger is his fear of losing face. For instance, a liberal or free-minded village gentry would not be particularly disturbed if a junior villager should unwittingly offend him. But if he were highly conventional or orthodox, he would be outraged and if the offender did not apologize immediately it would become a serious case. That is why ordinary villagers never dare to deal directly with this type of village gentlemen. Not a few self-made leaders are always in trouble with fellow villagers just because they care too much for their social prestige and are overly sensitive about it. This is especially true in cases in which middle-aged persons are involved.

Thus, age becomes a seventh factor in the problem of face. Young people have not as yet acquired much social prestige and therefore do not have much face to lose. On the other hand, old people frequently do not feel loss of face. They can easily be excused (and they always excuse themselves) on the ground that they are old, and besides, experience has made them too mature to be easily embarrassed. Only the middle-aged people, who are very careful to safeguard their social prestige, are serious about losing or gaining face. Lastly, a person's sensibility is also a factor. A situation that makes one person lose face leaves another unhurt. It is very easy to hurt a sensitive person's feelings and if the slight occurs in the presence of a third person he is certain to feel that he has lost face.

When a villager of note, a leader for example, is defeated in public affairs or is insulted at a social gathering by one of his rivals, he will feel great humiliation and swear to avenge himself. Thus, a bitter struggle ensues. If his family or friends say that he should not take the matter too seriously and that he ought to have tolerance, his answer will, in most cases, be like this: "Why? This is not a matter of insignificance. The safety of my face is involved. How can I maintain my respectable position in this community if I accept defeat from that bastard? Of course I must fight until my enemy is on his knees. Remember, we are upper-class people. We can sacrifice everything but our face."

When an upper-class family is attacked with bad words or violent actions by another of a similar social status, a serious conflict will arise. When village leaders come to settle it, the injured family very likely says: "Money, property, these are insignificant in comparison with our family's face! Just consider it from our point of view. How could we live on as usual if our face were lost to that infamous family? We cannot tolerate this. We must fight on till our enemy admits his guilt." If the mediators continue their effort, the family may finally give in, but say: "All right, we may give up the fight if you gentlemen will guarantee that our face will be safe." And the guarantee is given: "Surely, we will see that everyone's face is saved."

An individual villager or a family may behave immorally and yet not be subject to legal condemnation. If the misbehavior is repeated several times, the other villagers discuss it in social gatherings, saying: "Since he does not care for his face, what can you do about him?" "Yes, one can do mean things when he no longer pays attention to his face. It is too bad, indeed."

After some injustice has been repeatedly tolerated the injured party may warn the offender by saying: "Now, look here! I have several times given you face. I think I have done my best. If you mean that you really don't care for it, I will let you see what I can do. You should not complain that I am a man who does not pay attention to other's face." Or, if the offended person or family is too meek to wage a struggle, he may murmur to himself: "What can I do? I have given him face already several times, but he did not appreciate it. It seems that I will have to change my policy."

If a villager purposely reveals some secret of his neighbor before a public meeting, the neighbor will hate him and complain that he has been made to lose face in public. Or, if a person intentionally poses difficult questions to another at a meeting, the latter will also complain: "That son of a turtle purposely embarrassed me and made me lose face. I shall not forgive him."

When a villager is involved in trouble with his neighbor and is convinced that he must bear the blame, he will ask some village leaders to mediate the dispute. If the case is unfortunately revealed to the public, you may hear on the street corners these comments.

"Hear anything about Heng-sheng's case?" one villager asks.

"Not much. Only saw him running here and there. Guess he's looking for some face."

Another villager answers, "I just can't figure out what made Heng-sheng do such a foolish thing. It seems that there is no other way for him to get out of it except to find some important face. Guess he's doing that these days. Poor fellow!"

After a few days, these words may be heard in the village school: "Hey, know that Heng-sheng's case has been settled?"

"Yes, I heard that yesterday."

"How could it be?"

"Well, how would it be if not by Uncle P'an's effort? Of course, the opponent could not refuse Uncle P'an's face. Heng-sheng is lucky."

Another kind of circumstance in which face is involved is when a youngster offends a senior member in the village. When the offended man is about to punish the boy, other villagers may pacify him by saying: "For his parents' face, you may forgive him." Then the senior member may say: "All right. You are old neighbors. For your face and for his parents' face, I forgive him this time."

When two villagers are involved in a personal but not serious dispute or argument, one of them may ask the other: "Please stop it and give me a little face, will you?" When one villager asks another to do something but the latter is reluctant, the former will ask: "Please help me; it is a matter of face."

When a person or a family of the lower social class is involved in a dispute with one of the upper class and the latter has shown some generosity to the former, other villagers will say to the lower-class person or family: "He is a man of great face. Of course he would not see or do things like you would. He would lose face if he quarreled with people like you." On the other hand, when a person of high social status has intercourse with persons of low repute, the villagers will comment: "Too bad that he goes with that kind of people. His face and his family's face have been already greatly damaged."

Sometimes a family of the upper class may not act in accordance with the prevailing social customs in entertaining guests, in visiting relatives, in preparing a marriage or funeral, or in dealing with neighbors. The head of the family wants to save money by cutting the quantity and lowering the quality of the gifts or articles needed in these affairs. Then the villagers will complain: "A family like that should not be so stingy. They should pay attention to their face."

Village Leaders	14

VILLAGE leaders can be divided into the official and the lay leaders. Official leaders are elected by the villagers or appointed by the local or county government. They have specific duties to perform and are supposed to function not according to their own option but according to the fixed regulations. Under the old system there were four official leaders in a village of any size: the *she-chang*, the *chwang-chang*, the *hsiang-yueh*, and the *ti-fang*.

The *she-chang* was head of the rural district, the highest official post. No member of Taitou has ever been elected to this office. A member of the P'an clan held it two or three times, but he lived in a neighboring village. A *she-chang's* headquarters was his home, but he traveled with other village officers from one village to another and from his district to the county government to perform his duties.

The *chwang-chang* was the village head. He was always a native of the village in which he held office. He was elected for only one year but could be reelected continuously for a number of years.

The *hsiang-yueh* was the tax collector. Originally his chief duty was to convey to the villagers the Emperor's instructions as to how to be a filial son and to see that the social customs and the people's daily life were in conformity with the Confucian ethics. Gradually the *hsiang-yueh* became merely a political orderly for transmitting orders from the county government to the village and returning reports to them on village affairs. Finally even these circumscribed duties stopped and he became merely a tax collector, a position which did not command much respect. The *hsiang-yueh* was not necessarily an inhabitant of the village. Once the *hsiang-yueh* of Taitou was a man from a village three miles distant, for it seems that his jurisdiction extended over a territory that included several villages. Most often this job was in the hands of a member of the P'an clan.

The *ti-fang* was the policeman of the village. He had to arrest or detain any criminal, report the case to the government and help the government's commission in making the investigation. He also had to settle petty disputes and to organize the night-patrol system. This position was even lower than the *hsiang-yueh's* and no person of means or status ever wanted it. The *ti-fang* was often insulted or ill-treated by the government's servants who came to the village and, because he had no defense against such treatment, it was virtually impossible for him to retain the respect of the villagers.

Of the four officials, the *she-chang* and *chwang-chang* were elected by the villagers. Traditionally, anyone who desired one of these positions could make application to the government. Applications were so few that all those that were handed in had a good chance of success. Those in office acted as government representatives and consequently were somewhat dissociated from the village and generally disliked by the other villagers.

After the establishment of the Republic, the *Chu-Hsiang-Lu-Lin* system was installed. The rural district was organized into units, and each unit had its own leaders and councils. The *chu-chang* was the highest official leader of the rural district; the *hsiang-chang* was almost the equivalent of the old *chwang-chang*; and the other two officers, the *lu-chang* and the *lin-chang*, were subordinates of the *hsiang-chang* and generally acted as his assistants. All the officers were elected locally and were supposed to act on behalf of the villagers.

In spite of these changes, the official leaders in Taitou are still essentially of the old category and function in the old manner. A middle-aged man of the P'an clan now serves as the official head of the village. Older people still call him *chwang-chang*, while the young villagers who like to pick up new terms address him as *hsiang-chang*. He takes charge of all public affairs and acts on behalf of the villagers in dealing with the government or with other villages. This man has been in office about ten years. Before him, the *chwang-chang* was his father, and before that, it was a man of the Ch'en clan.

The village head, or the *hsiang-chang*, has an assistant. The present one is a member of the P'an clan and is a capable person. In the last few years, the government has started programs of road building, civilian training, land surveys, rural community organization, and so on. A capable leader was needed to impress the government's orders upon the villagers and to organize them for carrying out the new programs. This assistant has been able to handle the job with considerable efficiency. Many villagers, including his own kinsmen, did not like him, but nevertheless the people knew that no one else could do what he has done, and therefore he has remained in office for a number of years.

There is still a tax collector, though I do not know whether or not he is still called *hsiang-yueh* or by another term. Of late, however, most families have preferred to pay their taxes through a delegate chosen by them rather than through the official collector. A number of families, for instance, give their taxes to a responsible member and let him pay them in the county seat. In this way, they pay only the traveling expenses of their delegate and avoid the high commission due the tax collector for this service.

At the beginning of every year a meeting is held to elect a *hsiang-chang*, his chief assistant, and other subordinate officers. Those who attend are the senior members of the families. Every family may be represented by at least one member, though a number of families do not send anyone. Many of the representatives are not family heads, for the heads of the upper-class families do not attend the meeting. Many farmers are uninterested in village matters and assume that there is no necessity for them to go to these meetings, because the village will have its *chwang-chang* or *hsiang-chang* anyway. Ordinarily, however, some representatives of each of the four clans must be present or the election is not considered valid.

The election is conducted very informally. There is no ballot casting, no hand raising, and no campaign for candidates. The meeting is held in the village school or in some other customary meeting place. When several members of each clan have arrived, the person who presides over the meeting will stand up and say, "Uncles and brothers, now we are all here to discuss the public affairs of our village. As you all know, our *Chwang-chang*, Uncle P'an Chi has served us very well in the past year. He has worked hard and honestly to pacify disputes, to defend our village, to help families which have been involved in unfortunate controversies, to represent our interests in dealing with the government, and so on. As you also know, to be a public servant in these days is really a headache. Road building, military training for civilians, land surveys, school establishment, village defense, and what not, are all troublesome duties. We, as poor farmers, did not like them, because they cost us a great deal of money and time. But the government has insisted that they must be done, and our *Chwang-chang* and other officers have done their best in every one of these projects, so that we, as villagers, could live peacefully through these hard times. Now is the time to conduct a new election of our *Chwang-chang* and other officers. Uncle P'an Chi has recently said that he feels his age, that he is too tired to bear the heavy burden any longer, and would like to be relieved. I want to know whether we should let Uncle P'an Chi retire and elect another person to be our *Chwang-chang*, or should we ask him to continue. Since this is a matter of importance to our whole village, you are requested to express your ideas and let us know what your opinions are."

This opening address is followed by a moment of silence. Then one of the electors, usually a partially recognized village leader, will say, "Since, as Uncle Heng Li has just said, Uncle P'an Chi has served us well in the past, I cannot see why we should let him retire. I myself, and, I believe, many other fellow villagers, really appreciate Uncle P'an Chi's service, and I do not see any other person among us that is better for the office than he."

"Brother Heng Chun is right," says another representative, who is spinning his home-raised silk on a small spindle and has his long, thin tobacco pipe in his mouth. "We must ask Uncle P'an Chi to continue as our *Chwang-chang*. He has the ability and the experience. Who else can deal with those tricky government servants as he can? I know I couldn't."

A small farmer who does not have much social position in the village, might add, "I believe that any person who can be an official, great or small, must be born with an official star. The man who has such a star will be an official anyway. Uncle P'an Chi has been our *Chwang-chang* for a number of years. That means he was born to be a *chwang-chang*. He has his official star. Then, why should we bother to say yes or no?" At this everybody laughs. After a while, the chairman says again, "Now we have heard opinions which are for our *Chwang-chang* to continue in office. But is there anyone who has different ideas?" Nobody speaks, but the chairman wants to make sure that there will be no complaints later, so he addresses a member of the Yang clan: "What would you say, Lao San?" "I agree with the others that Uncle P'an Chi should continue." When several others ' ave been asked and given an assenting answer, the election is decided, and the village's *chwang-chang* is again in office.

Other officers, such as he *lin-chang, lu-chang* or *chia-chang*, are elected at the same meeting, but in a still less dignified manner. Every villager knows that no upper-class person wants to be elected to any of these offices and knows also that in each neighborhood there are two or three persons who would not refuse to serve. They simply tell one of these persons in each *hu-tung* that he is elected as the *lu-chang* of the neighborhood. The *chwang-chang* chooses one or two assistants, generally the persons who have already been his aides in the past.

The election is a relatively simple matter since there is no competition for office. On the whole, it may be said that the majority of villagers do not wish to serve in any official capacity and are glad to find among their number an individual who is eager to do so. This is sometimes enough to assure the election, for there are very few such aspiring persons.

The late P'an Chi was considered a successful *chwang-chang* in Taitou, and he may be taken as the type of person who generally became an official leader. He was a man of leisure. He had no farm business to occupy his time, nor was he a craftsman who had to work day and night when business was good. He was the head of a family of three grown sons who were capable of working the family's small holdings of land, so his help in the fields was not needed. He was a man who did not balk at petty deception when the situation warranted it, and he often admitted openly that, for the benefit of the village and for his personal profit, he had to play tricks every so often. He said that not all villagers were honest people and that not all honest villagers would see that some of the means by which the *chwang-chang* received compensation for his services were reasonable. In order to cope with those who were not honest and with those who were honest but unreasonable, subterfuge was necessary.

P'an Chi was a fluent and persuasive talker and enjoyed making speeches. When the villagers were indifferent or even hostile toward some government program, he was able to convince them of the desirability of participation in the government plan. His fluency made him invaluable in mediating disputes between important families or clans. When a conflict involved persons in high places whom P'an Chi did not dare reproach, he could be most ingratiating and conciliatory. He could also be threatening and often shouted aloud in the streets his criticisms of actions that displeased him. His abuses, however, were usually reserved for the poorer and weaker families. He considered that differential treatment and a glib tongue were necessary in the complicated social life of the village.

The *Chwan-chang* was a very sociable person. He had done a great deal of traveling in Manchuria. When he settled in Taitou, he made frequent visits to the market town. He was perfectly at ease in entertaining important persons, such as the local authorities, the county agents, district leaders, and leaders of other villages. He was energetic and brave. In Manchuria he had led hunting groups and had also been among a group of explorers who went into the interior.

Although he had ruined his parents' property by extravagances and his unwillingness to do farm work, he was not considered an unpleasant or immoral person by the villagers, but was regarded by them as a good sport. He did not hesitate to swear, he received commissions or took them when he handled public funds, but because he was genial he was not condemned for these practices. Another helpful trait, under the circumstances, was his willingness to admit that he was subordinate to the village gentry. He did not feel humiliated when ordered to do some business for them, and he fully recognized that he was only an orderly of the local authority or of the county government. He did not feel that he was losing face when he was insulted by the county officials but bore it with a good will.

The present *chwang-chang* of Taitou is P'an Chi's son, who is very much like his father. The chief assistant, also, possesses many of the same characteristics and he, too, has always been considered a capable village officer, though his moral standards are somewhat lower than P'an Chi's. This man is a member of the P'an clan, though he is poor. For a considerable time he worked as a cook or a domestic servant in Tsingtao, and failed to make much money. Since he had no land to cultivate and showed no interest in taking up any trade, the former *chwang-chang* picked him to serve as his orderly. Gradually he became indispensable and began to win the favorable opinion of the villagers. When he became chief assistant, he made enemies by attempting to squeeze too much money out of his deals. He married a woman who had already been married, which lowered his social status very much. But after they had a family and became prosperous, his wife gradually improved her relations with the neighbors and the people's resentment against her lessened. This man is still the *chwang-chang's* chief assistant and is playing an increasingly important role in village affairs.

Once such a person is elected, the probability is that he will remain in office for a long time. Some villagers may not be satisfied with him, but as long as he does not make serious mistakes they will not bother to elect someone else. If he himself really wants to retire, he informs the important villagers of his intention, so that the chairman of the ele_ion will make a different kind of opening address and the villagers will not reelect him. If he has done something inexcusable, then either he himself would not have face to hold office any longer or the influential laymen leaders would suggest his dismissal. In this case, the chairman of the meeting would also hint that a new *chwang-chang* should be elected and the villagers would follow the cue. The result of the election is therefore to some extent prearranged and the meeting is a routine matter. The real authority lies in the hands of the laymen leaders. Most villagers understand this and do not attribute too much importance to the office of *chwang-chang*.

The most important duty of the official leaders is dealing with the local or county government on behalf of the villagers. When a government order arrives, the local authority summons the *chwang-chang* of all villages in the district to the market town, where they are informed of their duty. The local *chwang-chang* returns to his village, sees the important laymen first, and discusses with them the way in which the order will be carried out. Then a tentative plan is drawn up. After this has been done, the *chwang-chang* calls a meeting of his assistants and all the other village officers, including representatives of some families of each clan, at which the government order and the tentative plan are presented. After some discussion, the final details for recruiting labor, sharing expenses, and planning the schedule of work are roughly formulated. Then the assistants and other subordinate officers inform all the families of what they are to do. In case some of the villagers complain about the plan or attempt to evade their responsibilities, the *chwang-chang* or his chief assistant will rebuke them on the main street or at a public gathering— provided they are not persons of importance. If many complain, the rebuke will be changed into an appeal. If an important person (or family) complains, the *chwang-chang* will go to see the complainant personally and try to placate him.

Occasionally a *chwang-chang* is required to make petition or explanation of certain matters to the government on behalf of the villagers—an appeal for exemption from paying of land tax when famines occur, or an appeal for protection when there are threats from bandits. In respect to neighboring villages, the *chwang-chang* is delegated to take up a federal defense project among a group of villages or in the whole market-town area; to discuss with one or two neighboring villages a collective sponsorship of opera practicing or religious parade; and to act on behalf of the villagers in controversies with neighboring villages. Within the village the *chwang-chang* and his assistants are active leaders in inviting an opera company to the village for a three-day practice session during the slack season; they are leaders in conducting a religious parade when there is a drought. They are also the responsible persons when collective action is needed to combat locusts, or to meet crop crises caused by hail, flood, or storm.

Sometimes they are asked by the schoolteacher to help in canvassing pupils. The official leaders, especially the *chwang-chang*, are mediators when two families or two clans get into a dispute. The official leaders are also charged with the protection of the village: night patrolling to guard against petty theft and fire; crop watching to prevent animals or thieves from damaging the fields; and also surveillance to keep gambling, opium smoking, and prostitution from becoming too serious. The *chwang-chang* and his assistants were the persons directly responsible in all these matters. When political order in the rural districts became decadent and the rural people were seriously threatened by bandits or other discontented elements, village and local defense became necessary, and the official leaders were again charged with the responsibility.

In acting as a leader of local defense, the *chwang-chang* of Taitou is a good example. We have already described the village defense organization and have pointed out that its success owed much to the leadership of the *chwang-chang*. He had learned to shoot and had acquired some knowledge of group organization when he was with his father in Manchuria. He put this experience into practice when, as *chwang-chang*, he organized the young villagers, built the defense lines and the fortifications, and, above all, led the defenders in actual combat with bandits. At night he was on patrol duty just as other villagers were. He led the men in chasing the bandits. He was the one who introduced military drill to the village. The entire village under his leadership was organized into one combat unit which sucessfully warded off all attacks.

Finally we see that the *chwang-chang* is often the chairman of the few significant village meetings that take place, such as discussions on how to participate in the government's rural reconstruction programs, or the organization of village defense, and so on. We also see that the *chwang-chang* is often asked to be present at the time of the separation of a family. His presence is not actually required in such an instance, but if the brothers have no important relatives or clan head he is the most suitable person to act as a witness to the proceedings.

The *chwang-chang* is often invited to dinner when a family entertains a guest for the daughter's betrothal, or for a son's wedding, or for the son-in-law's first visit to his wife's home, or for the celebration of a family head's birthday. Each of these occasions is planned in honor of someone, and the presence of important personages is a means of showing a guest that his hosts hold him in high esteem, for this is the equivalent of telling the guest that he is accorded the same treatment, and therefore held in the same regard, as this guest of assured and recognized status. The *chwang-chang* is the most easily available person to invite to a celebration when it is necessary to make this display of indirect respect.

The *chwang-chang* and his chief assistant receive compensation for their services in money or in entertainment and gifts. Formerly, the *chwang-chang* and other officers were not paid. Expenses were paid out of the public funds and the officers made a commission which took the place of a regular salary. If the actual expenses were ten dollars, for example, they would collect twelve and keep the difference for themselves. No villager ever bothered to make a fuss about this as long as the amounts were small. The cost of any rural reconstruction project is borne by the people of the locality. The *chwang-chang* and his chief assistant collect their village's share and here, too, they make a commission for themselves. This is an open secret. Within limits, the villagers tolerate it, but sometimes the exploitation becomes so flagrant that they are forced to take action. The only real means of reprisal is to put the *chwang-chang* and his assistant out of office and elect new ones.

At the time of the New Year Festival, each of the well-to-do families in turn invites the *chwang-chang* and other important leaders to dinner, but the *chwang-chang's* subordinates have few such invitations. If a *chwang-chang* does a favor for some family, he receives a gift from them on a suitable occasion. A popular leader may receive a considerable quantity of gifts and invitations during the New Year season, but his assistant receives very few.

In each village there are a number of persons who are in a sense leaders though they hold no official position. Their influence in public affairs or in the community life may be much greater than that of the official leaders, but it may not be evident. They are known essentially as respected laymen. The most notable of these are the village elders, those who have performed special services for the village as a whole, and the schoolteachers. These persons comprise the village gentry, so to speak.

In a Chinese village a *tsu-chang*, or head of a clan, has some influence over a designated group of families, but his influence is only recognized by the clan and opreates within its limits. He is usually an older member but sometimes may be the person who is the wealthiest family head in that particular community, for his wealth allows him to do things others cannot afford. A neighborhood leader is someone who can influence the five or ten families in his *hu-tung*, or small lane, by virtue of his personality or intelligence or general reliability. It may become customary for his neighbors to seek his advice and in this way he exerts more influence than anybody else in the vicinity.

A layman leader is not elected or appointed and is usually a man of a kind entirely different from an official leader. He is a leader largely because he is admired and respected or because he holds an important position in the social life of the village. A businessman who lived in Tsingtao was recognized as a top-ranking layman leader in Taitou all during the time he engaged in business there, though he was not a resident of the village. He is still an important leader, although he has retired from business now and lives on his small farm. When he was a young man, his father ruined the family's property by carelessness and neglect, so he had to go to work as an apprentice in one of the shops in the market town. He made a very humble beginning and what success he did achieve, which was considerable, was due entirely to his own efforts. The villagers admired his later fortune, representing as it did to them, hard work, thrift, and steadfastness. It was on the basis of this that he was sought out by them when there were local questions to be decided and was finally recognized by them as a most valuable leader. The Christian minister, who belonged to the Yang clan, and the present schoolteacher, who is a P'an, won their positions through a similar process. The Yang was the son of a poor farmer who had to struggle to achieve his present position. The teacher of the village school was also poor when he left home to become a worker in a machine shop. He and his brother learned the trade and came home to open a little foundry in the village. As the business went well, the brothers and the family both climbed the social scale. Later, the first brother went to the county seat to get the proper training for teaching in a new primary school. When he returned to Taitou, both the villagers and the government made him the teacher of the village school. His training is far from adequate, but since he has a degree, nobody can deny him his post. In addition to this, he is on good terms with all the decent and important villagers and they like him, so he is one of the important laymen leaders of the village.

A late Mr. P'an, as head of a wealthy family, was one of the village gentry. Though a rich man, he had himself worked hard on the farm during his younger years. With his brothers and cousins he studied as a boy in the old-fashioned school, but he applied himself with greater diligence than any of the others and as a result his academic training was superior. He later became the teacher of the village school. He was very mild in manner, behaved in strict accordance with the Confucian doctrines, and was respected and liked by almost everyone. When the new educational system was installed by the government and new schools were established in the villages, this man immediately saw the necessity of adapting himself to the new conditions. He went to the teachers' training school in the county seat, despite the fact that he was now over fifty years of age. On a cold winter day many years ago, this writer saw the old man carrying his belongings, beginning his twenty-five mile walk to the training school on foot. The villagers who were standing about on the street said to each other as they watched him, "Look, he's going to study again."

"It's silly for a man like him to undergo this sort of hardship. He has plenty to live on. What's the need of his going to teach in a poor school?"

"But he's a wonderful man. Just see what spirit he has and what a thrifty life he leads. I believe we all have something to learn from him."

After several months of training the old Confucian became a semi-modern teacher and the old clan school turned into a semimodern village school. This old man went frequently to the model primary school which was situated in the market town to seek the assistance of the younger but better-trained teachers who were there. Nor was he embarrassed when he sought the aid of a young high-school boy, the son of a Yang family who was spending his summer vacation at home. This young man taught the old scholar mathematics and the old man never hesitated to in-corporate what he learned in his own lectures to the students of the village school. After school, the pupils would jokingly say to the boy, "So, you are our teacher's teacher." Strangely enough, this did no damage to the old teacher's reputation.

There were several other types among the village gentry. One was the gentleman, distinguished by his handsome figure, neat dress, high spirits, good manners, humorous conversation and endless leisure. He was in sharp contrast to the other type of leisured villager who was aggressive, dominating, and inordinately fond of public hearings. Years ago these two types were well exemplified by the heads of two wealthy P'an families. One of them was admired and liked by all the villagers; the other was admired but was not liked because he often showed himself to be stingy in his dealings with hired laborers. These men were not ambitious to be leaders, but they exerted their leadership nonetheless, for it was forced upon them by the position they held in the eyes of the villagers. They were necessarily public figures. This was especially true of the more popular of the two. Because of his mild, impartial, and unassuming manner, he was sought after to mediate disputes that arose between families. He was known in the entire market-town area for his skill in arbitration.

Another man, also the head of a large and wealthy P'an family was of enormous build, active, voluble, and given to fierce gesturing. He was not a learned man, but had bought a military degree from the Manchu government. He was very ambitious but had failed to win a position in the government and this was a constant source of chagrin to him. He dominated all village affairs and insisted in having a voice in all administrative problems of the entire market-town area. On the whole, the village leaders and some of the local gentry made concessions to him and did not resist his attempts at leadership.

Age is not of itself a qualification for leadership, but it is usually true that the essential qualities manifest themselves in later life and people believe that aged persons have much valuable experience. Being an acceptable example to the younger generation is a condition for being a leader, and people look for models among the older people. A leader's successful functioning depends to a great extent on his knowledge of the people of the village, and such knowledge is more easily attained by those with the leisure to frequent wine shops and while away hours in conversation. The vague term "experience" includes much that the villagers think necessary for leaders and this term is closely associated with age. It is only since specialized training has become essential for certain types of leadership that the idea of experience has also become associated with the number of years spent in some particular area of training, and this new view to some extent threatens the former authority of the layman leaders. Formerly, as at present, leadership was something that was not sought but gradually became the accompaniment of certain other attributes—age, wealth, scholarship.

The laymen leaders remain in the background, but their role is so important that without their advice and support the *chwang-chang* and his assistant are unable to accomplish anything. The village gentry are also heads of the chief clans or families. If they object to a program, or even if they merely take a negative attitude, the administration faces an impasse. Laymen leaders do not, as a rule, deal with the government authorities directly. Sometimes the district leader or the county government invites them to a conference to hear their opinions regarding a certain case; not infrequently their advice influences government policy. In the old days there were various ways of determining public opinion in the countryside, but as a rule public opinion was created not by the small farmers but by the rural gentry and clan heads. The local officials were often ordered by the central government to listen to these laymen leaders, who thus played an inconspicuous but important role in local politics. In the written history of a county there can be found many pages devoted to the biographies of thousands of rural leaders which have been recorded carefully through hundreds of generations. It is a well-recognized fact that a great part of local history was made by them.

Laymen share a number of functions with the official leaders. In dealing with other villages or in discussing district-wide cooperation, the gentry of different villages meet in the market town as the official leaders do. In some cases, the two groups meet together. In mediating conflicts between families or clans, the laymen play a more important role than does the *chwang-chang*; they are more respected and consequently more influential. Their intervention in a case is highly valued and their words carry weight because of their position in the community. If important families or clans get into trouble, the *chwang-chang* does not have sufficient prestige or authority to settle the matter; the aid of the gentry must be invoked. Presiding at ceremonial occasions for important families or for the village as a whole is another function of the laymen leaders.

The relations between the laymen and official leaders is definitely a supraordinate-subordinate one. This was uniformly true in the past and is still largely true in the present. In public affairs the official leaders do the active work but laymen direct them. The official leaders are generally the functionaries or even messengers of the gentry and the clan heads. When the *hsiang-chang* and his assistants receive orders from the government, they cannot make any decision until they have consulted with the influential laymen, and in these conferences the official leaders are usually expected to be completely acquiescent. They relay the orders but their own opinions on how they should be carried out is of minimal importance.

Traditionally, the magistrate or his secretaries paid respect to the village gentry, schoolteachers, and the large clan heads, but would assume an air of superiority toward the official leaders. No villager of social rank or much self-esteem wanted to be an official, for he would lose face in dealing with those who outranked him in authority but not in social status. Besides, no one wanted to be at the beck and call of the government or to have to take orders. A Chinese country gentleman or a rural scholar might welcome a post in the district, provincial, or central government, but would nevertheless hate to bow to a lesser man. For this reason, village officials have generally been recruited from the poorer families; they are men who do not care overmuch for reputation or social status or who are exceedingly interested in the profits to be made. Naturally this has kept the offices low in the eyes of the people, who have never felt called upon to respect those who hold them. As far as can be remembered, the *chwang-chang* (or *hsiang-chang*) of Taitou has always been a man of an unimportant family and of little claim to village respect. The present incumbent is considerably esteemed, but this is because he has done unusually good work in organizing the village defense during the last ten years, a relatively new duty for the *hsiang-chang*. In the present system of organization of the local government, the office of official leader has been much enhanced and the people are becoming aware of the added qualifications needed for the job. The young officer now in charge is a junior member of the P'an clan and he still has to listen to the words of his clan heads. When official leaders are persons of the lower social ranks, they are conscious of their inferiority and the title of office is less instrumental in their relations than their family positions. This young man comes from a distinguished family but his youth is against him.

Formerly, if the land taxes were paid and no criminal case which had to be referred to the law courts occurred, the village and the government had little to do with each other. What collective activities there were in a Chinese village were largely negative or preventive in character and dominated by traditional procedures. Except in cases of necessity, no new measures were initiated. The duty of the leaders was to see that the existing order was not disturbed, and that any new suggestion which would threaten it should fail of accomplishment. Recently this has been changed. The government wants the village to do many new things and to eliminate many things which it has declared undesirable. Orders and suggestions come to the villages almost every day. The area has been reorganized, and the village officers have new authority. The old type of *chwang-chang* does not fit the new requirements, and trained people are replacing him. This has had its effect on the old pattern of subordination to the laymen leaders, who observe this change with a good deal of resentment. The old assurance of their status is gone and in the present insecurity lies the core of much of their antagonism to the new government. They are necessarily the "conservative" element of the population. Their criticism of the government is not specifically directed at policies or the plans for improving the rural areas, but rather at those appointed to carry out these changes.

There are also leaders who are not official, nor yet influential laymen, but who, by virtue of possessing some special skill, are recognized as being capable of leadership. Years ago a mason of the Liu clan became popular in the area. He trained an apprentice, who also became popular. A boy from a Yang family learned the trade with the second mason. In several years these three had trained several other masons in the village. The original master is still living. Although he has lost a great deal of prestige, nevertheless he still has some degree of leadership in that particular trade. The master-craftsman feeling still exists and the two masters can still influence the activities of the other four masons. When a piece of work of any significance has to be done, the younger masons usually go to consult their former masters and the latter give them the advice and help that they need to solve their difficulties. When there is a dispute among the masons themselves, it will be the two masters rather than the other village leaders who settle it, and their words are usually effective. When a young mason is not fully trusted by the villagers regarding his training in the trade, the master's recommendation is important if he is to obtain work. In return, the young mason recognizes the leadership of the master.

The two masters received from their followers three kinds of compensation. When the young masons were their apprentices, they paid a certain amount of what they earned to their masters. When the apprenticeship was over, payments stopped and instead gifts were given on special occasions. The two masters also would be invited to any special dinner that the families of the young men might give.

A similar relationship is seen among the four or five weavers, but the other trades, carpentry and blacksmithing, do not have this master-apprentice organization, because there are only one or two carpenters and smiths.

For many years it has been customary for a few people, young or old, to engage in some local trade as small retailers. The oil-pressing business which has always been confined to a few individuals is another example. Young men may also go to work as apprentices in the shops in Tsingtao. If one of these makes a great success, he is recognized by all the villagers and by many people of the market-town area as a businessman of the best type. There will be a group of people around him asking his recommendation or consulting with him about their plans.

Any problem regarding literature, ritual, children's school training, new laws or regulations passed by the government, and the news of the nation and the world is usually discussed with one or both of the schoolteachers. The villagers expect them to be able to answer questions relating to any of these topics. The preacher of the Protestant church and the leader of the Catholic group are also specialized leaders. The first is so far only able to lead the religious service and has done nothing, or very little, to answer the queries of church members on other subjects. This is probably because he is a man from the outside and there is little mutual understanding between him and the villagers. Another factor is that every one of the five or six successive preachers has been poorly trained and badly paid. The leader of the Catholic group has always been a villager. He seems to have led the group pretty well, because the members held services often and regularly for quite a few years though they had no preacher or subsidy from the outside. But this leadership also is largely limited to religious activities.

The teacher of the village school has been traditionally a person who occupied simultaneously several statuses. He was the schoolteacher, head of the P'an clan, a member of the village gentry, and a local scholar. The present teacher is no exception; he is an important layman leader, although he is too young to be his clan's head. The teacher of the Christian school has always been an outsider, so his leadership has not, as a rule, been widely recognized. One of these teachers, however, was a very influential person because he possessed the attributes of a real Chinese gentleman. In addition to his specialized training he was able to paint landscapes, write poems, carve wood and stones, conduct conversations, and appreciate natural beauties. He could also smoke like a gentleman and sip tea like an old scholar. He behaved very conventionally before women and old people, but was humorous when he talked with a group of young farmers. As a result he got acquainted with most of the younger villagers and all the old people spoke well of him. He taught in the school for six or seven years, during which time he exerted a significant influence on the cultural opinions and activities of the village.

There have been women who assumed leadership in a clan, the branch of a clan, or among the families comprising a small neighborhood, but their leadership was largely limited to influencing other women. Only one woman in the last fifty years showed a degree of leadership that affected the village as a whole. She was the first woman convert to the Christian church in the entire market-town area. She fostered Christianity in her village and frequently invited the handful of other converts to her home for worship and meetings. When a definite place was fixed upon for religious services, she was busy urging the women of the Christian families to come to worship with the men members, and made it a point to accompany them herself. This required great courage in a farm village of thirty years ago, and her initiative and daring much impressed her fellow villagers. She was among the leaders who organized the local Christians in a concerted effort to build their own church. While it was being constructed, she induced the other women to contribute their voluntary labor to it. By this time she was definitely recognized as a leader of the Christian group. Despite all kinds of complaints and counterarguments on the part of her relatives and all sorts of abuse directed at her by the villagers, she went to Tsingtao to attend a Bible School. When she came back to Taitou she was more devoted to the church than ever. Her success in achieving her aims, despite their unconventionality and the discouragement of others, made her a stimulating and perhaps disturbing example to the other women, who began to get from her an idea of what women might do. She was a particularly noteworthy example because she had a very pleasant personality and because she never allowed her varied activities to lead her to neglect her home and family. She managed her domestic affairs so well that her family rose in influence and importance during her lifetime. Since she was the only educated woman in the village, she won great respect from the important villagers, who also liked her high spirits and cheerfulness. Her leadership in her own clan, that is her husband's clan, was so great that even the head of the most ambitious family in it listened to her and occasionally conceded to her requests and opinions. At her death all the village leaders and the authorities of the church mourned her deeply. Two of her four sons became prominent professional men and the villagers credited their success to the energy and good sense of their mother.

TAITOU is closely related to Hsinanchen, the market town and connecting link between the various villages which surround it. The limits of the market-town area are set by the communication and transportation facilities and by the natural physical barriers of the region. There are points at which it may overlap that of another market town, and there are also some "neutral zones" between these areas, but, on the whole, although there is no clear-cut line of demarcation, each market town has a definite and recognizable area, and looks upon the people of certain villages as its primary customers; in turn, it is regarded by the villagers as their town.

Hsinanchen is much larger than any of the villages in its area, and has many good buildings, both commercial and residential. The important streets and avenues all meet at the center of the town to form a public square. The business section has broad streets lined with shops, drugstores, restaurants, and inns. At the northeastern end of the town is the Confucian temple and the new primary school. On the outskirts are the village-type houses of the farming families.

Since Hsinanchen serves more than twenty villages, it has a considerable volume of business. The five or six drugstores sell, in addition to drugs, sugar, oil, spices, and other things. There are also several blacksmith and silversmith shops, three or four bakeries, two hardware shops, one bookstore, two large wine-making establishments, two carpenter shops, three or four small inns and several restaurants. These shops are open all week but are busiest on regular market days. The owners and clerks came originally from the villages where their families still live, and customers patronize those from their own village. Shops are patronized by the same families for generations; farmers go to them because their fathers and their grandfathers went there.

Most of the trade still takes place on the six regular market days, which occur on the first, fifth, tenth, fifteenth, twentieth, twenty-fifth, and thirtieth day of every month These dates were arrived at in cooperation with the other four market towns in the adjacent areas, so that traders in the region can go to market in one town or another every day, with no conflicting dates or marketless days to interrupt their routine. On market days the business life of the town is in full swing. On the evening before the market opens, the professional itinerant traders begin to pour in with their wares; early in the morning come the village butchers with their dressed hogs; the country merchants with their bags of wheat flour, cans of petroleum, bales of spun cotton yarn; and the carpenters with their homemade furniture and farm implements. Later come the traders who deal in dried foodstuffs, fish and seafood, fruits, pottery, chinaware, and scores of other merchandise. Then the farmers begin streaming in from the surrounding villages with their loads of grains, beans, fresh vegetables and fruits, animal feed, and firewood. Some also drive in livestock which they hope to sell or exchange. Later come the people who have nothing to sell but only want to buy. Some member from almost every household in the village is in the town on market day. In the morning every road leading to the town is crowded with people. Very few women go to market, with the exception of some old women from poor families who carry eggs, or chickens, or baskets of seafood for sale, or some of their handiwork which they hope to exchange for a little money.

All the available space in the town is crowded with booths, counters, and platforms heaped with merchandise. Traders dealing in similar commodities occupy the same section, thus forming more or less specialized markets. The livestock market and the fuel market are located outside the town on the riverbank. People crowd the streets, shouting, bargaining, greeting friends, yelling, and swearing. The excitement reaches its peak at noon and then begins to decline. Soon the roads are filled once more with homeward-bound villagers, but the marketing continues until late afternoon.

Besides the six regular days there are usually two occasions set aside every year for special marketing, generally in the late spring and autumn. These fairs, which last from three to five days, draw people not only from the local villages but also from neighboring communities and even from other counties. The schools are closed for one or two days, and everybody, young and old—except the young ladies—comes to town. Dramas are performed, the wine shops are crowded, and large quantities and great varieties of commodities are assembled. Here the local people can buy things which are not available on the ordinary market days—fine cloth, silver for weddings, furniture and farm implements, imported furs, special medicines. Trade in livestock is lively.

Thus far, China has not become a country of modern industries, but she has numerous small-scale rural industries operated by farmers and their families or by rural artisans. As a center for selling what the farmer makes and for supplying him with raw materials, the market town is indispensable. It has been reported, for example, that the cloth-weaving industry in many parts of the province is still essentially the old type of

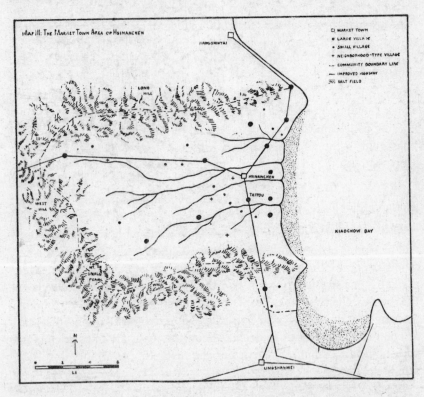

Chinese rural industry; that is, it uses the market town as a center where families buy cotton yarn for weaving, and sell their cloth for local consumption or for export to distant markets. In this part of China there are many market towns dealing primarily in the distribution of manufactured cotton yarn to the rural families and the assembling of the cloth woven by them.

The market town also finances the rural families. A regular customer of a certain store does not have to buy with cash; credit is usually extended to him for periods up to one year. In general, the villagers pay their debts on the three large festivals, the *Ch'ing-ming*, *Tuan-wu*, and *Chung-chiu*, or at the end of the year. Some farmers may even postpone all their payments to the last month of the year. Since most of the store proprietors in the market town have families in the surrounding villages, they are usually related to the farmers or know them well. It is customary for farmers who have surplus money to deposit it in the store run by a kinsman or a fellow villager; the store, in turn, lends the money to its good customers, thus taking the place of a pawnshop. There is no pawnshop in Hsinanchen, therefore, the villagers cannot raise money by pawning their valuables.

The market town provides opportunities for farmers from different villages to meet one another, and is in fact one of the few places where they can meet. Chinese farmers always have friends and relatives in other villages and these meetings in the market take the place of visits, which would be more expensive. When the farmers return home they report to the whole family what they have seen and heard and, in this way, people are kept informed about one another.

Most of the leaders in a Chinese rural community have leisure time, which they are apt to spend in the wine shops or the teahouses in the market town. They talk or argue in the stores on current affairs or historical events and discuss community problems. Many community programs, good and bad, come out of such informal gatherings and many problems have been solved, wisely or not, in these discussions. A score of villages are linked together or separated in conflict whenever their leaders take measures to avoid each other in the market town.

A group of separated villages may appear isolated from the larger rural community, but it is easy to see in the market town on market day, how their integration is accomplished. When the local government proposes some desirable but not mandatory program, leaders of all villages of the area will be called to the market town to confer with the authorities and offer their opinions. Back in the villages the official leaders go to the important laymen leaders and the villagers to tell them what has happened in the market town. Villagers are not in a position to propose anything definite, but they talk the matter over among themselves. On the following market days, the official leaders find out from each other the opinions of their respective villages regarding the particular matter. The laymen leaders do the same thing and sometimes meet with the official leaders for a general discussion. After two or three weeks, when the case has been discussed again and again, the local authority summons the leaders of the villages and important men of the local area to the market town for a final decision. Then every village starts to make plans for the program. Sometimes a program may be initiated by two or three influential persons of different villages. When this is the case, the initiators will advocate and discuss their ideas with leaders of other villages when they meet in the market town. After several such meetings a final decision may be made and a definite program started.

In general, every large market town is crossed by a main road on which persons from the outside world travel. They bring news from distant places. In the town there are telephone and telegraph offices. The post office brings mail into the town to be distributed to the villages. Commercial agents from the county seat or other large cities bring information from their headquarters, which travels to the villages immediately. Teahouses and wine shops generate rumors which are widely spread. There is an old saying that statesmen should listen to the talk in these hidden corners. Public opinion and social attitudes take form in them and there are numerous historical tales of Chinese officials who visited them in disguise in order to discover what the common man was saying about current affairs. It is well known that the farmer does not have much to say at home but is a good talker whenever he finds himself in the market town and sits with his fellow villagers in the teahouse.

A model school was opened in the market town several years after the revolution, and the market-town area became known as a school district. The school in the market town is a six-year primary school. In each large village there is a four-year primary school. Students may come here to finish the second part of their elementary training in order to enter the high school in the county seat. The village schoolteachers come to discuss their teaching and administrative problems with the teachers of the town school, and students from different villages come to know each other in the schoolroom. On Sundays or other holidays, teacher and students of one school may organize groups to visit those in another. Thus, the town school forms a nucleus for a larger community organization.

Adjacent to Taitou are four villages, three small and one large. The children of the three small ones have for generations attended the school in Taitou, those from the large village also went there occasionally. Since the establishment of the Christian school, which is believed by many people to be better than any other school in the vicinity, pupils have come from many near-by villages. The distance from Taitou to these villages is not great and the boys walk back and forth without any difficulty, except when during the rainy season the rivers are in flood.

A collective system of local defense among a group of near-by villages has been in existence for a long time. Recently, because of the threat of bandits, this system has been greatly strengthened. Each village in the market town area was organized and equipped as an independent unit. Then all the units joined together making the market town their headquarters. Should any one village be attacked by bandits, the village would use all its resources to defend itself, but at the same time all the adjacent villages would help, and the distant villages would be ready to send aid should they be called upon. Once in a while an armed parade of the whole federation is held to search the highways and mountainous areas where bandits might take refuge. This organization succeeded in driving out two or three powerful groups of bandits who had entered the area. At one time eight armed outlaws who came from Tsingtao to kidnap a family in an outlying village were caught. When the alarm was given, men with their modern weapons were immediately called together from all the villages of the area to form a huge group. They scattered over all the roads leading to the besieged village, and when the bandits saw them, escape was already cut off. The fight between the bandits and the local people lasted for some time until the bandits were outnumbered and driven to the seashore. By noon, all of them were captured. At the market town the captives were tried and executed by the authorities of the federation, who neglected to inform the county government of the trial. Later, the local people realized that they had acted illegally and worried a great deal about it, but fortunately the political authority was then too weak to take action and the case was ignored.

How closely a market town is related to people of the surrounding villages is shown in a story * about a new teahouse in a village near Soochow, Kiangsu. It is true that this story represents the situation in east central China, but it might have happened in Hsinanchen.

Mr. Shih, a social worker in a village, noticed that the local farmers usually traveled three *li* every day to the market town to have a cup of tea. He realized that this was a great waste of time and labor, and to remedy the situation he and several villagers started a "Central Teahouse" in the village temple. They hoped in this way to bring about closer contacts among the villagers. Since they knew that the farmers who went to drink tea in the market town also bought some of their daily necessities at the same time, they added to the new teahouse a trade-service department equipped with the articles in most frequent use. Furthermore, they knew that villagers always got information on the prices of their

* Shih Chung-i, "Village Life in My Rural Service," in *Experiences in Rural Work*, by Hsu Pao-Chien (Shanghai, Y.M.C.A. Press, 1936), pp. 40–45. (In Chinese.)

farm products and news of local affairs in the market-town teahouse, and they therefore invited several community leaders who were interested in social improvement and who possessed knowledge of commerce and industry to give these people news and to talk about contemporary social trends in the new teahouse. Since the market-town teahouse provided old-fashioned recreation, such as the telling of superstitious stories and singing, they also supplied a phonograph, musical instruments, popular magazines, newspapers, chess games, and many other recreational facilities. They also invited people who could recount the historical tales popular with the country people. Since they knew that the market town teahouse is a place where many community disputes and neighborhood quarrels are settled by drinking the so-called "mediating tea," they invited the village leaders and community elders to conduct their mediating tasks in the new teahouse. In short, they tried to equip their teahouse with everything that the market-town teahouse had, paying special attention to quality and educational value. What was the result of their effort? At first, only a small number of curious young people came. When their curiosity was satisfied, they stopped coming. The teahouse owners were surprised at this. Seeking an explanation, they were told that it was because the teahouse was in a temple and no farmer likes to drink tea in a temple. This seemed reasonable, so they moved their enterprise to a new place, which was much more comfortable than the temple, and hoped for better success. Alas, after a short period of prosperity, they were again rewarded with empty rooms. After this they made still another try, but with no result except more money lost.

This time they decided that they must find out the real reason for their failure. They learned that many of the farmers who go to drink tea every day at the market town do so because they feel they must. Everybody has followed the custom for generations and they dare not break it. Many can ill afford it, but should they fail to present themselves for a few days running in the market-town teahouse, they would immediately become the object of rumors and their financial credit would be suspected by everybody in the community. The market-town stores would refuse to delay the payment of debts or deny any extension of credit. Their friends would avoid them or greet them coldly. Finally, they would be in danger of bankruptcy. Therefore, in order to maintain their social prestige or to hide their economic weakness, they have to go to the market-town teahouse every day. This is why a villager may sometimes go to market town when he has no business there. He is seen sometimes just wandering in the town or going to and from the market town with an empty basket.

Intervillage religious activities near Taitou are rare, but there are two temples and two shrines, besides the two Christian churches, which are frequented by villagers of the whole district. One temple is located at the northeastern end of the market town. The deities in it are Kuan-kung and Tseng-sun. The former was a loyal general, also a sworn brother of the first emperor of Shu of the Three Kingdoms. A symbol of loyalty rather than a divinity, he has been worshiped for generations here. Tseng-sun, one of Confucius' seventy-two apostles, is worshiped because he was praised by his Master for his filial piety. This temple is not frequently patronized by the farmers but rather is a meeting place for the rural scholars. At the second large temple which is Buddhist and is located near the market town, farmers seek divine blessing and protection. The monk performs Buddhist services at funerals for the village families, and thus is more familiar to the villagers than are the heads of the Confucian temple. The two shrines are located on the northern mountain and the southern hill. One is a shrine to the King of Cattle, the other is visited once a year on the ninth day of the ninth month, mostly by women. These temples and shrines are controlled by a group of local leaders who appoint the head of the Confucian temple and govern the duties of the monk. Each temple owns a certain amount of land, the rent from which pays for its maintenance. The two shrines are maintained either by the revenues from the annual fair or by public funds.

When there is a drought, the local leaders organize a religious parade to the Dragon King, who is supposed to dwell in an old spring or well. If rain comes within ten days after the parade, the farmers feel that the Dragon King has answered their prayers. In giving thanks, a sacrifice is made to the god and the date for an opera is set. It is interesting to note that the Chinese farmers as well as the old-fashioned merchants and handicraftsmen have for long used the opera as the chief feature of religious thanksgiving. After several months, when the farm does not require so much attention, the village, or villages, have an opera which lasts three days and is attended by people from neighboring villages.

For generations Taitou has cooperated with a village just across the river in the production of an opera. The stage was usually built on the southern bank of the Taitou River, so that the people of both villages could reach it conveniently. In the evenings, men, women, and children of the two villages and of other near-by villages mingled together as if they were members of one community, enjoying the show. Unfortunately, this cooperation has been frequently interrupted, when the leaders of the two villages disagreed on the location of the stage and the sharing of expenses. One year Taitou had its own opera, the next year the other village followed suit. Sometimes each village staged an opera in the same year and rivalry ran high.

Since commercialization and industrialization have gradually penetrated the countryside, the farmer becomes increasingly dependent upon goods not produced by himself. He produces only the primary foodstuffs on his farm and in his vegetable garden, and everything else must be bought from the market town or other cities. This means that he depends more and more on the market town, that its stores play an increasingly important role in the rural economy, and that its trade service is becoming an essential factor in organizing the local community. It also means that the village and the outside world are becoming more interdependent through the agencies of the local market town, the market towns in the outlying areas, and the growing contact with Tsingtao.

There are a number of market towns immediately beyond Hsinanchen. In the north and northwest lie Hungshihyai and Wantai, each about ten miles distant. The former is a small seaport serving a considerable rural area, while the latter is an inland town of some importance. In the south and southeast are Lingshanwei and Hsuehchiatao, the latter at the main road junction between the rural area and Tsingtao. Because Wantai is a much larger place and supports numerous small industries, shops with luxury foods, and, periodically, large supplies of livestock, villagers go there when they want to buy special things, such as the Moslem biscuit, Yenshan chinaware, Tsingchow furs, and so on, or when they want to buy good mules or big oxen.

Hungshihyai is known for assembling grain and peanuts from the surrounding rural areas. Our farmers sell their wheat, soybeans, millet, and other cereals to the dealers in Hsinanchen, from where they are transported to Hungshihyai and from there shipped to Tsingtao. Some of the villagers and a number of the merchants in Hsinanchen opened business shops or agencies in this market town. Formerly goods manufactured or bought in Tsingtao were first shipped to Hungshihyai and then to Hsinanchen, so that the latter was almost a dependency of the former. To a certain extent this was true of Wantai.

Lingshanwei is also a place where our farmers could occasionally sell their farm products, but the most important business is dealing in fish.

The town is near the southern sea where great quantities of swordfish are caught every year. In the late spring a big fish market is held and fish is transported from there to many inland towns and cities. Villagers from Taitou go there themselves to buy the fish, but a family or a group of families make such a trip only once a year, and it is an unusual affair.

Hsuehchiatao has recently become an important seaport for a large rural area southwest of Kiaochow Bay. Because of the shorter and improved highway, people of our district have gradually altered their route to Tsingtao to lead through Hsuehchiatao, which is a great market for vegetables, fruits, poultry, and the young sweet-potato plants produced or raised in our district. In the spring and summer, numerous loads of vegetables and fruits are transported from our village to the Hsuehchiatao market and thence distributed to surrounding villages. The prices for these products are higher in this market than in Hsinanchen and therefore villagers carry their products the extra distance rather than sell them in the near-by market. Fishing and sea-going commerce are important occupations in this area. Most of the men fish late in the spring so that they cannot seed their nursery of sweet-potato plants. When they come home it is already time for planting the crop, so they have to buy the young plants. It is the farmers of our districts, especially those of Taitou who supply the fisher's needs. During the planting season one can see every morning hundreds of sweet-potato plant sellers traveling on the road between Taitou and Hsuehchiatao.

The economic relations between Taitou and the county seat of Kiaohsien have greatly decreased since the development of Tsingtao into a commercial and industrial city. Transportation to Tsingtao is much simpler. In spite of this, when our villagers want to trade articles used for the New Year celebration, such as the *nien-hwar* (scrolls and posters), firecrackers, incense sticks, candles, money paper, lanterns, old-fashioned cakes and candies, and so on, they still go to the county seat, because the new city does not produce these things.

Economic relations with Tsingtao are on the increase, both in trade and in the employment of villagers. Every year large quantities of farm products are sold to Tsingtao either directly by the farmers themselves or through the grain dealers and vegetable merchants. The farmer's inclination for growing special crops and raising certain livestock for the market in Tsingtao is becoming more obvious day by day. The increased acreage for growing soybeans, wheat, certain vegetables and fruits, and the increased amount of poultry and hogs is all due to the new market. In return, Tsingtao supplies the farmers with an ever-increasing amount of manufactured goods. In every rural market town one can see huge quantities of factory-made wheat flour, cotton yarn or cloth, cans of petroleum, boxes of matches, soybean cakes for animal feed, and hundreds of other articles. The self-sufficient economy of the village as well as of other villages has become an historical fact.

Taitou's population has been in the past relatively stable. Nevertheless there has always been some movement, notably between the village and the Northeastern Provinces, or Manchuria. Several decades ago, a single man of a Yang family went to work in Manchuria. Because of his special ability in reclamation and farm management, he succeeded in acquiring a large farm of several hundred acres. He married there and had three or four children. Recently, however, the head of the family decided to move back to his ancestors' place. So, five or six years ago, a new family was added to the village of Taitou. But unfortunately, the local people, including his own kinsmen, and the land situation very much disappointed the once successful farmer. He could not buy the amount of land he wanted because land is more scarce and expensive here at home than in Manchuria. He could not even get the kindness which he had learned to expect from his own clans people. People who understood the difficulties and losses he has suffered said that he should not have come back, and he, too, has come to realize this. However, the northern Chinese peasants have, through generations, developed a deep-rooted passion for the place of their ancestors. They cannot resist the idea of coming back home, unless a whole family or a group of families have moved out simultaneously and sold all their properties, so that they would have nothing to live on if they should come back. Almost all the single men who went to Manchuria, or elsewhere, have come back sooner or later after they have made some money. They come back to marry, to buy land, and to settle down. More than a dozen men have come home from Manchuria in the last ten or fifteen years. But not all of them came back with fortunes. Unlike emigrants from Hwanghsien, Penglai, and other counties on the eastern Shantung Peninsula, who, by and large, went to Manchuria as merchants, people of Taitou went there as farmers, vegetable gardeners, or other kinds of laborers. Therefore, this village has not been conspicuously benefited by those dozen adventurers, except in the case of two or three families.

Another case was the moving of a Hsueh family to the Northeastern

Provinces. Forty years ago a Hsueh family moved to Taitou from Hsintao, a village six miles to the south. The move took place because a sister of the head of the family was married to a family in Taitou. The family head was a fisherman. When he came, he brought along his wife and four children. The wife died not long after they settled down. They had bought a house but had not been able to buy any land. The family head kept on fishing and the two sons were hired by the neighbors as farm hands. Life became very difficult for the family head, because he could not make much income by fishing during the long winter. His sons were also out of work after the farming season. Lack of a woman to take care of the home and the children, especially the two young daughters, added greatly to the family instability. At this time somebody told the fisherman that life was easier in the Northeastern Provinces. Despite his reluctance to separate from his kinsmen, he made up his mind to follow the advice. The scene on the morning when the family gathered together all their possessions and started on the journey was similar to that described in *The Grapes of Wrath*.

Recently the movement of people between the village and Tsingtao has risen sharply. This is especially true among the young generations. Some have left the village seeking work other than agriculture, others to get new or advanced education, still others, just because they are attracted by new things. As a result, the old stability of population can no longer be maintained. While the old generation still resent the so-called "foreign devil" and fathers and grandfathers still insist that no way of life can be better than digging the earth, the sons and grandsons are thinking in terms of factories, railways, machine shops, a business career, or higher education. The young people want to see the new world, to live a new life, and this new life, as they can see, is not in the village but in the big city. So they are ready to go whenever opportunity comes. This is the situation in the village. In the city, cotton mills and other factories, transportation services, commercial enterprises, and a lot of domestic services, have created a great demand for manpower which can only be supplied by recruiting young men and young women from the country. When the first group of city-goers came home to visit their relatives, they brought more new attractions to the village. Their new dresses and new luggage, the money they brought back, the stories they told about the fancy things in the city all had much effect on those who still remained in the village. Gradually, as the villagers saw their neighbors profit by the money sent back by sons or daughters working in Tsingtao or other cities, fathers began to encourage their sons to leave home and seek opportunities elsewhere. Consequently, each year more and more young people leave the village.

T'ien-tzŭ (T'ien-tzŭ) 天

BP: Taitou, Shantung
SB: per present family
Source: "the story of T'ien-tzŭ" in: Yang, Martin C., A Chinese Village;
楊懋春 (Yang Mou-ch'un); n.y. [Col. U. Press], 1945, pp. 202-228

"the story of T'ien-tzŭ" in: Yang, Martin C., A Chinese Village;
楊懋春; n.y. [Col. U. Press], 1945, pp. 202-228

parent ... the "small" name ? the person ... the "small" n pet name / a small child used only by family members

No real names given ... p. xiii

Context: purpose in writing this "auto" ... whose style differs its celebration ? the life of the subject — is explained, and to make the picture real, though the eye of a person who actually grew up in the "village", experienced most of what is described, & closely is concerned with the story ? a village's boyhood. p. xi

the author, a small, underprivileged child, multiply used by parents who occupied by form and older ... indulged dreams of frequent idleness w/ true wealthy told his life — as elaborated ... illusion ... two brothers (viewed the youngest ? children) & the village lavishing on ... to help or harm "village" fortunes, & relatives, he is accepted to help or harm "village" fortunes, & this

He's pensive & over-indulgent, & still childless, & this "depreciation" was compensated for by Tien-tzŭ's wit & cleverness. This familiarity seems to have predestined / other conversion to Y'j, w/o told plan — w/o any explanation; after Tien-tzŭ proved age 6. Tien as a child, his mother had sought dueling to Tien-tzŭ from counting ... in a village ... setting p. 203 that differed from the villagers & Nagmaros & the village priesthood & follow Xian. Amongst most long after p. 219. Fiat fights were quite common to Tuesdays, & apparently not uncommon to others in his group. p. 205, 213, 221. His relation to others in the village — popular in central role — to him in his group, & was sent work & to the other children & to his parents — is described in some detail. Being bravest man among two, Tsën — axis; village was overwhelmingly in enemy & businessmen, & was in II part of the area occupied & punishedly looted by Japanese soldiers pp. 222 – 23. trained to school he "usually drilled to act as a soldier all the time" p. 225 &

of part of an enemy, anti & consciousness prevented him from education by teachers. Was on the same play, ed in drills & exercises & speeches of arms & drums the object of praise from teachers, leaders carry these stories to the village home, after him as a model to younger students, & an interesting process of myth-building begins to emerge, at least so after another. Yang describes it p. 225–

a scrappy & stubborn, but intelligent boy, who, after repeated & diff villages - to whom in his villages school & a no. of years working, & was sent to a "new" where in the market at the wharf & his selling broken pots from et the ways? who & others in the enemy worked his poverty. He excelled in, his prosperity, & his grown enjoyed estimates, & suppressed reputation in the com'ty, preventing his family & and him their hi & acting first to explain that he completed college, meant it & part of his claims, & was on the whole of a university — contributing to the extension & reputation of his family.

TIEN-SZE" was the small name of a boy who was born about forty years ago in Taitou. The name expressed the great gratitude of his parents to God for the fortune of his birth. Tien-sze was the fourth child and the third son of his parents. The family had four boys and two girls, but one of the girls died when she was a very young child. The first child was a boy, the second a girl, the third and fourth were boys while the fifth was a girl. After the death of the second girl came the sixth child, a boy. Tien-sze was separated by a number of years from both his next oldest and next youngest siblings. The death of the second daughter indirectly influenced his life greatly, as we shall see later.

It is said that Tien-sze suffered a great deal from illness in his early youth. Twice his parents gave up all hope for his recovery and laid him upon the dirt floor to wait for his last breath, but each time he recovered. His frequent illness was due to the lack of adequate care from his mother. When he was an infant the family was very poor, although it was growing. The parents had only young children and no adults to help them, so the mother as well as the father was kept busy all the time and did not have much time to devote to any one child. She had to let her small son lie in bed or on the floor by himself while she worked. Tien-sze was frequently wet, bitten by insects, and his feedings were hurried and irregularly timed. This was not because his mother was indifferent to his existence, but because she literally was unable to do more for him and she was grieved on this account. When he was sick she sought help from the country doctors and when they failed, she turned to the various gods. A spirit-possessed woman who lived in an isolated house in a large graveyard was twice invited by the family to practice her witchcraft on behalf of the sick child. Once an extravagant religious procession was organized for him. But the child remained sick. Another time the witch-doctor tried, and again it had no effect on the child. Finally the parents abandoned all their efforts and left him to his own fate, but somehow he did not die, but grew stronger as he got older.

When Tien-sze was only five or six years old, his self-centered and domineering tendencies were already very obvious. He claimed as his own everything which happened to please him. If he was denied, he was not only hurt but bewildered as well. When he wanted anything, that thing must be his. When he wanted to do anything, his action must not be checked. His extraordinary stubbornness was probably due to his former illnesses. His parents and siblings did everything possible to please him while he suffered, and tried to satisfy his wants and to tolerate his ill-temper and crying.

There is an interesting story about Tien-sze's first trip to school. His mother was an ambitious woman. She came from a family of farmers and students and she wanted to improve the position of the family. She and her husband had agreed to work hard and live frugally so that they could buy more land and houses and send the children to school. The first boy studied in the village school for four or five years; then the second boy joined him and, finally, Tien-sze. But Tien-sze did not like the school, and he refused to go. At first, the mother tried to overcome the boy's objections by persuasion. She gave him good food, candy, and interesting things to play with, but these methods were not effective; the boy still did not want to go. Then harder measures were tried. The boy started to attend school again, but only three days out of five. The other two days Tien-sze spent neither at home nor at school. On the way from his home to the schoolhouse there was an empty house that belonged to a neighboring family. In the house there was a huge empty basket. Tien-sze would leave home shortly after his brothers had gone and would proceed to the empty house. Here he turned over the basket and crept under it. After about two hours, when his brothers and the other boys passed by the house on the way home to dinner, he would come out of his hiding place and run home behind them. His parents supposed that he went to school; his brothers thought that he was permitted to stay at home, and so his hiding place was not suspected. But he was finally caught by his brother, and his parents discovered what he had been doing. Tien-sze was severely punished. Depressed and ashamed he went to school again for a few days, and then he began to hide in a neighbor's vegetable garden. It was not long before he was discovered and he got another beating. This put an end to his truancy. He went to school regularly, but made no attempt to study. He would fall asleep even when the teacher was present, but when the teacher was absent, he was the most mischievous of all the pupils. Gradually both the teacher and his parents came to the conclusion that it was useless to compel the child to study. When the school year ended, Tien-sze's schooling was also over, at least for the time being.

In order to punish him for disappointing their ambitions in him and also to make him realize that work on a farm was not as pleasant as studying in school, his parents made him work in the fields. In addition he was ordered by his mother to take care of his baby brother and a small niece, the first daughter of his eldest brother. His younger brother and his niece were of the same age and needed the same care, and Tien-sze was the only older child in the house. His mother and his niece's mother were constantly busy with housework, and his older sister and brothers were busy helping at home and in the field. His younger sister was dead. Therefore, he was the only one available for this task. He did not like it. Looking after young children was considered girls' work and he was a boy. As a boy, he wanted to be free, so that he could run wild and join the other boys in their play, but his task kept him at home and away from them. He had the opportunity to play only with girls who were engaged with the same task he was. He had to carry the children to the street and back home several times a day, and this he found both difficult and shameful. He was very tired of it and cried frequently.

When Tien-sze was eight or nine years old his parents began to let him do the work of an older boy. He assisted his second brother in taking the cow to the field to graze. Tien-sze liked this job. He could run in the fields, over the hills and down the valleys, he could catch fish in the streams, collect flowers, hunt eggs or young birds in their nests underneath the bushes or in the trees. He would dig out the clay from the holes in the weatherbeaten rocks at the foot of the South Hill and from it, fashion toys and other objects to give to his sister and her friends. Sometimes they traded these things for the small fragrant bags that were distributed at the *Tuan-wu Festival*. South Hill yielded still another underground treasure—a kind of quartz of very low quality. Boys liked to use the small pieces they picked up for making arrow points or playthings.

Nobody expected the boys who took the cows to the fields to behave as adults. They raced along the road or the edges of the fields, and fought among themselves, splashing water in the stream or, when the fight was between them and a group of boys from another village, throwing stones. They roasted birds they had caught, or peas, beans, peanuts, and sweet potatoes that they picked up in the fields. Swearing, teasing the smaller boys, and plotting against a villager they did not like, were frequent activities of the cow-boys. Tien-sze always got very excited in these adventures. He was a mischievous and stubborn child, but he was intelligent and full of wit. Although he was still young, his tricks were highly appreciated by the older boys who therefore forgave him his age somewhat.

His second brother was too meek to deal with them and when the other boys tried to take advantage of him, Tien-sze came to the rescue.

Tien-sze was also ordered to cut grass as feed for the family's animals. Generally he liked this work too, but when the kaoliang field was hot and humid under a blazing sun, he cursed his lot and wished he had been born rich. Boys assigned to this job usually went out in groups. They would annoy the crop-watcher, steal melons, fight the boys from other villages, chase or embarrass the girls who came out to pick the string beans or to help the men in the fields, or they would hunt birds and rabbits in the woods. The amount of grass cut by Tien-sze in a day was seldom enough to merit his father's praise, but the boy did not care.

Tien-sze was frequently assigned to take care of the donkey used to transport the harvested crops from the field to the threshing ground during the harvesting season. He liked it best when he could ride on the back of the beast and beat it until it ran. This was, of course, forbidden by his parents and brothers. When he had to make numerous trips a day and several days in succession, he could not but tire of it. Then he would complain with tears in his eyes and bitterness in his heart against the necessity of the burdensome work. In midsummer his bare feet were burned in the hot dust on the road, and in the late autumn, when the water was already icy cold, he had to cross one or two streams on every trip. No doubt his parents took pity on him, but since he was a boy he had to undergo the disciplining effects of unpleasant work. Working hard and living frugally were principles to which Tien-sze's parents were completely devoted.

Tien-sze was put to work at tasks as difficult as his strength would permit. Even in the bitterly cold winter he was awakened early in the morning and ordered to collect fuel on the riverbanks and in the woods, together with his brothers. His ears, hands and feet would be frozen after the first hour, and only after two or three hours of hard work would he begin to feel warm again. Tien-sze was too young to bear this exposure well. One of his ears was frozen and has shown the scar ever since. The skin on the back of his hands became as coarse as that of an old man. After breakfast he went with his brothers to the West Mountain, which was about five miles distant from the village. There they spent the day collecting wood, leaves, and dry grass. They had to climb mountains and cross valleys, a difficult trip for a young boy, but in general Tien-sze enjoyed it because he was with others. When the weather was fine, groups of ten, twenty, or more left Taitou for the mountains. They sang the local songs and joked with each other on the way. When they reached their destination they scattered into smaller groups of five or six, so that each could find ample fuel. At noon they ate whatever they had brought with them and drank the spring water. Before the sun set they packed up what they had accumulated, carried the burdens by a pole across their shoulders and started for home.

During the trip Tien-sze found wild honey on the thick pine trees, and frost-bitten berries, and as he ate them he looked at the huge rocks on the ranges or the streaming water at the bottom of a deep valley. He would have a strange feeling, but he could not tell about it. Occasionally, when he was lost in the woods, or separated from his brothers among the rocks, he would feel a mixture of excitement and fear. The sounds in the mountains delighted Tien-sze very much, particularly the echoes. The fuel collectors shouted to locate each other, or just to hear the echo. Some rocks were hollow and the boys would beat upon them so that the sound could be heard at a far distance. It was very beautiful up on the mountain. He could hear the dogs barking in the villages down at the foot. When Tien-sze and his brothers were in the woods, or among the rocks, or in a deep valley, he felt that he was lost in a wilderness, and the barking made him realize that the human world was still close to him. He felt a great relief. Another sound that Tien-sze liked very much was the ringing of a bell in a temple beyond the horizon. He was not religious, nor was he musical, but he liked the sound. There were also frightening sounds. When a strong wind swept over the mountains, the valleys, and the woods, a sharp and fearful sound came out of the pine trees. Tien-sze was always bewildered by it. If he were alone in the woods he would immediately run out to a high and open spot, or look for his brothers.

When the time came to go home, all the small groups either met at the foot of the mountain or gradually came together on the way. But now everybody was tired and hungry, and the older boys had a burden on their shoulders. They did not want to speak, except when they stopped for a rest. Tien-sze was too young to carry the fuel, so he walked with his empty basket and bamboo rake. He also was tired and hungry. He walked silently behind his brothers. He did not feel ashamed because other young boys also walked with empty baskets. When they reached home, Tien-sze found his mother and sister awaiting them with smiles and the announcement that supper was ready.

This was his parents' principle of working hard and living thriftily, which applied also to him. It was true that Tien-sze had never been starved nor suffered a shortage of food. His mother knew well that enough food was essential if the men were to work well, nor did she want to hear her daughter-in-law complain of hunger to her parents or to the neighbors. Moreover, when Tien-sze was still very young, his family had the help of a hired laborer. Tien-sze's mother insisted that the man be fed well, so that he would work honestly and efficiently and not say bad things about the family. The meals in Tien-sze's home were always better than in the families of a similar economic status.

Nevertheless thrift was still a hard-stressed virtue in the family. Unnecessary spending of money was forbidden. Tien-sze and his brothers and sister were never allowed to spend one penny for candy, toys, or a good time, except on the New Year Festival or when he went to see an opera in a distant village. On the last day of the old year, there was a special market day in the market town, and the mother would say to the father: "Since the boys worked diligently during the winter you should give them a little money, so that they can buy firecrackers or other things they would like on this special occasion." Meanwhile Tien-sze would fix his pleading eyes on his father's face and hold his breath. His father reluctantly handed fifteen coppers to Tien-sze, and his second brother also received the same amount. His first brother was already grown-up, he might have received more, though not much more. Fifteen coppers was the only money Tien-sze got for the New Year Festival! In some years he was lucky enough to be sent to visit his paternal aunt after the Festival and there he would get another fifteen or twenty coppers. Parents in other families gave "New Year Money" to the children when they formally greeted them, but Tien-sze's family did not observe this custom. He got nothing when he greeted his parents. Tien-sze could not buy candy, could not play the "money-game," and could not go to the market town in high spirits. He envied other children when he heard them boasting of how much they had received from their grandparents and parents.

His father's stingy attitude made Tien-sze too timid to ask for money even when it was necessary. When Tien-sze was in school for the second time, the superintendent told the students one day that each boy should contribute twenty coppers for their teacher's traveling fee from home to school. All the boys accepted this readily but Tien-sze's heart became heavy. At home he did not dare tell his parents. He had only one day in which to get the money. Tien-sze could not find any solution, and the next day he wept and hesitated to go to school. His mother asked him what had happened but he would not tell at first. When he did tell. his mother pitied him so much that she asked the father to give him the money immediately, and told the boy to speak freely when he needed money. Another time the school had a holiday for a special occasion in a rather distant village. The teacher and students had planned to attend the opera there. The teacher had been invited to a luncheon and the boys bought themselves bread, cake, candy, and other goodies. Tien-sze could not buy anything for he didn't have a penny. His schoolmates, when they found out, helped him. In the evening he told his mother and she had pity on him, but scolded him for not having asked for the needed money. But Tien-sze had thought of it in another way. He feared that if he told of the holiday and the trip first, his father would certainly not permit him to go but would send him to work on the farm. He also knew too well that his father would not give him money without pouring upon him harsh words.

This restricted allowance kept Tien-sze out of many kinds of recreation and amusement which were indulged in by others. Tien-sze could not join the money games that were played on New Year's Day. Other boys went to the temporary gambling houses, but Tien-sze could not go there either. A few boys used their small capital to buy sweets in the market town which they would then retail to the gamblers. From this they could make a small profit, and besides they enjoyed it. Some parents encouraged their children in this because it was a trade. Tien-sze desperately wanted to "be in business," too. He appealed to his mother but she would not give him the "capital," nor would she let him go to the gambling houses. This was because she knew very well that the "business" and the gambling houses would be a bad influence on the boy, but she did not scold him. She did not tell him that she could not grant permission because the houses were bad places, but said, "My boy, so you want to do business, to make profit. That is a good idea. Every boy ought to learn to do business, to earn money. But a boy of great prospect should think of big business. He should prepare himself for large profits. Don't you think that the profit made from selling candies in the gambling houses is only as big as the point of an embroidery needle? I want my boy to work and to study for a big fortune instead of a needle-point profit. What do you think?"

Every year there are two special fairs in the market town at which there are numerous amusements. Villagers usually attend the fairs with a little extra money to spend. This custom was not observed by Tien-sze's parents. They let their children go, but did not give them money

unless it was needed for books or paper. Tien-sze could only enjoy him
self in ways that cost nothing. He could walk on the streets and look at
the toys and other interesting things displayed in the booths on the sidewalks, with a covetous light in his eyes. The fair usually included a most
exciting circus that Tien-sze never saw. He could only stand at the outskirts or hide among the adults to steal a look. There were also two or
three *Hsi Yang Ching* * of an immoral nature which had great appeal to
the boys and young men. Tien-sze was safe from their influence because
he could not afford to see them. But he could stand there and watch the
man who managed the show, and he learned the speeches of the manager.

Tien-sze and his brothers were not only prevented from taking part in
the commercial amusements, but the restriction unwittingly extended
to activities which did not cost money, or cost only a little. Boys like to
catch birds in the spring and keep sparrows in the summer, and they
like to fly kites on the *Ch'ing-ming* Festival or knit bird nets in the winter.
These things were not encouraged by Tien-sze's family. A singing bird or
a sparrow was never in the house. Tien-sze had no net and never caught
birds by himself. When he did go, he went with other boys and was only
a follower. Nor did he ever have a kite of his own. These activities were
considered a waste of time and money, and a means of spoiling the children. As his mother used to say: "To let a boy catch birds in the fields may
not be wrong, but how can you guarantee that the boy would not damage
the crops when he is excited at seeing his prey in the net? It interferes
with his regular work and is dangerous, for a boy will climb walls, or
roofs to search for young birds, and chasing them he might be hurt. How
can responsible parents let their children take this risk just for some fun?
Have you seen any person of a respectable calling wasting time and
energy in keeping or hunting birds?" Tien-sze could not openly defy his
mother, but he was bitter when he saw other boys carrying their birds.

Tien-sze's first older brother, Sung-chun, was twelve years older than he
and the two boys had had little to do with each other during their early
childhood. Tien-sze could vaguely remember that once his first brother
had worked in Tsingtao for the Germans. One day when Tien-sze and
his parents went to attend the Sunday service in a Christian church of a
distant village, people told his mother how the Germans mistreated the
Chinese laborers who worked for them. The mother and father were
extremely worried about their eldest son. Tien-sze could not understand

* Showing modern but cheap pictures in a box. Customers could see the pictures
through small holes in which microscopes were fixed. The pictures were Western.

the real situation but he was impressed by his parents' anxiety and by the words "German," "Chinese laborer," "work," "beating," "escaping." A few days later his first brother was home. He told the family what he had seen in Tsingtao and how he had escaped. But what interested Tien-sze most was the story about how the Germans made their bread, transported their food on horse carts, and how they only ate the central part of the bread and threw the rest away. Tien-sze wondered what kind of people these Germans were and what happened to the bread they threw away.

Tien-sze remembered a day he and his brother spent on the South-western Mountain. They had gone to collect grass for smoking out mosquitoes that were a pest in the summer months. Without knowing it they had gradually climbed to the highest part of the hill. It was a mid-summer day and there were no trees where they were, and they suffered from the heat. When they began to descend they found that the slope was steep and there were no projecting trees or bushes upon which they could hold for support. They were both badly scared. When they reached level ground, they felt a great relief. Both long remembered the climb.

It was Tien-sze's eldest brother who first taught him to do farm work. The brother himself did not like farming and had little patience in teaching the young boy. One hot day when they were hoeing in a sweet-potato field, Tien-sze found the heavy hoe too much for him. The work was badly done and some of the plants were injured. At first, his brother corrected him but as he kept on hurting the plants his brother lost his temper and shouted harsh words at the boy. Since Tien-sze was already greatly annoyed with himself, the brother's scolding could only bring the tears to his eyes. He was depressed for the rest of the day and had no appetite for luncheon or supper.

Once the two boys cooperated in helping to build the Christian church in the village. Tien-sze's family were Christians. All the Christian members in the village had planned to build a church by having every family contribute something to its construction. In addition to other materials, Tien-sze's parents promised to supply small stones for the walls. These stones were abundant at a place below the West Mountain. It needed a considerable amount of labor and time to carry them to the site of the church. Tien-sze's first brother decided to do the work in the winter before the construction was to begin, and he asked Tien-sze to help him. They took with them two baskets and a wheelbarrow drawn by a donkey, the brother took care of the wheelbarrow and Tien-sze tended the donkey. When they reached the foot of the mountain they picked up the small stones and then rolled the filled wheelbarrow home. They could only make three trips during the short winter's day and it took them about a month to finish the job. In the course of their work, the two brothers were drawn more closely together than they had ever been before. The place where they picked the stones was a vast sand bed in a big valley, and in the winter very few people ever came there. Big trees, high peaks and awful cliffs, and the wind whistling through the trees made the spot a very desolate one. Tien-sze would follow his brother closely, or keep him in sight if he had to leave his side for anything. He felt his brother to be his protector and the brother, realizing Tien-sze's attitude, treated him tenderly. One day Tien-sze found a small bag in which were a dozen or so coins and a small pocketknife. It had probably been lost by a cow-boy or a hunter. Tien-sze was delighted. Added to his pleasure was the praise of the villagers who customarily followed the two brothers as they rolled their barrow through the streets.

Though Tien-sze's first experience with school had ended in failure, he was nonetheless a bright boy. This was evident in his mischievous behavior, in his domineering over his second brother, in his play with the other children. A distant uncle used to say that he was the most brilliant of all the children, that he had a very promising future if he could develop his talents. A member of the wealthy P'an family told Tien-sze's mother several times that the boy had a fine intellect, that his eyes showed his brightness and that if he were put in school he would make a good student. Tien-sze's mother was influenced by these remarks, but not so his father. By this time new schools had been introduced into the area. Several of the young men of the community had attended the teachers' training school in the county seat. Tien-sze's first brother was very much interested in these new developments. He went to the market town quite often, and there he heard the talk about the new Republic, the new education, about the establishment of a new school in the market town, and about the new ways of getting official positions. Being a young man, he found himself attracted by these things. He had his wife and sister make his clothing in the modern style, and he joined a political group to learn how to vote for the local representatives. He wanted to reeducate himself, but he was too old to become a primary-school student and his father needed him on the farm. Since it was impossible for him to go to the new school, his attention turned to his third brother. He observed that Tien-sze's presence was not essential on the farm and he was old enough to enter a primary school, so he decided that Tien-sze should go to school and become a scholar or an official in the world that was rising around them. With this in mind he began to persuade his parents, telling them all that he had heard in the market town. The mother consented and the father did not oppose. His sister helped him because she was fond of their brother too. Consequently, one morning shortly after the New Year Festival, Tien-sze was dressed up and taken to the new school in the market town. There his brother told the teacher that Tien-sze had been a cow-boy for several years, and that his manners were rude. He asked the teacher to have patience with the boy. He asked several of the town boys to look after his younger brother. Later, when Tien-sze's father complained of the heavy burden the school expenses had laid upon him, and the shortage of labor on the farm, the brother did his best to pacify him. Fortunately, Tien-sze's mother and sister were in league with the brother and Tien-sze's education was not further delayed. This was a turning point in his life. Tien-sze later became a highly educated man and his mother's ambition was fulfilled. This was largely the result of his elder brother's efforts, though these indicated a fatherly interest, rather than just personal affection for the younger boy.

Tien-sze's relationship with his second elder brother, Pei-chun, was quite different. The difference in their ages was not very great—they were only five years apart. They played and worked together often and, when they were quite young, slept in the same bed. In spite of all this, no great ties of affection existed between them. The second brother was very meek and submissive. He could only withdraw or cry when other boys insulted him. For this reason, the boys purposely annoyed him and took advantage of him whenever they could think of ways of doing so. This involved Tien-sze in numerous fights on his brother's behalf, for he felt it incumbent upon himself to protect his brother in these encounters. If he was beaten, he not only cursed the boys but at the same time was angry with Pei-chun for being so weak. Sometimes this gave rise to quarrels between the brothers. Tien-sze did not like to be with his second brother, though his parents always ordered him to stay with him.

At home Tien-sze used to boss his second brother who tolerated it with little display of protest, and conceded to his younger brother's appropriations of toys quietly. When the two boys slept together, Tien-sze used to tease his brother and this sometimes led to fights which disturbed their parents. At first they blamed Pei-chun because he was older, but later realized that it was always Tien-sze's fault, and they directed their anger toward him. Sometimes when he was beaten severely, Pei-chun would be very sad and bewildered. One night when Tien-sze was lying trembling in bed, awaiting his father's punishment, Pei-chun got up and appealed to their angry father, asking to be beaten in Tien-sze's stead. The mother was very much moved, and persuaded the father to forgive the children. Unfortunately, Tien-sze was too young to appreciate his brother's kindness. The parents liked Pei-chun because of his honesty and generosity, but were disappointed in his weak and submissive personality, and on this score they preferred the bravado of Tien-sze. This was true though he often angered them with his precocity. The two boys were too different from each other ever to become fast friends, or perhaps if the difference had been reversed, if the elder were the dominant and the younger the submissive one, the difference might not have prevented their friendship.

There was great affection between Tien-sze and his sister, Ts'ung, who was ten years older than he. After the death of the second daughter, this sister was the only girl in the family. She could only occasionally go out to play with other girls, and this threw her and her young brother together often, and made them dependent upon each other for company. She liked making flowers, embroidering fancy designs on boy's shoes, jackets, aprons, and hats, making clay toys, or the small bags used at the *Tuan-wu* Festival, and all kinds of charms. As a rule, when a girl is working on such things she likes to have another girl with her because they can talk about what they are doing, appreciate each other's accomplishments and amuse themselves by exchanging news. Tien-sze fulfilled the role of friend and companion for his sister. She asked him to help her in many small ways. When she made a flower or some fancy work, she showed it to Tien-sze, or perhaps gave it to him. If she needed material, she asked Tien-sze to fetch it for her. Being a bright and active boy, Tien-sze could satisfy her needs and appreciate her work. The mother usually discouraged or even forbade the girl to make fancy things because she thought it a waste of time and Tien-sze always helped his sister to fool their mother. Once some very fancy flowers made by the girl were discovered by the mother. She was very angry and was going to punish her daughter but Tien-sze appealed to her and persuaded her to forego her anger. The sister and brother became more and more intimate. When the girl grew older, she spent more time and thought on Tien-sze than she did on any other member of the family. She took a lot of trouble to make the prettiest shoes, clothes, hats, and other things for him Tien-sze appreciated most of them. Only when he was dressed up too much like a girl and was teased by the other boys, would he refuse to wear the shoes and things she made for him.

After Tien-sze entered school, he became an informal teacher to his sister. The young girl's fiancé, a student in a new school in Tsingtao, wanted her to study and at least learn how to read and write. It was still impossible at that time to send a girl to school, and besides, her family could not spare her. The first brother, the mother, and Tien-sze became her teachers and her home her school. Tien-sze was the chief instructor because he was the most advanced in learning of the three and because he had the most time to give to his sister. Tien-sze liked to tell others what he had learned. He was doubtless most eager to tell his sister and he had become accustomed to teaching, since he often assisted his teacher at school. With so many courses, a single teacher could hardly do the teaching without help, and qualified students were relied upon for assistance. This task fell to Tien-sze's lot very often. He preferred to teach at home, for his words were so much more appreciated there. He never tired of it, never became impatient with his student. As a younger brother and a little boy, he was no doubt proud of himself. His sister was very eager to study and the lessons went well. Besides, Tien-sze was still a young boy and had deep affection for his sister, so the latter could, without embarrassment, confide in him her dreams and hopes about her fiancé. Tien-sze had no jealousy. Instead, he learned to like the young man too. By the time the girl married, she could read and understand all the textbooks and do the arithmetic problems that were taught in school.

Tien-sze continued to help his sister after her marriage. Whenever she came back to stay with her parents, Tien-sze was ready to do anything she asked. When she had her first baby, Tien-sze was the only person in the family she could turn to for help, for their mother was dead by that time. Tien-sze's sister filled the place for him which his mother had left.

Once, after the death of their mother, when his sister was very ill and Tien-sze saw her suffering, he had the same sad and frightened feeling that he had had while he was watching his mother die. Tien-sze's brother-in-law worked in a business firm in Tsingtao and later in Shanghai, and he gave a great deal of material aid to Tien-sze. Later they became good friends. Marriage did not interfere in this case with the intimacy between brother and sister.

Tien-sze's relations with his parents were in no way out of the ordinary. When he didn't go to school, he was out of favor with them for quite a while. It was only when his mother discovered again that the boy was bright and was eager for work that he began to build up new hopes for him. She began to love the child again, though her belief in discipline and hard work restricted her demonstrations of it. The father seemed as distant and careless of Tien-sze's future as he had ever been. Of course, he had taken him to the field and had taught him to work, but he had never bought toys or candy for him, nor taken him to any amusement or played with him at home or on the street. The father's interest in saving money, his insistence upon frugality, gave Tien-sze a good deal to bear and widened the breach between them.

This situation changed when Tien-sze was studying in the county high school. By this time his mother had died and his sister was married. When he came home for his vacations, especially in the winter, he used to sit in his father's room and talk with him through the long evenings. The father knit on a straw raincoat while the son told him of Chinese history, the famous ancient characters, and the new things he had learned in school. The father was greatly interested in the stories. He listened attentively and occasionally put questions to his son. Tien-sze's father had for long been given to severe depressions, sometimes lasting for several days. He worried unreasonably about his farm business, his family, and his life. Tien-sze's mother had been the only one who could encourage him when he felt this way, and after she died there was nobody else who could help him. His daughters-in-law could not, because of the social proscriptions that kept them at a distance from their father-in-law. His sons and daughter could not because they were either fully occupied with their own problems or were not aware of their father's trouble. But Tien-sze was educated and had insight into the problems of others, so that he could sympathize with his father and comfort him. Thus, Tien-sze had, to some extent, taken over his mother's ministrations to his father. As the father aged, his appreciation of Tien-sze grew deeper and deeper. He also became proud of his son's good reputation in the school, and used to talk about it with his neighbors. Thus father and son became friends. The grown-up Tien-sze was always very sad that his mother had not lived as long as his father, for their intimacy might have developed in the same way.

There is little to say about the relationship between Tien-sze and his younger brother, Feng-chun. Tien-sze had to look after his young charge while the latter was yet a baby and this contributed very little to the development of brotherly feelings between the two, for the task was decidedly irksome to Tien-sze. Later, when the younger brother did not require this care, Tien-sze was in school all the time, and did not have much chance to play or work with him. But when they were watching their mother die, they were both heartbroken and cried a good deal. Suddenly Tien-sze put his arm around his younger brother's neck and said to him, "Don't be afraid, I shall take care of you. I shall protect you from any danger." Fortunately, Tien-sze did not have to fulfill his pledge because his younger brother was adequately cared for by his father and other brothers, but the emotion that existed at the time had its effect.

We have mentioned before that Tien-sze had been severely punished by his parents during his boyhood, and frequently because he had refused to go to school. Other beatings resulted from his quarrels with Pei-chun. Once Tien-sze was playing before the front door of his home. He saw a neighbor's dog devouring the manure. He chased the dog away, but it came back again. After several attempts the boy became greatly annoyed. He caught the dog (it was small) and almost beat it to death. This made their neighbor's wife very angry and she came to Tien-sze's home and cursed the boy and fiercely protested to Tien-sze's father. The father had been working hard all day and was very tired. The cursing of the woman was like oil on a fire. He knocked the boy down on the ground and then lifted the spade he had been holding in his hand. Tien-sze's life was momentarily in danger, but his sister rescued him. Tien-sze was very bitter after this and he hated his father's ferocity, for he felt that it had been unjust. The animal manure was very important to the family's crops and he thought he had been doing his family a service. The father's anger appeared to him to be most unreasonable.

When Tien-sze was a boy of six or seven, he suffered from enuresis. *bed-wetting* His parents thought that he was too lazy to get up at night and they punished him for it. This punishment too seemed altogether unjust to him. He hated his difficulty more than any one else did. Every night he remembered to go to the toilet before he went to bed. He was annoyed and even frightened whenever he made his bed wet. When he woke up and found the damp sheet underneath him, he was afraid, humiliated, and would reproach himself severely, but his parents did not know. They punished the boy continuously and with ever-increasing wrath. Tien-sze felt that no humiliation could be greater than this. When he was being beaten he cursed himself with the most violent words he knew, and hated his parents intensely. Had he been a little older he might have committed suicide. He thought that he could never forgive his parents' refusal to recognize that his trouble was beyond his control.

Because of his father's great thriftiness Tien-sze was denied many things that a school boy loved to possess. A pocketknife, a pair of bronze weights for pressing the paper down when practicing calligraphy, a vessel for holding water, and other customary objects never graced Tien-sze's desk. Needless to say, he was always envying the boys who had these things. One day he saw that the preacher of the Christian church owned a small knife and he asked permission to borrow it for a few days. The preacher, who was very fond of Tien-sze, consented. Once the knife was in Tien-sze's hand, he was reluctant to return it and kept it for another two or three days without asking permission. When he finally realized that he had to return the thing, he could not find it—it was lost. The boy was so frightened that he did not dare to tell the preacher or anyone else. The preacher told his parents about it, and the father became very angry and shouted, "What's the use of his going to school if he learns to do such shameful things?" The mother also was quite astonished, her hopes for the boy again seemingly vanished. They both felt that they had to punish him severely or the preacher would think they were lax. The father thought he should beat his son, but the mother objected on the ground that he was already more than ten years old and reputedly a good student. Tien-sze's sister kept her brother in her room when the time for the punishment came. The father scolded the boy through the closed door and while the mother also complained that the family's reputation had been ruined by his misbehavior, she secretly blocked the father's path to the boy. Finally, it ended with only scolding and complaining, but to Tien-sze, this was the worst punishment he had ever sustained. His guilt was terrible and he felt utterly disgraced. For a week he could not hold his head up. He was so self-conscious that he felt that everyone in the family, except perhaps his sister, was blaming him. He was only relieved when his sister said to him one day, "Cheer up, you little stupid. Mother knew that you never intended to steal the knife. We knew that you were covetous of it and that you failed to return it on time as you had promised. But Mother and Father are still blaming you for having coveted a thing which was not yours and for having kept the knife too long. Remember, never do this again. By the way, I picked up the knife on our threshing ground and have returned it to the preacher, so don't worry about it. Why didn't you tell me when it was lost? Did you forget that I could help you?" After hearing this Tien-sze smiled miserably at his sister and ran away.

Tien-sze's boyhood was also influenced by illness, sorrow, and death

among his family and kinsfolk. First, he witnessed the death of his little
sister, Hsiao-mair. He could never forget his mother's and sister's weeping
and the Christian burial. Three days after it Tien-s   and his older sister
went together to see the little tomb. His sister told him that Hsiao-mair
was sleeping there and that her house would not be disturbed by wild
dogs. Tien-sze did not understand why his little sister had died and why
she was sleeping in a tomb instead of at home. Later he saw his second
brother suffering in his long illness. The brother had chronic stomach
trouble. Tien-sze was terribly sorry for him because they had been close
companions. Several times his mother invited the Christians and the
preacher of the village to pray for her sick son. While the group prayed
or sang the hymns the boy lay moaning in his bed. Tien-sze was still
too young to understand the meaning of the ceremony. But he did
wonder why Jesus did not come immediately to help his brother.

When Tien-sze was about ten years old he saw his father in a terribly
depressed mood. It was a summer day. It had been raining for five or
six days, and the fields were either flooded or soaked and the crops completely ruined. The father lay in his bed without speaking to anyone.
Tien-sze's mother sat beside him and tried to console him, while the
frightened children went about silent. The dark clouds, the sickening
rain, the starved animals, the fallen walls, and the muddy courtyard and
street intensified the gloom of everyone's mind. The mother and sister
had no spirit to prepare the meal. The brothers were secretly quarreling
with each other. Tien-sze was starved, scared, and depressed, too. He
never forgot the scene.

Tien-sze's mother had a long illness before her death, and during it
he frequently rubbed her legs or massaged her back. Because his sister
was already married by this time and out of the house, he also had to
help with the housework. Tien-sze's father sat with his wife at night.
In the day a daughter-in-law, Tien-sze's first brother's wife, was the chief
person upon whom the sick woman depended. When the situation became serious, the married daughter was called back. Tien-sze, his second
brother, and his sister could not sleep for several nights, but just wept
continuously. One night, the mother suddenly sat up and summoned all
her children to her bedside. She told them that if she should die it would
be nothing but a call from Jesus Christ, so that her children should not
be too sorry and that they must not spend too much for her funeral. She
told Tien-sze's first brother and his wife to take care of their younger
brothers and see that they were all married; and to carry out the family's

objectives. She also said they should continue to be devout Christians
and serve the cause of Jesus Christ. Then she turned to the father and
said: "If I should die, please don't be too sorry. You know that God
will sooner or later call everyone of us back to His home. We will see
each other over there. We have been together through a long struggle.
I am glad that we have these children and that they all try to be good
children. They will not fail you and God will bless you, too." Tien-sze
could not understand all these words, but he, as well as all the other children and the father, knew that this was a farewell. They all wept miserably and Tien-sze was altogether astonished at them. He did not cry
but just sat there. A few days later his mother died. In the last few days
Tien-sze as well as his brothers and sister were completely exhausted
and bewildered by the confusion in the house, so he was insensible to
his mother's death. Only when he realized she was really gone did he
begin to cry.

Tien-sze had been much impressed by the Christian activities of the
family. Both parents were Christians, but his mother had always taken
the more active interest in it. It was she who taught Tien-sze to read the
Ten Commandments. Tien-sze would be asked to watch the donkey
which was pulling the stone quern in a little hut, and meanwhile to learn
one of the Commandments. For this he would receive a certain kind of
potato which was generally not given to older children. When the New
Year Festival was near, Tien-sze could read all the Commandments. Of
course Tien-sze could not understand what he had read, but he did
remember that he should not steal from a neighbor and that he should
obey his parents.

Tien-sze was also taught to say grace at table and was taken to the
village church on Sundays. When he was a little older, he was told the
stories from the famous "Pilgrimage" (Chinese edition) and the Bible.
He also learned to sing a few of the simple hymns. At that time two
Chinese versions of the Christian songs were popular with the small Christian group in Taitou. One of them Tien-sze's mother and sister could
sing well, so Tien-sze was also taught to sing it. On Christmas Eve, gifts
were distributed to children of the few Christian families, but they did
not understand the meaning of the festival.

When the church had just been built, an evangelist was invited to
preach in it. One day Tien-sze's mother took him to visit the evangelist.
She said to the preacher: "Tien-sze has said several times that he wants
to be a teacher or a pastor of a church. Do you think he will be able to

do that? I would be glad to have your help." The preacher's answer was: "Very good. I know he is a bright boy. Surely he can be a teacher if he likes to study." Tien-sze was embarrassed, but secretly he was encouraged. Three years later, a new peacher was invited to the church. Tien-sze's mother called on him. This time she told the preacher: "I want to dedicate this child of mine to our Lord Jesus Christ. I know you have heard that he is a good student in the market-town school, and I know that you are fond of him. Will you help him to improve his character and develop his knowledge?" Although Tien-sze was still very young, he remembered his mother's words.

Outside the family Tien-sze had relations with young and old in the village. When he was a boy attending his father's cow or cutting grass, he formed a special friendship with another boy of the same neighborhood who was about his age. They had attended the old-fashioned village school together, and after they left school, they continued to see each other, to play together and sometimes even sleep together. They never quarreled and never engaged in the usual fist-fights. When Tien-sze went to school again, his friend became a farm hand. But the friendship between them continued until Tien-sze went to the high school in the county seat.

Several of Tien-sze's cousins were specially fond of him. They played together after supper or when they were free from work, but these cousins were much older than Tien-sze and assumed the manner of an older sister with him. With one of these girls Tien-sze was on intimate terms, reminiscent of his relationship with his sister. Later he played very often with a particular girl who almost became his "girl-friend," but they separated when they were older.

Once during Tien-sze's boyhood a high-school boy came to the family to deliver a message to Tien-sze's mother. The boy wore modernized clothes and had his hair cut short and arranged in the new style. He was young, handsome, and cheerful and therefore attracted Tien-sze's attention. His haircut had special fascination, for at that time men and boys in the countryside still wore their "pigtails." The day after this boy's visit Tien-sze's "pigtail" was gone. His parents and brothers were all surprised, but not his sister for she supported him in this. This made him the first boy in the village who had rid himself of one of the symbols of the Manchus. The villagers insulted him by calling him "Little Monk," but he did not care. Only three or four years later the practice of cutting hair became general and Tien-sze's hair style ceased to be conspicuous.

When Tsingtao was seized by the Japanese during the first World War, the Christian churches in the city were temporarily closed. Preachers, evangelists, and Bible women became unemployed. One of the Bible women and her children came to Tien-sze's home to stay during the emergency. By that time Tien-sze's family had adopted Christianity and his mother was well acquainted with this woman. Her two daughters were students and were comparatively modern. No doubt they experienced a great deal of inconvenience living with a country family, but they had to stay there for quite a period. During this time Tien-sze no doubt learned a lot from the girls about the new city, and therefore when Tien-sze first entered the new school he already knew more new things than other boys did.

Tien-sze formed an early impression of foreigners, especially Germans and Japanese. Because the village was close to Tsingtao, German soldiers and businessmen used to come across the bay to the country area for hunting or exploring. Tien-sze was impressed by their appearance and the things they brought with them. Their proud spirit prejudiced the local people against them. Tien-sze did not know how they had ill-treated the people, but he still did not have any sympathy for them. Toward the Japanese Tien-sze was especially bitter. Later when they were attacking Tsingtao a great part of the Shantung peninsula and the land surrounding the city were forcibly occupied by them and taken as strategic bases. Tien-sze's village was in the occupied area. Nominally, the area was borrowed from the Chinese government for military purposes, but in fact it was treated as Japanese territory. They looted and seized everything they wanted from the local people. At first the villagers tried to resist the foreign army, but their resistance only caused more looting and even atrocities. Finally, the poor peasants had to flee or evacuate their women and children and grain to the mountains or to places outside the occupied area.

Tien-sze had personally witnessed his people gather together to resist the first small group of soldiers who came to the village. The villagers succeeded in scaring them away, but the next time a larger group of soldiers came. The villagers' resistance was broken and the village experienced its first looting. Then the enemy came almost every day. All the families of means were evacuated and only the men, who could run away when the enemy was in sight, remained. The village was almost deserted. Tien-sze's mother, sister, and sister-in-law also fled to a village in the West Mountain, taking with them great quantities of grain and other foodstuffs. Tien-sze stayed at home with his father and brothers, but they had to run and hide once or twice a day. This made everybody in the village, as well as in the whole occupied area, bitterly antagonistic toward the Japanese. During the period when the Japanese were the authority in Tsingtao, they fostered every evil that could destroy the Chinese economically and morally. The most evident evils were the bandits and the sale of opium. The bandits were protected in Japanese territory and were not prevented from their forays, kidnapings, and attacks. Tien-sze, as well as all the other villagers, had personally experienced the effects of the bandits' destructiveness and they knew all too well that it was purposely planned by the Japanese. Tien-sze knew very little about the sale of opium and other drugs, but he did see a number of suspicious Japanese "doctors" or "traders" who lived in the market town, and noted that the poeple who came to their places of business were all opium smokers or opium sellers. All the people in the area surrounding Tsingtao had the firm conviction that the Japanese were their enemies and that sooner or later they would be involved in a life and death struggle with them. Tien-sze was still too young to visualize what this meant, but he did not have any doubt that he should hate the Japanese.

The invading Japanese left another impression with Tien-sze, that of the mounted soldier. The horse was so tall and grand, the soldier on it so enormous! We have mentioned that Tien-sze was a stubborn and aggressive child and the kind of boy that is usually fond of heroic fighting men. When looking at the wall pictures at the New Year Festivals, other boys and girls would find themselves interested in the flowers, birds, and beauties hung there, but Tien-sze had always been attracted by the warriors dressed in armor, astride their horses or standing on the fortress of a city gate. His favorite had always been the picture of Chao Yun, the most popular warrior of China. Chao Yun was fully dressed in armor, and with bow and spear in hand, stood on top of the gate of Ching Chow, the city that figured so prominently in the story of the Three Kingdoms. According to the story, this warrior had protected the city when it was in great danger and had defeated the huge and proud army of his enemy. Tien-sze had been so impressed that he had secretly wondered if he would himself be such a warrior. When he saw the mounted Japanese soldiers, his desire was again greatly stirred.

When Tien-sze was again in school, he received a great deal of praise from the village elders. A most respected head of the P'an clan who was also the teacher of Taitou's school, heard of Tien-sze's reputation in the market-town school. He brought back the news and broadcast it among other villagers. Because his words carried so much weight with the villagers, all the other leading persons in the community began to take notice of Tien-sze. When the boy was in a group that gathered on the street corners, an elder member, either of the P'ans or Ch'ens, would for one reason or another say to the other young people that Tien-sze was not the seed of a plain farmer but that he was to be a great official some day. Upon hearing this, everybody would look at Tien-sze, who in turn, would be greatly embarrassed. An interesting point was that the people who praised him were mostly members of the P'an clan. This had much to do with the gradual improvement in relations between Tien-sze's family and the leading families of the P'ans. Of course, Tien-sze as a young boy was not aware of them.

Tien-sze's second entry in school had a great deal to do with the future course of his life. The new school life had really changed him to a great extent. He learned the elementary facts of national history and geography. He learned new explanations and information about nature: the plants, the animals, the birds, the mountains and the waters, the stars and the globe. He was much surprised to learn that the earth was round and not square. He discovered that there were other foreign peoples in the world besides the Japanese and Germans. He was told that all the peoples on the earth could be divided into five groups, the yellow, the white, the black, the brown, and the red. Of course all this knowledge was pretty vague to him but it made him dream and wonder about the expanding world he was discovering, and it gradually separated him from the boys with whom he had cut grass and tended cows. This was not only realized by Tien-sze but also by the other boys. Only when he was called back to work on the farm during the long vacations could he again mingle with his former playmates.

The physical education program in the new school made Tien-sze a young patriot and encouraged his admiration of soldiering. Physical education was at that time a kind of military drill. The goose step, marching, saluting, and the terms were all similar to the procedure of a military camp. Even the athletic exercises were aimed at making the boys into good soldiers. The teacher's addresses at such times contained words which stimulated the young boys' national consciousness and taught them to know their nation's humiliation, and also carried the appeal that they must wake up and make themselves strong in order to defend their homes and their nation. The education inspired Tien-sze so much that he secretly decided to act as a soldier all the time. He began to sit and stand with great erectness of carriage and to walk to school with a marching step. The only difference between his present image and the earlier one was that instead of armor his hero now wore a modern army uniform, and instead of a spear, he carried a big sword and a pair of field glasses. By this time the national flag also came to Tien-sze's mind. He learned to salute it and gradually formed a great feeling of pride for it.

Through his school contacts, Tien-sze became aware of the whole community of the market town, and no longer considered himself as belonging only to Taitou. On the other hand he came to be known to many. He was one of the best students in the school and had been made an assistant in his class by his teacher. He was also recognized by his classmates as their leader. By assisting his teacher in physical education, he was at times in charge of the whole school. In addition, his writing skill drew praise. At that time Chinese and composition writing were leading courses. If a boy was good in these, he was particularly liked by the teacher. Tien-sze's teacher talked of him to other teachers and to most of the people in the town stores. The community leaders came to know of this leading student. When the village teachers addressed their pupils, they cited Tien-sze as an example to follow. Thus the schoolboys in every village knew the boy too. He himself never tired of attending school and never let the weather or anything else interfere. He always arrived before the other boys, despite the fact that his home was much farther away. Tien-sze was much interested in the stories about the ancient worthies and how they had studied hard when they were poor boys. His insistence upon going to school even on a bitterly cold day in the winter was due to a story about the boyhood of Lord Nelson.

One day Nelson and his brother were going to school. The road was long and the wind was terribly cold, so the brothers returned home. Their father asked them why they had returned, and they said because it had been too cold for them to proceed. Then the father quietly said to his sons, "Yes, it is cold but no boy can grow up to be a worthy man if he is scared by a cold day." The boys were greatly moved and started for school again immediately. Nelson became one of the greatest statesmen of England and a famous admiral. When Tien-sze was walking in the cold on his way to school, he would think of this story.

The boys who came from the market-town families or town stores lived somewhat differently from Tien-sze. They had better clothing, they always had pocket money, and they had candy or sweets all the time.

Their conversation was about things unfamiliar to Tien-sze. All this made a gradual change in the country boy's way of life. Sometimes he was ashamed of his coarse and unfashionable clothes. Other times he was embarrassed because he shared his friends' candy but he could never offer them any. When he was first taken to the stores or to the town families, he felt uncomfortable. Later, however, when he became one of the best students in the town school, he was admired by these boys and he became used to the new situation. The student body of the town school was not very large. About a dozen of the older and upper-class boys formed an intimate group and Tien-sze was one of them. Several of the town boys were rivals for his friendship and tried to win him to their side. One of Tien-sze's intimates was a town boy who competed with him in all the lessons except physical education. They were good friends throughout their school years. He also had several friends among the boys who came from other villages. They liked each other because they had similar family backgrounds and were all ambitious about their future. Among the upper-class group there was one boy whom Tien-sze and the other boys did not like. He was very much older than the others and a very domineering person. He was a brilliant student and good in all his lessons, but his composition writing was inferior to Tien-sze's, according to the teacher. On the other hand, he excelled where the others failed. He could paint, and his calligraphy was already famous in the country district. He was well-built, wore good clothes, had polished manners and was something of an orator. His reputation overshadowed Tien-sze's, but curiously the schoolteacher never said that this boy had a promising future. Tien-sze and the other younger boys were not jealous but they were afraid of him, and this may be the reason that the boy never became a real leader, nor even a real member of the group.

Tien-sze's mother had not been able to see her son graduate from the primary school. She knew of his good reputation and had had occasion to be proud of him. Tien-sze was at one time selected by his teacher as one of a dozen boys to participate in a contest in the county seat sponsored by the county government. This was a completely novel event for Tien-sze's family. It was nothing less than a government examination. Tien-sze's mother and sister were excited. Even the usually indifferent father was pleased. On the morning of the departure, the family rose very early. The mother was busy preparing the meal while the sister did her best to dress Tien-sze up. He had no dress suit, so his sister tried to put on him her silk garment. It was not too large but the color was a bright red. Tien-sze felt very shy of wearing it, and they decided to cover it with a blue jacket. They found the finished effect pleasing and all was well. Father and son started off while mother and sister waved to them from the front door. The mother murmured a prayer to God with joyful tears in her eyes. Tien-sze and his father went to the town school first, in order to join the teacher and the other boys. Each boy had a relative to take care of him, so that the teacher, the boys, the boys' relatives, and the beasts of burden formed quite a parade on the country road. On the way, Tien-sze's father was very happy and was, consequently, very kind to his son. When a farmer on the roadside asked him what was going on, he told him cheerfully that his son was going to win a name on the government's honor roll. However, even on this occasion he did not forget his frugality. At luncheon-time in a roadside inn, he did not buy anything for his son or for himself except a handful of roasted peanuts and a pot of tea. Tien-sze was hungry, but he did not dare to ask his father for more. After luncheon all the boys' relatives were to return home while the teacher and the boys went on to the county seat. There was still a ten-mile walk ahead. Tien-sze was very tired and hungry by the time they reached their destination, but he was excited for it was the first time he had seen a city. The boys had a good time in the city for about a week. They had not been very bothered by their primary task, the contest. Tien-sze, as he looked around the city, began to wonder if he could come to the city school after his graduation. Back at the market-town school, the other boys looked upon them with envy. Tien-sze won a certificate of government honor besides a number of other rewards. Everyone in the family was very happy. The neighbors and the village schoolteacher congratulated the boy and the family. It was probably due to this success that Tien-sze's mother, first brother, and sister decided to see him through high school.

Tien-sze's graduation from the market-town school took place the year after his mother's death. Tien-sze had to decide whether to continue studying or return to the farm, or perhaps apprentice himself in a market-town store. His brother talked over the problem with the evangelist of the Baptist Church who knew of the boy's good record. He recommended the boy to the high school operated by a Baptist mission in the county seat. The school was tuition free and Tien-sze's father did not oppose the plan. The day on which Tien-sze was to take the entrance examinations in the city was very cold and he had to walk eighty *li*, for there was no other way of getting there.

Tien-sze was accepted as a student in the high school and studied there without interruption, getting good marks in almost every course. After his graduation he was appointed a teacher in a primary school. Because of his good work and reputation he received the means to study in college. During Tien-sze's years in high school and college he visited his village every summer vacation and renewed old friendships. After his graduation from college, he married a girl of his own choosing and paid for the wedding out of his own savings. He is now the responsible head of a small family. Though he has not made a great fortune, he has held important teaching posts in high schools and is now a member of a university staff. Not only has he lived well but he has helped his father and brothers at home buy some land and build a new house. His family's position has been raised a great deal in the village because of his success.

The Village of Tomorrow 17

THE village of Taitou is fortunate in its geographical location. The climate is mild throughout the year and there is usually sufficient rain in the growing season. There are occasional droughts or floods but these are never of a serious nature. The soil is only of fair quality, but it is varied and can produce diversified crops, an important point in a community which must be economically self-sufficient. The nearness to the sea lane and to the modern metropolitan center of Tsingtao is also an advantage, although Tsingtao has given very little help to the village. Yet the modern influences which radiate from the city are being increasingly felt by the rural people and there is little doubt that the new civilization will eventually overthrow the old traditional ways of life. This process of change will be hastened by the development of modern means of communication and transportation between the city and the country and by the penetration of the modern economy.

In most countries, when men leave a rural community and find work in the city they settle there permanently with their wives and children and sever connections, for the most part, with their relatives back home. In China, however, most of the villagers who seek work in the city maintain close ties with their relatives and send their surplus earnings back to their homes to be used to buy land and build houses for the family. If they are married, the wives and children remain in the family home. If they were single when they left the village, they usually return to marry a girl chosen by the family.

This custom makes it possible to have a society existing in a state of balance between city and country life. Such a population movement has advantages both for the village and the city. Returning villagers bring new methods, new ideas, and new wealth to the village, and, since most of those who go forth to seek their fortunes eventually return, the countryside is not depleted by the lure of the city. It is advantageous to the city also for it provides needed workers without creating the congestion found in European and American industrial communities where the workmen's families are crowded together in a residential slum. However, it must be admitted that the Chinese migrant returns to his home place and leaves his family there not because he feels that country life is better for them than a city slum, but because he is bound by a series of ancient traditions. Young people of today who have adopted new patterns of thinking and who have no deep sentiment for the old ways are very likely to change this pattern and to settle down permanently in the place where they earn their living. Therefore, if this traditional, home-loving character of the Chinese migrant is to be preserved, the countryside must be made more healthful and desirable, and the rural districts must be more accessible to the amenities of modern civilization.

Farming is the chief source of livelihood in Taitou, but it has numerous drawbacks, the greatest of which is the low production per worker. Although there is intensive cultivation, production is held back by inefficient equipment, insufficient fertilization, ignorance of soil conservation and of the control of plant and animal pests and diseases, inferior seeds, and inferior methods of animal breeding. Another serious drawback is the insufficiency of capital. Many of the farmers know about modern methods of agriculture and would like to put them into operation but they have no cash with which to buy fertilizer, insect sprays, or proper equipment. A third factor is the density of the farm population. A primary problem of China's agriculture is the smallness of individual farms. This can be met only by adding new cultivatable land or by removing a large part of the population from agriculture. Since it is impossible to produce additional land, a population shift seems indicated and it is generally believed that such a shift can be effected by developing urban and rural industries.

China's land problem, however, is one not only of quantity but of method. The system of fragmentation and the practice of scattering pieces of land over a wide area are wasteful and uneconomic. Much good land is lost in the innumerable boundary lines, and the farmers' time is wasted in boundary disputes. The smallness of the individual fields increases the difficulties of irrigation and renders the use of modern machinery impracticable. Furthermore, the worker wastes time and energy in going from one plot to another. Various remedies have been suggested. The government has worked out a drastic policy, in cooperation with which the writer offers the following plan.

Briefly, a policy of repartitioning the land is needed. Under this policy, the government would buy on credit all the land owned by farmers and landlords and then sell it in one-piece units to the farmers who actually till the land. A farmer would buy his land in one piece no matter how large or how small the unit might be. The procedures necessary in carrying out this policy can be roughly stated as follows: First, the government makes a careful survey of the land of each farmer or farm household. The total amount of land and the number of fields, the size of each, together with its location, land classification, and current value, and the total value of all of the fields is very carefully and accurately recorded. The farmers must participate in the planning and surveying, so that they may be convinced of the advantages of the new system. After the surveys are completed, the repartitioning should be started on maps in the Land Bureau. First, for each household of a village the total amount of land and its current value must be found. Second, the total amount of land of a village or a district must be divided into units according to the number of farm households. The size of the units should be determined by land value, classification, location, and communication facilities. In partitioning the land, the size of the farmer's new unit must be equivalent in value to that of his original land. The following tables may serve as an example.

SURVEY OF CURRENT VALUES OF LAND OF DIFFERENT CLASSES

Land classification	Values in $ per mow	Description
Class I	25	
Class II	30	
Class III	40	Located at short distances
Class IV	58	from villages, with good
Class V	85	communication
Class VI	100	
Class I	20	
Class II	25	
Class III	35	Located at medium distances
Class IV	50	from villages, with ordinary
Class V	65	communication
Class VI	85	
Class I	18	
Class II	23	
Class III	34	Located at long distances
Class IV	48	from villages, with poor
Class V	65	communication
Class VI	85	

LAND HOLDINGS OF FARM HOUSEHOLD X

Class	Distance	Communication	No. of mow	Value per mow	Total Value
I	Medium	Ordinary	2	$ 20	$ 40
II	Long	Poor	5	23	115
VI	Short	Good	3	100	300
V	Medium	Poor	2.5	63	157.50
VI	Medium	Ordinary	1.5	100	150
			14		$762.50

Since the total current value of Farm Household X's original land is $762.50, it can buy back from the government a new farm unit valued at $762.50. In the same manner the Land Bureau works out the total value of land of every household. Then it divides the cultivated land of the whole district on the map into units corresponding to the various total values. The total value of all the units must be equal to the original total value of land. The units of land of good quality and good location naturally will be smaller than those of inferior quality and inferior location. If a household originaliy owned 14 *mow* of different classes of land together valued at $762.50, under the new system it would be compelled to buy a farm of 11.7 *mow* of Class V land and located at medium distance from the village, or a farm of 33.15 *mow* of Class II land located at long distance from the village, or a farm composed of 4 *mow* of Class V land, 10 *mow* of Class II land, and 5 *mow* of Class IV land, all located at a medium distance from the village. In any case, the total value is the same. Theoretically, there should be no objections from the farmers, because they will get back land of the same value as their former holdings. However, tradition and old ways are strong among the farmers and they may be reluctant even to trade in a poor farm for a better one. Therefore it is probable that force will be necessary in carrying out this policy.

Farmers of Taitou have other agricultural problems. First, their crops are often seriously damaged by several kinds of plant insects. The three most dangerous are the larva of *Mimela lucidula* (locally called *tu-tsan*); *Aphis mali* (locally called *mi ch'ung-tze*); and the cutworm. The first does great damage to the peanut and sweet-potato crops. The *Aphis mali* feeds mostly on cabbage, green vegetables, and beans. A few years ago, the damage inflicted was so great that the villagers were without vegetables. It is not uncommon to see a whole vegetable garden stripped bare by these insects. Sweet potato is not only subject to damage by the larva of *Mimela lucidula*, but also by insects that wither the leaves and vines. The cutworms are mortal enemies of the young plants of millet and other grains. In fact, every crop is threatened by one or more of these pests. It is true that the problem can be completely or partially solved by applying scientific methods of insect control, but so far no such methods have been introduced. The farmers have their old methods, but these are ineffective.

Another problem is the lack of irrigation. Vegetable gardens are watered by hand, but there is no irrigation system for the fields. When drought comes, the farmers can only wait and hope, or perhaps put on a religious procession. They are equally helpless when there is too much rain. People of this village have seen the irrigation systems and methods of other places, but have not followed suit. The belief is current here that by sinking wells in the north of the residential area the *fung-shui* of the village would be broken. Actually, however, the soil is too loose for well-sinking and the water level too far below the surface of the ground to make the building of wells practicable. Unless cooperative irrigation is developed among farmers who have fields in the same locality, the area cannot be irrigated, for no one could afford to sink a well to water his one *mow* of land.

The last point to be mentioned in regard to the agriculture of Taitou is the role played by women. Except in the very poor families, women work on the farm only when sweet potatoes are planted and when sweet potatoes and peanuts are harvested. They may also occasionally pick string beans or other vegetables which are grown in the field. Women are frequently asked to work on the threshing ground or in the vegetable garden. Indeed, they are important workers in threshing wheat, millet, and peanuts. In the ninth month when men are so busy in the field, most work on the threshing ground falls upon the women.

In summarizing, it can be said that the condition of the villagers is not very bad. They have enough to eat, except in a rare case of drought in the growing season. From a nutritional point of view the diet is not too well balanced, but there is considerable variety, except for the few months of winter and early spring when there are no green vegetables, or in the case of a few very poor families. In discussing the conditions of housing and clothing, the writer has stressed the social and cultural aspects rather than the economic. The sanitary conditions are admittedly bad. Especially in the summer, the filthy streets, dirty courtyards, and overcrowded houses make living not only uncomfortable but unhealthy. The arrangement of the family privy and the disposal of night soil and animal manure are fertile sources of disease. The prevalence of tuberculosis and diseases of the eye are direct results of the unsanitary condition in the homes, and children suffer from stomach trouble due to the unsanitary ways of preparing food and cleaning dishes. The villagers want to be healthy and decent but too many things stand in the way. They are ignorant concerning hygiene and health preservation; they don't understand the relationship between dirt and disease; they are hampered by superstitions, prejudices, and traditions which compel them to do things in the old way instead of adopting new and better methods; they do not have the means to install improvements in the home; and in working on the farm are necessarily dirty much of the time but are kept so busy that they have no time for personal cleanliness, for preparing food properly, or for ridding the house and courtyard of accumulated filth.

It is obvious that public health improvement in the village will be a tremendous task. It is not simply a matter of having more money, or one of education or village administration. It is a task which requires a co-ordination of all these efforts. In other words, the economic condition must be improved, the people must be educated, and the village as a whole must be effectively reorganized before a high standard of public health can be attained. And this will require gradual but steady pressure; there is no possibility of making great changes overnight.

As regards family life, the writer wishes to make these important points. First, most of the economic and social structures are still based on the family rather than on the individual. Agriculture is entirely a family enterprise: the family as a whole owns the land and all other means of production; in the process of producing, all the family members participate as one unit. In practice as well as in principle every member does his or her best to increase the family income. There is no sharp differentiation: if one member works harder, he does not get more; if another slacks, he does not get less. In other words, the whole business is a communal affair. In an American farm family a son may work as a partner to his father. He gets a share or a wage more or less according to his work. Although both are members of one family, they are separate economic units; the land and most of the property belong to the father or the parents, not to the family as a whole. In a Chinese farm family, unless parents and children are legally separated, such a situation never exists.

Second, if a family has a member or members working outside or in occupations other than agriculture, the family unit remains unbroken. The member still works for the family and not for himself. He does not own what he earns but must turn his surplus over to the family. For instance, a family has a son who works in Tsingtao as a mason for a period every year. He must spend part of his wages for his keep, but in his mind he never thinks that the money belongs to him or that what he spends is entirely under his control. His attitude is exactly the same as if he had worked on the farm at home.

Beside the family, there is the neighborhood or village economic organization. This, too, is based on the family unit. There are many instances of neighborhood families cooperating in plowing, sowing, harvesting, or threshing. Families help each other financially in weddings, funerals, and other special affairs. Thus far, no independent economic organization has been founded by any individual members of the different families. (Once two young persons did form a small but temporary partnership for the buying and selling of chinaware without any financial ties with their respective families, but it was a temporary venture, only.) Any kind of a village organization is but a federation of family units— the strength or weakness of a village is determined by the number and kind of families in it rather than by the number and kind of individual leaders. Also, in a farm village like Taitou there are very few organizations or structures other than the family which can be considered as strictly economic. What we actually see are the independent family units, each carrying on its own business of production, consumption, and saving. There is, of course, the organization for executing government programs and sharing the expenditures which such undertakings cost. But the fact that this kind of organization is absolutely based on family units is beyond doubt.

Social structures or activities in Taitou are also organized on family units, save those belonging to the sphere of recreation or personal amusement. The family itself is a most complicatedly interacting group; it is a primary ceremonial group; it is a primary and completely important center for training the young, sustaining the adult, and taking care of the old. It is true that the family in every country and among every people can be considered as a social group. But that the Chinese farm family is a social structure wherein the members can conduct social activities is more apparent and is of more necessity. When a social activity is extended to the village scale, the organization is based on families, not on individuals. As a matter of fact, the village is organized or divided on the different associations of families. In public affairs only families are represented. Village defense, the village school, the religious parade, the Christian churches, the selection of leaders and officers, the carrying out of government programs, the social control, and other matters of like nature, are all based on the family, not on the individual. Thus, the family is the foundation of village social life just as it is the foundation of the village economic life.

There is an interesting point in regard to a family's biological evolution. In many a Chinese family, there are five continuous stages in the process of development. The first stage, which constitutes the family in the Western sense, is a primary kinship group—husband, wife, and offspring. When one of the sons is married, the family reaches the second stage and thereafter it is not a basic family but a household. When the married sons have children but still live with their parents and unmarried brothers and sisters, the unit enters its third stage. When all the children are married and have children, but one or both parents still live and hold the whole group together, the family is in the fourth stage of development. When the parents are gone and all the sisters are married, the brothers will, as a rule, separate from each other. In some cases, however, they try to keep the large structure from breaking up. This we may call the fifth stage. But the holding-on cannot last; eventually the structure will break up. When it breaks, a number of small families and households of the first stage emerge. Each one of them is the beginning of a new process of family development. This kind of family development is different from that of a Western family. The development of a typical American family can be represented graphically.

An American family always remains a conjugal family. Its components are always parents and unmarried children. Whenever a son or a daughter is married, he or she will have a family independent of the parents. A married son or daughter is no longer a member of the original family, as far as dependence is concerned. After all children are married, the old parents will live alone. They return to the condition in which they were when first married. They may go to live with a married son or daughter, but they are treated as guests and not as members of the family.

The development of a Chinese family can also be illustrated by a graph. Not every Chinese family goes through all five stages. In many cases, the family breaks up when it reaches the fourth stage. When all sons are married and all have a number of children, it is very hard for the wives and children to live together without quarrels and friction. When once the brothers begin to quarrel they are no longer able to work together amicably and the household splits into several conjugal families. The parents, if they still live, will either live independently in the original home, or be taken care of by the sons alternately. Very few households are able to reach the fifth stage, unless for special reasons—economic problems, social prestige, an especially capable household head, sentimental attachment between the brothers, one or two brothers living outside with their families, and so on. In Taitou, a Yang family has undergone exactly the five stages shown in the graph. Here is a brief story about it.

American Family

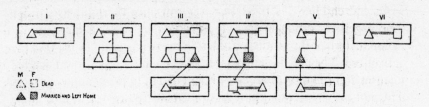

M   F
△ □ Dead
▲ ▨ Married and Left Home

Chinese Family

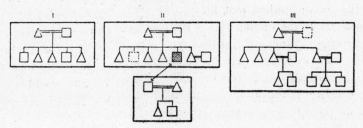

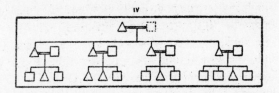

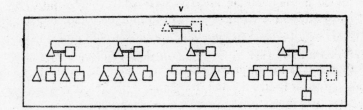

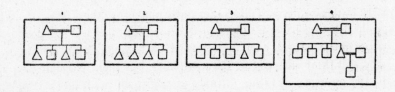

The family at the fourth stage was made up of four brothers with their wives and children. As the father was still alive the brothers naturally lived together, although quarrels were frequent among the wives and children. Two of the brothers had left home to engage in work other than agriculture. They could send some money home to help the household finances and to buy several *mow* of land to add to the common property. This not only prevented, to a certain extent, the rise of trouble among the brothers, but also made the people at home believe that the holding together was an economic advantage to the household as a whole. One of the absent brothers took his own family to live outside. This helped, too, to lessen the friction among the wives and children. Another reasc. for staying together was that the brothers and the wife of the first brother all sentimentally held that any early separation of the household would be sadly against the will of their deceased mother and would also be a great distress to the old father. Besides, they were Christians. A Christian family should act as a good example for other villagers, as the eldest brother was wont to say. He used to tell the family that a good family is one in which the members love one another, by which he meant they should live together in spite of many difficulties.

After some years, the father died. Most of the villagers predicted that the household would certainly break up this time. But the brothers insisted on remaining together. This time the economic reason was especially emphasized. They believed that none of them could have a secure livelihood if the common property were to be divided into four parts, because each part would be too small to support a family of six or seven persons. Besides, the two remaining brothers would find it hard to work the fields without each other's help. Realizing these critical problems the brothers succeeded in silencing their wives' desire to divide the household and continued to live together for almost a decade. It was not until very recently that they separated into four basic families.

Holding a large household together may be advantageous for certain large farm families and altogether undesirable for others. First, the large group does not have so unified an attitude regarding the economic prosperity of the group as a whole as does a basic or small family. The brothers may still think in terms of the household, but their wives are occupied by the present and future fortunes of their own small units. Ever since they married into the family, they have been looking forward to the time of separation from it, and they want to grab as much as they can from the common income in order to make the economic condition of their own group more secure. This gives rise to many apparent or potential troubles in the family, breeding jealousy, suspicion, misunderstanding, resentment, and selfish anxiety. At first, these troubles exist only among the wives, but later the brothers are drawn into the general ill-feeling. The children of one brother quarrel with those of another. Finally, the family is held together only by the single roof over their heads; it has already broken spiritually. With morale so low, cooperation in the division of labor will also decline. The wives quarrel over the housework and the children continue the strife. Cooperation is thus undermined at home. The wives' complaints and selfish ideas reach their husbands' ears and take root in their hearts, and finally the brothers also begin to feel prejudice toward each other. Gaps, overlapping, wasted time and labor and materials can be seen both at home and in the field. Efficiency is decreased, and the very unity of the economy is threatened. A strong father or an exceptionally capable mother may be able to restore order, but the spirit of oneness is gone.

Socially the trend is toward a reduction in the number of large families. People of the younger generations have no sentiment for the orthodox family teachings and do not look with favor on five generations living together, with the hall and chambers full of children and grandchildren. A frequent complaint from younger daughters-in-law is that they would prefer a poor and independent family of their own to a rich and troublesome household. Quarreling about dividing a large family is almost everyday news in the village. Old people have their hearts broken, but young members think it is a matter of course.

In regard to marriage, critics of China condemn the custom of keeping the couple apart until after the wedding. They charge that this ignorance of one another is the cause of many marital failures and tragedies: since love can only be generated by mutual understanding and sympathy between two persons, it is ridiculous to assume that a woman can love a man she has never seen; and without love no marriage can be successful. According to the writer's careful observation, this is only partially true. The young couple's lack of knowledge of one another may make an early adjustment difficult, but it does not prevent successful marriage. When a husband and wife have worked together, raised children together, tried to build up the prosperity of the family, shared happiness and sorrow, they feel that they have had a successful marriage, be it romantic or not. In a rural community such as Taitou, although a young couple may not know each other personally, their backgrounds, their attitudes toward life are so similar that there is no danger of conflicting ideologies or patterns of living. A marriage based on mutual attraction between young people of different standards and ways of thought often calls for greater mutual adaptation than in the case of the traditional Chinese marriage, which is arranged by the parents but in which the parties concerned know exactly what is expected of them, and have similar traditions and ambitions.

Divorce is almost impossible in rural China and if it can be accomplished, it invariably carries a strong social stigma. Some critics regard this also as a great handicap, but when divorce is easy, young people often ruin their lives by breaking up their union over some slight quarrel or temporary unhappiness. The Chinese wife, knowing that divorce is impossible for her, makes the best of her situation, uses tolerance and kindness even if she is ill treated, and tries to subdue the man's harshness with patience and love. Her goodness bears fruit in love and respect, and instead of knowing the loneliness and sorrow of the divorced woman, she is an honored wife and mother. Of course, many marriages are happy from the start and the wife does not have to endure any initial harshness. But the writer feels that disapproval of divorce is not always a disadvantage to a temporarily unsuccessful marriage, while, on the other hand, ease of divorce breaks up many marriages which could have been made happy by the mutual exercise of patience and self-control.

Turning from the family to the village as a whole, the writer wishes to make three points regarding village organization. The first characteristic of village organization in Taitou is that its purposes are negative: the leaders' duty is to guard the traditions and prevent any new ideas which would threaten the old ways of doing things; an attitude which has been typical of China's political philosophy since the establishment of the Chinese Empire. The village has no organized recreation, no village-wide social group, no community means for keeping the streets clean, supplying pure water for drinking, or for any community welfare or betterment. To be sure, it once maintained a well-organized system of defense and a corps of crop-watchers, but these were only to prevent evils, not to create something that would enrich the common life. In short, the village organizations have not, to date, done anything to improve and reconstruct, they have not attempted to destroy the undesirable and build the desirable for the people.

The second characteristic is the intravillage division. There are practically no village-wide associations; the groups are all based on particular interests, locality, kinship, or religion. So we have the clan groups, the neighborhood groups, the two Christian groups, Protestant and Catholic, and groups based on similarity of economic status. The closely knit structure of these groups tends to prevent any joint action of the village as a whole. If use could be made of the various groups as representative bodies in village administration, the situation could be improved, but so far no move has been made toward this.

The third characteristic is the clan interest. All the village organizations, except possibly those based on economic status, are determined directly or indirectly by clan relationships. A glance at the village map shows that neighborhoods are largely made up of families of the same clan. Thus the association of these families is based on neighborhood as well as on clan relationship. The Protestant group formed by the Yang and Ch'en families has been interpreted, rightly or wrongly, as an organization of the two clans against the P'an clan. The P'ans wanted nothing to do with it, not because it was an alien religion but because it was an affair of the Ch'en and Yangs. The village school, on the other hand, belonged practically to the P'an clan. The teacher was a member of the clan and they felt obligated to support him and send their children to his school. The Yang and Ch'en families sent their children to the Christian school, thereby setting up further clan rivalry.

Many people believe that China is a democratic country, but its democracy is of a negative sort. It is true that the villagers, after they have paid their taxes and fulfilled other occasional obligations, are almost completely independent of governmental administrations, and to this extent can be considered self-governed. But a closer view of the public life of the village shows it to be far from democratic. Local affairs have always been dominated by the village aristocracy, the clan heads and the official leaders. Individual villagers, or individual families, have never taken an active role in initiating, discussing, or making plans. By and large, the people have been ignorant, docile, and timid as regards public affairs. A real democracy is based on participation by the people in community affairs, and the purposes of the democratic process are designed to improve and enrich the daily life of the people themselves. Neither of these conditions is true of Taitou, which therefore can scarcely be considered a democratic community.

In an effort to relieve this unsatisfactory condition, the government has recently initiated a series of rural reconstruction programs. The authorities are anxious to modernize the villages and rehabilitate the rural districts, but this program presents many problems. It calls for a new type of leadership, and China does not have enough well-trained and well-qualified people to fill the need. Moreover, the old village gentry, clan heads, and other dignitaries will not willingly and without a struggle yield to a young upstart, even though he is backed by political authority. The influence of the old in the public affairs of the village is too deep-rooted to be overthrown by any outside force. The success of the new programs will be jeopardized on the one hand by too much overt conflict between old and new and by too much compromise on the other. It is a matter for delicate adjustment and wise leadership.

In a Chinese village, conflict and lawlessness have always been settled by private mediation backed by the force of public opinion. Formal legal power is seldom invoked. Since prejudice and tradition operate too strongly in this system, injustices frequently occur and the government, in an effort to establish greater social control and a more clearly defined legal power, has adopted the *Pao chia* and the New County systems. When these become really effective, the rural people will enjoy greater security of life and property.

However, the writer feels that it would be unfortunate should the traditional social controls of village life be entirely replaced by a series of fixed formal laws. Law provides well-defined security but it also permits injustices which shake the foundations of a closely integrated community. In a large city a man knows little or nothing about his neighbors or whether their wealth has been made honestly or through corruption; but in a village, where people are aware of the smallest details of each other's economic and social doings, it would be very disillusioning for the neighbors to see a man accumulate property by exploiting the poor or doing business with a national enemy while the law protects his property as vigilantly as the hard earned savings of an honest man. The poor but decent farmer would feel bitter resentment at such injustice in the functioning of the law. The problem of rural administration is how to combine the advantages of a modern legal system with those of the old system of control through public opinion and tradition.

"A rural community," says Professor Taylor, "consists of the people in a local area tributary to the center of their common interests. Up to a certain point, the larger that community the better, since the numbers should be great enough to allow the formation of groups with special interests and occupations which enrich the common life and to admit of the collective provision of services and amenities which a smaller community could not afford. But it must not grow too large or the sense of community weakens." * Other writers point out that social feeling assumes its most binding and powerful character when the community is large enough to allow free play to the various interests of human life but is not so large that it becomes an abstraction to the imagination. In predicting the future of the American rural community, Dr. Dwight Sanderson also emphasizes the relation between the size of the population and the social service it can achieve. At the larger centers, more institutions and services can be established which will enable rural people to have advantages similar if not equal to those enjoyed in the cities. Only the larger communities can support the services demanded by farmers as a result of increased contacts with cities and a rising standard of living.**

In considering the territorial size of a community, two factors must be taken into account: population and communication. A dense population with a high standard of living can maintain itself in a small territory, for it has the means to provide itself with the necessary services, schools, public utilities, fire protection, recreational facilities, and the rest. A sparsely settled and poorer region will need to take in a larger territory in order to raise the funds for the same services. Transportation methods also have considerable influence on the size of a community. Common interest is a most important factor: the public services mentioned above are the concern of the whole community; the success or failure of these enterprises will cause happiness or disappointment to all who depend upon them and have a share in them.

According to these principles, an effective rural community organization in this part of China would not comprise a single village or even several villages but would include the market town and the agricultural villages which surround it, as the market town area described in Chapter I. In the case of Taitou, it would include Hsinanchen and all the villages on that piece of level land (see page 1). Low standard of living and lack of capital create the necessity for a rural community organization of this size. One American farmer may be able to contribute a hundred dollars toward improvements in his community, but the Chinese farmer could probably not spare more than two dollars from his meager cash surplus; therefore the ratio of population needed to support a similar enterprise in a prosperous American farm community and in rural China would be

---

* J. B. Taylor, *Aspects of Rural Reconstruction* (Peiping, Yenching University, 1934), pp. 9–10.
** Dwight Sanderson, *The Rural Community* (New York, 1932), pp. 564–566.

50 to 1. Where fifty families can support a school in America, it requires 150 or 200 Chinese families to do it. An effective rural community in China today should have a territory with a radius of from three to four miles, because only a territory that large can support the 20,000 or 30,000 people necessary for carrying out rural reconstruction programs. With improved roads such an area would present no difficulties to the Chinese farms, which may be expected to use bicycles and rubber-wheeled carts in the future. The market-town area is the most natural and reasonable organization of a rural community, as it represents the traditional relationship between villages of the same locality.

It was believed that the introduction of better roads and modern transportation, in offering the farmer easy access to the larger centers, would cause a decline in the local market towns, but this has not proved to be the case. For one thing, although the farmer now goes more often to the larger centers for the goods he cannot buy locally, nevertheless the social life of his own market town and the weight of tradition make him continue to go there. Also, the sharp and rapid reduction in his self-sufficient economy in the present century has compelled the farmer to buy more goods. He no longer weaves his own cloth or makes his own tools; and with his new and varied wants has come a greater temptation to buy manufactured articles from the outside world. Therefore, although he may go more often to the big centers of trade, his business in the market town does not fall off. Undoubtedly the market town will play an important role in organizing the local community within its trade area.

The Chinese government has recently been devoting much attention to rural community organization. Although, as mentioned before, the primary purpose in the adoption of the *Pao-chia* system is social control, the rural organization under the New County system is designed to carry out the rural reconstruction programs. Under the New County system, the county (or *hsien*) is viewed as a local political unit for future self-government. The New County administration is divided into four grades: *Chia*, *pao*, town (known as *hsiang* in the rural area and as *chen* in the urban area), and county. As in the *Pao-chia* system, a *chia* consists of ten neighboring households and a *pao* consists of ten neighboring *chia*, or one hundred households. But the County system provides for a greater number of officers with more duties for each. At the head of a *pao* are a master and a number of administrative assistants. The *pao* master is concurrently president of the *pao* hall, principal of the citizenship school (primary school), and head of the civilian defense corps.

In a more advanced *pao* he may appoint a full-time school principal and also a deputy to take charge of local police and militia. In less developed areas two or three *pao* may jointly establish a citizenship school. Ten *pao* comprise a town (*hsiang* or *chen*), whose officials are the mayor, the deputy mayor, the principal of the central school (high school or higher primary school), the captain of the town militia and police, and the head of the town cooperative society. Above the town is the county itself. The magistrate of the county is still appointed by the provincial government. When the lower administrative units are well organized, the magistrate will be an elective officer. Under the magistrate there are from four to six departments: civil affairs, military affairs, finance, education, economic affairs, and social affairs. All the heads of these departments will be elective officers when the county is completely reorganized on the new basis.

We see several disadvantages in this system. One of its most distinctive features is the use of ten as the standard number in determining the size of the various units—ten households to a *chia*, ten *chia* to a *pao*, and ten *pao* to a town. For the purpose of social control, small units of ten households are satisfactory. But from the point of view of rural reconstruction, the *pao* and town should not be limited to ten *chia* and ten *pao* respectively, because such small units cannot supply sufficient money or personnel. Another disadvantage is that a village of three hundred households is, by the *pao* unit, split into two or three factions, whereas traditionally, it has always acted as a unit. Now it must act as three units: it must have three schools, three civilian defense corps, three cooperatives, and so on. To see how this works disadvantageously in the community, let us examine the school situation. In rural China of today, and perhaps for a long time to come, one good school is all that a village of 300 households can maintain. Educational leaders in China contend that 300 children are the most economical number for a primary school. If there are less than 100, the efficiency is greatly lowered. Therefore, rather than split one village into several units with a number of poor schools, a better policy would be to preserve a large village as a single unit and to combine two or three smaller villages as a unit with one good school for all. This principle applies with equal cogency to many other community programs.

Organization by towns also has disadvantages. Since a town consists of only ten hundred households, it includes only a part of the villages in a market-town area, and as the *pao* breaks up the village unity so the town splits the unity of the larger area. According to the new system, there are two kinds of towns: the rural *hsiang*, composed of farm households in the villages and the urban *chen*, composed of households in the market town or in the city. Thus, the market town and the surrounding villages are separated into two political units. Economically, socially, and traditionally, they are one unit or organism; the former is the head and the latter the body. Under the new organization, however, one has only a head, the other only a body; neither functions effectively without the other.

On the contrary, a market-town community organization would be well-suited for the purposes of the rural reconstruction programs. First, it would be effective in agricultural improvement. When it is possible to mechanize China's agriculture, the pattern of mechanization will doubtless resemble the much-advocated collective farm, with machinery and tractor stations established in central places to serve groups of villages. The natural and ideal location of such a station undoubtedly is the market town, which will eventually be transformed into a center of power supply and agricultural aid in a broad sense. Tractors and other machines will roll out to the surrounding villages to do the farm business. The farm households will not need to own the machines individually. They will come to the central station to engage the use of the publicly or cooperatively owned machines and other kinds of mechanical aids. They will come here to make or to repair their smaller farm implements.

Such a rural community would be effective for organizing farmers' cooperative enterprises. In order to secure sufficient capital for agricultural operation and improvement, the farmers of each village should be guided to organize themselves into one credit cooperative society. The village societies should in turn unite in a community federation with headquarters in the market town and with sufficient standing and authority to get funds directly from the banks. Village societies can borrow from the federated association and lend to their own members. Thus, the whole community becomes a unit of a credit cooperative association, and the market town becomes a center of farm credit. The larger a farmers' marketing cooperative is the better, because only a large one can provide the necessary volume of business. However, since success also depends on community interest, the basic unit should not be too large. In general, the market-town community is about the right size. The farm products of each community would then be assembled at headquarters and thence shipped to the outside markets or factories by the federated organization. In this way the integrity of an individual community is preserved, while at the same time the advantages of a large organization are realized. The farmers' purchasing cooperative should be organized in the same manner, with headquarters in the market town. Thus, the farmer could make one trip to transport his products to the market town and bring back his supplies.

A large rural community is necessary for many other aspects of agricultural improvement. Cooperative irrigation and drainage, collective control of insects and diseases are best put into operation through the combined forces of a large community. Moreover, the market-town area would be ideal for agricultural extension work and the market town a good place for broadcasting agricultural information either by radio or through other channels. In regard to rural industries, it would be the center for various manufacture; for assembling finished products from the villages to be sold locally or to be shipped to outside markets; for gathering raw materials; for financial supply; and above all it would be the headquarters of the producing cooperatives. Regarding the first point, it would be desirable if the rural workers could work by day in the market-town factories, returning to their own homes in the villages in the evening. In this way, the small industrial center and a number of residential or agricultural villages could exist side by side to form an ideal rural community possessing both the natural advantages and the amenities of urban life. Improved transportation facilities, such as bus services and bicycles, would be practical means of carrying the villagers within a radius of five miles back and forth between the market town and their homes.

A market town rather than a village should be a center for gathering raw materials and assembling finished goods because it is crossed either by a highway or by a railway, or both. Thus, it can be reached by trucks or freight cars. There is another way in which a large rural community is better than a small one for the development of rural industries. The industries owned by farmers' cooperatives will not be large, but, according to industrial principles, if they are too small operation costs will be too high. The new rural industries in China should not be confined to household manufactures and handicraft. But a single village or a few villages together would not be able to run a good-sized modern industry, yet it is undesirable to have rural industries owned and run by outside capitalists. Therefore, the most desirable method is to organize a larger group of villages to run an industry cooperatively for themselves. The larger community would have the capital, manpower, and raw materials to feed the industry and the capacity to consume the product (as, for example, commercial fertilizer, feeds, and building materials). It is interesting to note that the Chinese Industrial Cooperatives have developed in a manner very much like that which has been stressed here.

The development and improvement of rural education would also require a large rural community. "A village school will function most vigorously when it is not an isolated unit but when its teacher is the member of an educational association through which he receives constant stimuli, and when the school itself is part of a local system," writes Professor Taylor. "Within the community we are envisaging the principle of association will best be served by treating the schools and less formal educational activities of the area as a system managed by a committee representing the community. If that system is to be as complete as financial resources allow, it will probably include Lower Primary schools in all but the smallest villages; High Primary schools in the market towns and in a small but growing number of the large villages, so located as to reduce the distance which the students have to travel to a minimum. In addition, we should hope to find a Vocational school of Junior Middle grade at the center; and to have these supplemented by adult education with a much wider and more permanent function than the removing of illiteracy." *

It has been discovered that in a Chinese rural community the area of medical service generally coincides with the area of trade. Rural people have been long accustomed to consult the doctor or buy medicine in the market town. The half dozen or so physicians also traveled within the market-town area to visit patients at village homes. A public health program recently established by the government is organized vertically from the lowest unit, the village health worker, through the District Health Station, up to the County Health Center. The village health worker serves one village, the County Health Center serves the whole county from the county seat. The District Health Station serves a district—of no prescribed area. It would be ideal if the district could be the traditional market-town area. Granted that a population of from 20,000 to 30,000 people (supposedly the size of the population of an average market-town area) needs a good hospital, one or two well-trained physicians, two or three nurses, the market town might well be the seat of a community hospital and headquarters of the district health administration. Several dispensaries, or branch hospitals could be established in some of the larger villages in favorable localities. These should have one or two

---

* J. B. Taylor, *Aspects of Rural Reconstruction*, pp. 17–21.

itinerant physicians and two or three itinerant nurses to meet emergency calls and to conduct public health extension service. The village health worker should be well trained and should be at least partly paid from public funds. If it is possible, he or she should be a part-time staff member in the village school. It would be desirable to have the system run on a cooperative basis by the whole community, otherwise it should be administered by the county government.

In organizing social recreation, a single village can do a little, a group of villages can do more, but a community as large as the market-town area would be able to sponsor many large programs—a community fair, a community concert, a community athletic club. The market town has always been a recreation center for the whole rural area. The teahouses are there, the story-tellers are there, the annual fairs are there, and the most colorful New Year celebration is also there. In organizing new programs one needs only to change the contents and the techniques of the old ones and to add to them the new ones. The most important point is to organize the people, men and women, old and young, into different interest-groups, and into different local units, and then unite them all into a community-wide federation. Each small unit can conduct simple programs in a small territory, such as a single village or a group of villages. But whenever a community program is needed all the units can come together readily. Take the new drama for example. In ordinary times, each larger village or each group of neighboring villages can maintain a small band of young farmers and play simple dramas to entertain their own fellow villagers. But on special occasions, such as the annual fair, the New Year Day, the Spring Festival (Ching-ming Festival), October Tenth (Chinese Independence Day), and so on, all the village bands of the community should be organized together to have big programs at the market town. This will greatly enhance the community consciousness, and the unity of the local people.

Appendices

I. DEVELOPMENT OF FARM IMPLEMENTS

THE plow (Figure 10) consists of seven parts: the handle, the down-curved beam, the horizontal base, the upright board (sometimes called the guide-board), the side-peg handle, the moldboard, and the share. The moldboard and the share are made of cast iron, the rest of wood. The handle is about three feet long; its lower end is connected through the horizontal base to the upright board. The beam is about six feet long. At one end is inserted a wooden pin on which the whipple-tree swings; the other end is squared to fit loosely into a rectangular slot at the middle of the handle. The upright board, which is about two feet long, is the center of the plow. The lower end is firmly mortised into the horizontal base while the upper end goes through the beam. The horizontal base is pointed at the front to fit into a socket at the end of the share. It is about two and one half feet long. The cast-iron moldboard is oval shaped with twisted blade and long slotted projection. In use it is tied upon the upright board and stands on the share. Its purpose is to throw the earth over the furrow. The share is slipper-shaped and ends in a socket into which the horizontal nose of the plow is driven. The purpose of the share is to underslice the furrow. The side-peg handle is a wooden pin about one foot long which is inserted horizontally into the rectangular slot in the handle of the plow. It serves to change the depth of the furrow: it is pressed down to cut deeper into the earth.

In this part of the country, the plow is used both for preparing the field and for sowing. (For sowing, however, the moldboard is taken off.) Sometimes it is also used in cultivating the sweet-potato field, if new earth is needed on the ridges. Then it is guided by a plowman and drawn by a team composed of a donkey and an ox. The present cost of a plow is not known, but it cannot be more than five dollars. It may last about twenty years

It is interesting to note that a plow is not used for sowing in Taitou. This is probably because of the particular local methods which have the advantages of saving seed and concentrating the fertilizer around the plants. Our farmers must have decided that these advantages outweigh the saving of labor made possible by sowing with the plow.

The harrow (Figure 11), locally called *pa*, is another important implement for preparing the field. It is composed of a strong rectangular wooden frame, and has twenty-three iron teeth and two horizontal wooden boards which are crosswisely connected to the sides of the frame. The length of such a harrow is about six feet. The teeth are about eight inches long and are driven through the bar evenly with about one inch showing above it and four inches beneath. The function of the harrow is to break up the clods of earth and to soften the soil after the field is plowed. In the spring, when the preparation of the fields only requires slicing a thin layer of the hard surface, a harrow, drawn by a team, is used instead of a plow. If deeper cutting is desired, the harrow is weighted with a rock or other heavy article, or a boy rides on it. The cost of the harrow is about four dollars and may last for about ten years.

A second kind of harrow, also drawn by a team, is locally called *lau* (Figure 12). It is used to level the furrows and cover the seeds after they have been sowed and to smooth the surface of a plowed field, if there are not big clods. It is made of a wooden board and a number of shrub branches. The wooden board is about five feet long, eight inches wide, and four inches thick at one side, but only two or three inches thick at the other. On the middle of the board a line of wooden pins are firmly mortised. The branches must be long enough so that they can be bent into long, narrow, U-shapes. They are firmly tied onto the wooden pins and then lashed together with strips of ox-skin or string until the whole thing looks like a big flat brush. On it is a wooden cross brace. The team driver stands on the cross brace to create the pressure needed in leveling the surface. He must also frequently lift up the wooden board a little so that the earth does not pile up under it. This can easily be done by swinging one's weight from one leg to the other, making the two ends of the harrow also swing back and forth. If the driver is experienced in this work, his movement, the movement of the harrow and the plodding of the team all fall into a harmonious rhythm. The cost of such a harrow is about three or four dollars.

At the edges of a field the hoe and rake are needed. The hoe (Figure 16) is composed of two parts: a wooden handle and an iron head. The handle, a pole about five feet long, is inserted into the head and held there by a wedge. The angle between the handle and the head is governed

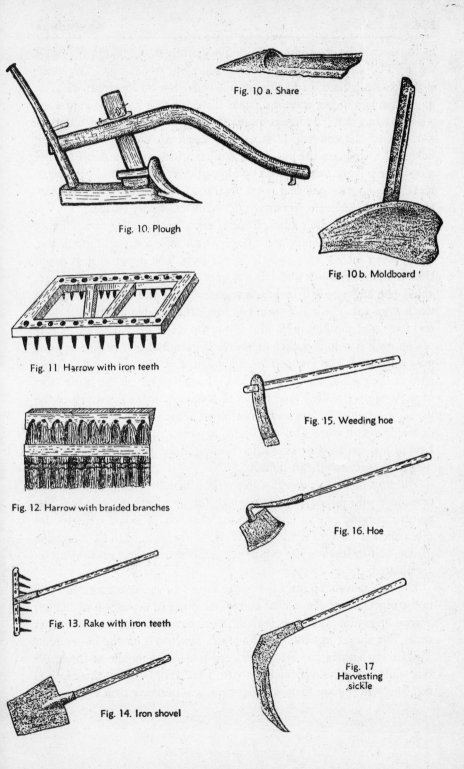

Fig. 10 a. Share

Fig. 10. Plough

Fig. 10 b. Moldboard

Fig. 11 Harrow with iron teeth

Fig. 12. Harrow with braided branches

Fig. 13. Rake with iron teeth

Fig. 14. Iron shovel

Fig. 15. Weeding hoe

Fig. 16. Hoe

Fig. 17
Harvesting
sickle

by the work to be done and is adjusted by putting in or taking out a small wedge. The head is about a foot long and three inches wide. The blade is thicker near the eye and thinner but wider toward the edge, which is more than two inches wide and made of steel so that it can be reinforced when it wears out. The hoe is the most useful of all farm implements in our part of the country. It is used to break up the big clods in the field and to prepare the vegetable gardens which are too small for the plow. The poor farmer who has no plow or draft animals uses the hoe to make the ridges for planting sweet potatoes. In harvesting sweet potatoes and peanuts, the hoe is the most important tool in my village.

For weeding, another kind of hoe is used, locally called *ch'u* (Figure 15). This also has a handle and a head. The head is a wrought iron blade, about seven inches wide and six inches long. The upper edge is much thicker than the lower and has a square socket in it. The lower edge, about one and one-half inches, is made of steel and can be reinforced when worn out. The handle is in two parts: the wooden pole, about three feet long, and the iron neck, also about three feet long. The upper part of the neck is a long socket in which the pointed end of the wooden pole is inserted. The lower part is a gooseneck of solid iron with a hook-nose at the end. The nose is inserted into the socket on the blade. The angle between the blade and the neck is important for the depth of the hoeing, and must be frequently readjusted. This is done by putting into or taking out of the socket on the blade one or two small wedges. This kind of hoe can be large or small according to the age of the person who uses it. It costs about two dollars.

The iron rake (Figure 13) consists of a handle ending in a wooden crosspiece with drilled holes into which the iron teeth are inserted. The points emerging on the upper side are clinched. It is indispensable for preparing the manure fertilizer and it is also much used in the vegetable garden and in leveling the top of the small ridges when sweet potatoes are planted.

The iron shovel (Figure 14) is also a farm tool widely used in the field, in the vegetable garden, and at home. It is made of wrought iron and has a wooden handle. The blade is about fourteen inches long and ten inches wide. The socket in which the handle is inserted is on the upper edge. To give strength to the blade a ridge is left in the middle of the upper side while the under side is left smooth. The handle is about three to four feet long. On the top there is no crosspiece or iron ring such as is seen on

Fig. 18. Stone roller for threshing

Fig. 19. Grain scoop for winnowing

Fig. 20. Wheelbarrow

Fig. 21. Flail

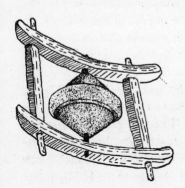

Fig. 22. Stone roller for pressing the earth after millet is sown

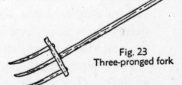

Fig. 23
Three-pronged fork

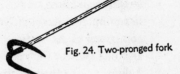

Fig. 24. Two-pronged fork

Fig. 25. Bamboo sweeper

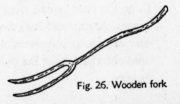

Fig. 26. Wooden fork

Western shovels. When in use it is pushed with the hands with the whole body's strength behind it. Only occasionally it is foot-driven, that is, when the farmer has his shoes on.

Because of the particular kind of sowing practiced in my village, a special fertilizer holder is used. Locally it is called *pa-doo-tze*. It is woven of dried hemp stalks and has a braided strap which hangs over the farmer's shoulders suspending the holder in front of his chest. The holder should not be too deep and the opening at the top should be wide.

For harvesting, the sickle (Figure 17) is an important tool. It is generally used for cutting crops such as soybeans, rice, and sweet-potato vines. There is not much difference between a Chinese sickle and a Western one. The local people call this implement *lien*.

The stone roller, the two-pronged and three-pronged forks, the wooden rake, the flail, the wooden shovel, the bamboo sweeper are all used for threshing, and the grain scoop for winnowing. The stone roller (Figure 8) is about two feet long, and ten inches in diameter. The surface is smooth. In the center of each end there is a round socket made with a chisel. In use, a bowlike whippletree is put on it. At the two ends of the whippletree two pins made of hard wood are loosely inserted into the sockets on the roller to serve as axles. A rope is tied to the middle of the whippletree and the draft animal is driven by it. There is a corrugated variety of the stone roller which is used for the same purpose. It is better than the first one when the layer of stalks on the ground is thick or hard.

The two-pronged and three-pronged wooden forks are shown in Figures 23 and 24. They are used for moving the stalks from one place to another. The first is made of a two-armed branch. The fore points of the two prongs are sometimes covered with iron to make them last longer. The wooden rake is similar to the iron rake, but the wooden teeth are much longer than those on the iron rake. The flail (Figure 21) is locally called *lien-chin*. It consists of two parts: a swingle and a handle. The swingle is composed of six sections of strong shrub branches, each two feet long and one-quarter inch in diameter, which are knit together with strips of hide in two or three places. The handle is made of wood about four feet long. On the top end is an eye through which a hard, smooth cross brace passes. At one end the cross brace terminates in a knob and on the other the swingle is connected with strips of ox hide. It must fit very loosely into the eye so that the swingle can be swung freely when the implement is used.

An important implement used in transportation is the wheelbarrow (Figure 20). The principal parts of the vehicle are the large wheel; the framework which covers the upper part of the wheel and guards it from contact with the merchandise or persons transported; the two long shafts, held at a proper distance from each other by two cross-pieces, to the central sections of which the framework is attached; the two handle-bars which are the terminals of the shafts; the two carrying frames formed by curved bars and attached to each side of the shafts by the cross-pieces; and the axle, made of very strong wood. The whole wheelbarrow is made of solid wood; occasionally the wheel is capped with an iron tire.

When the merchandise is bulky, it is loaded on both the framework and the carrying frames; but if it is grain in bags, or persons, only the carrying frames are used. A braided suspender is tied crosswise on the two handlebars. The operator puts the suspender over his shoulders and grasps the handlebars. The barrow and its load are supported by the wheel and the man's shoulders. The man pushes the barrow from behind while a mule or a donkey pulls it from the front.

II. PRACTICAL APPLICATION OF KINSHIP TERMS

A. *Patrilineal Relatives*

1. PARENTS AND OTHERS OF PARENTS' GENERATION.—As a child, ego calls his father Da-da and, as an adult, Dieh. Ego calls his mother Niang always, but occasionally Nian-niang when he is a child. When ego is middle-aged and his parents are still alive, he may refer to his father or mother as Lao-Jen-Chia (the Old Man or the Old Lady) or Chia-Li-Ti Lao-Jen-Chia (the Old Man or the Old Lady of our family).

Ego calls his father's elder brother Ta-yieh. If his father has a number of elder brothers, then the first one is Ta-yieh, second one, Erh-Ta-yieh, third one San-Ta-yieh, and so on. (Erh and San mean second and third, respectively.) Ego calls his father's younger brother Shu. If his father has a number of younger brothers, then the first one is Shu, or Ta Shu, the second Erh Shu, the third San Shu, and so on. If the last one is very young, and the same age as ego, he may be called Hsiao Shu. (Hsiao means little.) This term should be changed when they are grown-up, or after the uncle is married. These terms can be similarly applied to the father's male cousins in first and second degree.

Ego calls the wife of his father's elder brother Ta-niang, adding the appropriate number if there is more than one brother. He calls the wife of his father's younger brother Shen-tze, similarly adding a number if necessary.

Ego calls his father's sister Ku, regardless of whether she is older or younger than the father. If there are a number of Ku, they are numbered according to their ages. The eldest is Ta Ku, the second Erh Ku, the third San Ku, and so on. If the last one is very young and the same age as ego, she may be called Hsiao Ku. This term too is changed when they are grown-up, or after marriage. These terms can be similarly applied to father's female cousins to the first and second degree. Ego calls his Ku's husband Ku-fu. If there are a number of them, they are numbered according to the Kus' numbers.

The application of the terms for ego's father and mother is exclusive, no other persons can be called by the same terms, except step- or adopted-parents.

2. GRANDPARENTS AND OTHERS OF THEIR GENERATION.—Ego calls his grandfather Yieh-yieh and grandmother Ma-ma. If the grandfather has an elder brother, he is called by ego Ta Yieh-yieh; if younger, Erh Yieh-yieh. If there are more than one, they will be numbered according to age, regardless of their age relation to the grandfather. The same terms can be applied to the grandfather's male cousins of the first degree. Ego calls the wife of grandfather's brother Ta Ma, or Erh Ta-ma, according to her husband's number.

Ego calls his grandfather's sister Ku-ma. If there are more than one, then they are numbered according to age, regardless of the grandfather's age. Ego calls his Ku-ma's husband Ku-yieh, according to the Ku-ma's number.

3. BROTHERS, SISTERS, AND OTHERS OF EGO'S GENERATION.—Ego calls his elder brother Ke-ke. If there are several older brothers, they are numbered according to their ages. Ego calls his younger brother Ti-ti, or Hsung-ti. If there are several younger brothers, they are numbered according to age. The same terms can be similarly applied to ego's male cousins of the first and second degree. Ordinarily, however, ego can call by name a younger brother who is not more than twenty and is unmarried; if he is older or married he should be addressed by the proper term. When brothers and cousins are all middle-aged, ego can address the younger ones by number alone, adding the prefix Lao. For example, if ego is the eldest, he may call his next younger brother Lao Erh, the second Lao

San, and so on. These terms can be similarly used by people of the senior generation to address the grown male children.

Ego calls his elder sister Chieh-chieh; if more than one, they are numbered according to age. Ego calls his younger sister Mei-mei. If there are more than one, they are numbered according to age. When younger sisters are under fifteen, or so, ego can call them by their names. But when they are grown-up, they should be addressed by the proper term. These terms can similarly be applied to ego's female cousins of the first and second degree.

Ego calls the wife of his elder brother Sao-tze. If there are more than one, they are numbered according to the elder brothers' age. Ego calls his younger brother's wife Ti-mei. But for everyday life in the same household these terms are considered too formal and are seldom used. The usual practice is to use no term at all. If ego is married and has a child, then he calls her T'a Ta Shen-tze, or T'a Erh Shen-tze. (T'a means of the child; in a possessive case. T'a Shen-tze means child's Shen-tze.) Ego's wife may address the younger brother-in-law's wife in the same way.

Ego calls his elder sister's husband Chieh-fu. If there is more than one elder sister, their husbands are numbered according to the sisters numbers. Ego's younger sister's husband is Mei-fu. If there is more than one younger sister, their husbands are numbered according to the sisters' numbers. Terms for addressing ego's brothers' wives and sisters' husbands can be similarly applied to the wives of ego's male cousins and the husbands of ego s female cousins respectively.

There are no proper terms of address for ego and his wife. When they are young, or before they have any child, the word Ni (you) is frequently used by both of them. When ego wants his wife to bring him something, for instance, he may yell: Ni Pa Na Ko Lan-tze Tai Lai (you bring here the basket). When they have a child, they may still use the same term but gradually they begin to address each other through their child. Ego calls his wife Pao T'a Niang. (Pao is the name of the child, T'a is a possessive case. So, the whole phrase means the child's mother.) Wife calls ego Pao T'a Da-da (child's Daddy). There are also no proper terms of reference for a young couple when either of them is conversing with parents or with any one of the senior generation. The word T'a is frequently used in reference. Here it is a third person pronoun, but it is specially used for referring to either man or wife. When a young wife says T'a in conversation with her mother-in-law or her own parents, they understand that she means her husband. The word is used in the same way by the husband. There is always shyness on the face of the young wife when she says T'a. But in talking to a junior member, neither the young wife nor the young husband will feel embarrassed if they refer to each other. Thus, ego can very freely call his younger brother Ni Sao-tze, and ego's wife can address her younger brother-in-law as Ni Erh Ke.

4. YOUNGER GENERATIONS.—Until their children are married, or reach middle age, ego and ego's wife call them by small names. Some parents do not drop the practice; this does not necessarily mean that they are rude people, but only that they retain the earlier sentiment for their children. Usually, however, when a son is married and has a child, his parents will address him and his wife as "child's father" and "child's mother."

Ego addresses his brothers' and sisters' children just as he does his own. He may speak of his sister's boys as Wai-sheng and her girl as Wai-sheng-nu. Villagers who are inclined to observe formalities may use the term Chih-er in referring to a brother's boy and the term Chih-nu in referring to a brother's daughter. The most common usage is by name when the children are young, and by number with the prefix Lao when the boys are grown-up or married. Ego's wife can act in the same way.

Ego addresses his son's children by name when they are young and by number with the prefix Lao when they are married or middle-aged. A granddaughter is not called by name by her grandparents or by number when she is married or middle-aged, but by the collective term for grown-up girls, that is, Mair. This is also used frequently by the girl's parents. The literary term for a grandson is Sun-tze, for a granddaughter is Sun-nu. But these terms are very seldom used by the farmers, except on an occasion of congratulation. When a grandson is born, the neighbors may congratulate the grandparents by saying: "*Hao Ming Oh, Tien Sun-tze La*" (How fortunate you are, you have a grandson now). In reference, a grandfather calls his daughter's son Wai-sheng Sun-tze, his daughter's daughter Wai-sheng Sun-nu. The prefix Wai-sheng means kin-children of the sister's or daughter's family.

Except for a very few cases, ego does not meet with people of the third generation above or below his, so there are no terms of address for them. In a big clan there may be one or two persons of a generation above the grandfather's then he or she is called by ego, Lao Yieh-yieh or Lao-Ma-ma respectively. Here Lao means great.

B. For Matrilineal Relatives

1. BROTHERS AND SISTERS AND THEIR WIVES AND HUSBANDS.—Ego calls his mother's brother Chiou. If she has several, they are numbered according to age, regardless of whether they are older or younger than ego's mother. If the last one is young and of an age with ego, he may be called Hsiao Chiou. When he is grown-up or married, he should be addressed by the proper term. Ego calls his Chiou's wife Chin-tze. If there are several Chiou, their wives are numbered according to the Chiou's number.

Ego calls his mother's sister Yi. If there are several of them, they are numbered according to their age. Ego's mother is also counted within the series. If the last one is very young and similar in age to ego, she may be called Hsiao Yi. This is changed to the proper term when she is grown-up or married. Ego calls his Yi's husband Yi-fu. If there are several Yi, their husbands are numbered according to the Yis' numbers.

Terms for mother's brothers and sisters and their spouses can be similarly applied to mother's male and female cousins and their spouses.

2. PARENTS.—Ego calls mother's father Lao-yieh, mother's mother Lao-niang. If mother's father has a number of brothers, they are called by the same term but numbered according to their ages, irrespective of their age relation to mother's father. The wife of Lao-yieh is addressed with the same term for mother's mother, but numbered according to her husband's number. Ego calls mother's father's sister Ku Lao-niang. If there are more than one, they are numbered according to their ages. There is no term for the husband of Ku Lao-niang and he is not looked upon as kin.

3. BROTHERS' AND SISTERS' CHILDREN.—Ego calls a son of mother's brother or sister Piao-hsung, if he is older than ego, and Piao-ti, if he is younger. (Piao means outside.) Ego calls mother's brother's or mother's sister's daughter Piao-chieh, if she is older than ego, and Piao-mei, if she is younger. Sometimes a differentiation is made between them. The son or daughter of the mother's brother is Chiou-chia Piao-hsung or Chiou-chia Piao-chieh, while son or daughter of mother's sister is Yi-chia Piao-hsung or Yi-chia Piao-chieh. (The character Chia means family. Thus, by Chiou-chia Piao-hsung means a Piao-hsung of Chiou's family.) These terms may also be applied to children of father's sisters. Thus, ego calls a son of father's sister Ku-chia Piao-hsung or Ku-chia Piao-ti, a daughter Ku-chia Piao-chieh or Ku-chia Piao-mei.

Cousins with the prefix Piao may marry each other. When they do marry, only the terms of the two parties are affected by the husband and wife relationship. All others remain the same. Of course the wife must address her husband's family members with proper terms no matter how she has addressed them before.

C. For Wife's Relatives

1. PARENTS.—There are three terms which ego can use to address his wife's father: Yueh-fu, Chang-jen, or Dieh. The first is too literary and no farmer would use it. The second is considered too rude by the local people and they do not use it either. The last one is also seldom used, except by a few young husbands who love their wives very much and wish to show affection by addressing her father or mother in the same terms which she uses. But the dignified husband would not do this. As a result, a son-in-law addresses his father-in-law very rarely. The father-in-law understands the situation and makes no fuss about it. For addressing his mother-in-law, ego can also use one of three terms: Yueh-mu, Chang-mu-niang, of Niang. Actually, ego does not address his mother-in-law just as he does not his father-in-law. If a young man addresses his mother-in-law precisely and frequently with the term Niang, he pleases his wife very much, but all his relatives and friends will tease him or sneer at him.

2. SIBLINGS.—Ego addresses his wife's brothers and sisters exactly as he does his own brothers and sisters. But in reference, ego can call a brother-in-law Chiou-tze, a sister-in-law Yi-tze. He adds the prefix Ta to the terms for those who are older than his wife, and the prefix Hsiao for those who are younger. These terms can be similarly applied to wife's male and female cousins respectively.

3. NEPHEWS AND NIECES.—Ego uses the same term for children of wife's brothers as he does for his own brothers' children, but in reference he calls the boys Chi-chih and the girls Chi-chih-nu. (Chi means wife, a literary term, Chih means nephew. Chi-chih means wife's nephew, Chi-chih-nu means wife's niece.)

A wife addresses her husband's parents and brothers and sisters by the same terms her husband uses. In reference, she calls her father-in-law Kung-kung, mother-in-law P'o-P'o. She calls her brother-in-law Ta-pei, if he is older than her husband, Hsiao-shu-tze, if he is younger. She calls her sister-in-law Ta-ku-tze, if she is older than her husband, Hsiao-ku-tze, if she is younger. If she has a number of brothers-in-law and sisters-in-law, they are numbered according to their ages, and each sex is a series. She calls the children of her brothers-in-law by name or number just as her husband does. She calls the children of her husband's sisters Wai-sheng, if a boy, and Wai-sheng-nu, if a girl. A wife uses the same terms as her husband does to address her husband's cousins and all other siblings.

D. Piao-cousins' Children

Ego calls children of all the Piao-cousins, Piao-chih, for boys, and Piao-chih-nu for girls. In practice, the kinship relationship between ego and these people is negligible.

Index

評內版台叢年第〇五四三號 高號

發行人：林在　　

發行所：台北市重慶南路一段一四四號　出版社

總　經　銷：中央圖書供應社　台北市重慶南路一段一四四號

地　　址：台北市重慶南路三段五一七二六〇號　

印　刷　所：郵政劃撥明定印刷二〇三二號

地　　址：台北市〇

CAVES BOOK CO.

99 CHUNG SHAN RD, N. (2)

TAIPEI TAIWAN CHINA

TEL. 44754